BURIED NEW JERSEY

UNDERGROUND ADVENTURES IN THE GARDEN STATE

JANICE L. PHILLIPS

AMERICA
THROUGH
TIME

To my parents, who taught me how to find the answers to my questions even when they didn't have the answers themselves.

America Through Time®
An imprint of Sutton Publishing Inc.
www.through-time.com

First published 2025

ISBN 978-1-63499-562-7

Typeset in 10pt on13pt Sabon
Printed and bound in the United States of America

Contents

INTRODUCTION

I've loved cemeteries for as long as I can remember. I think part of this love came from my love of ancient Egypt. I don't remember when I first read about mummies and pyramids, but I was fascinated. This led to a lifetime fascination with how different cultures deal with death. Death causes a problem besides grief: it leaves a body—a body that you have to do something with because it can quickly become unpleasant. I never realized that I was a cemetery explorer when I was young, I just knew that my mom and I would pull over to look at any interesting cemetery if we had time.

My love of New Jersey came later. I was born on Staten Island and spent a good amount of time there even when my mom and stepdad moved to New Jersey. My parents had shared custody, and I was in Staten Island every other weekend. It wasn't until I'd left the small town that I grew up in that I realized I loved New Jersey. I love this state because there are so many cultures here living side by side. Our burial history extends far beyond the colonists who came here, back to the Lenni Lenape whose burial grounds are still being found. Our state is built on the dead.

This book is a small sampling of burial culture in New Jersey. There are some cemeteries included here that I could have written an entire book about. How did I choose which cemeteries to write about? First, there had to be a story. I learned that lesson the hard way. I pulled over at a cemetery when this project was first pitched to me and spent over twenty minutes photographing it only to find it had no story. More accurately, I suppose that every cemetery has a story, but this cemetery's story was very regular—a group of Episcopalians had a church and needed a place to put their dead. I'm intrigued by the very old, the abandoned, the forgotten, the remote, the possibly haunted. Second, it had to photograph well. I'm not religious but I love mortality icons. I love the Victorian language of cemeteries. I love cemeteries that are broken, forgotten, or left behind. This book isn't meant to be an encyclopedia or a list of famous headstones or celebrity burials. I very much want this book to encompass the strange and unusual.

1
Little Lost Cemetery

60 Littleton Rd., Parsippany-Troy Hills, NJ 07054

Little Lost cemetery is located behind the District Six Firehouse in Parsippany-Troy Hills. The cemetery is small, just a 20- by 30-foot plot of land that was forgotten by the town's residents until Interstate Highway 287 construction threatened its removal.[1] There are small white markers, some of which are too weathered to read. One central marble marker with a plaque lists the names of the known children buried here. There are stone benches with statues of children, and a wooden bench. There are fourteen marked graves of children who died at the Morris County Children's Home.

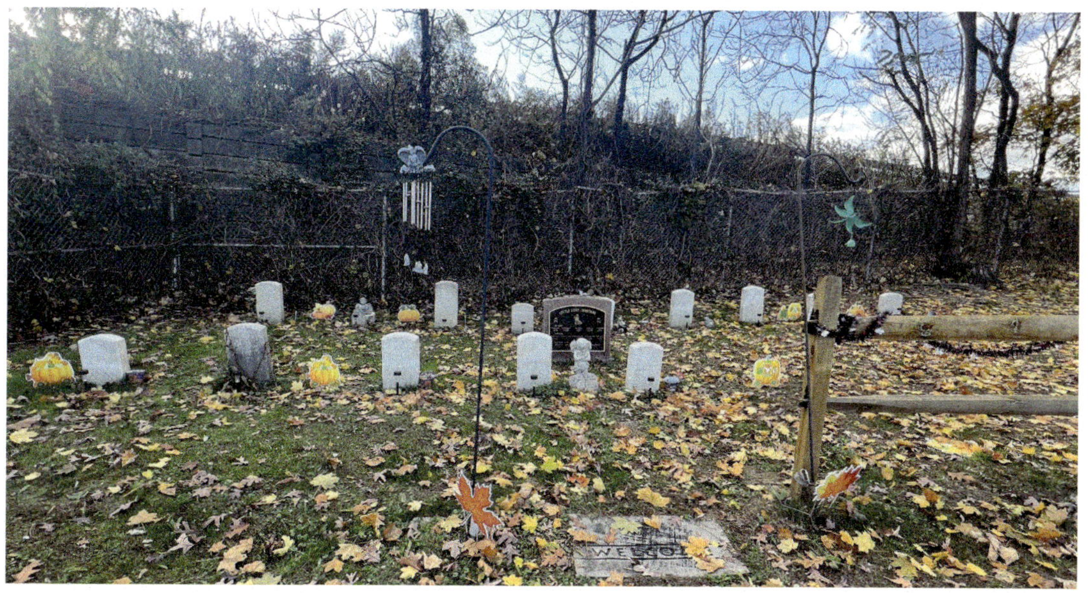

Efforts from the local community have made Little Lost Cemetery a welcoming place to honor these children. The fence, sign, windchimes, and decorations are all from concerned locals.

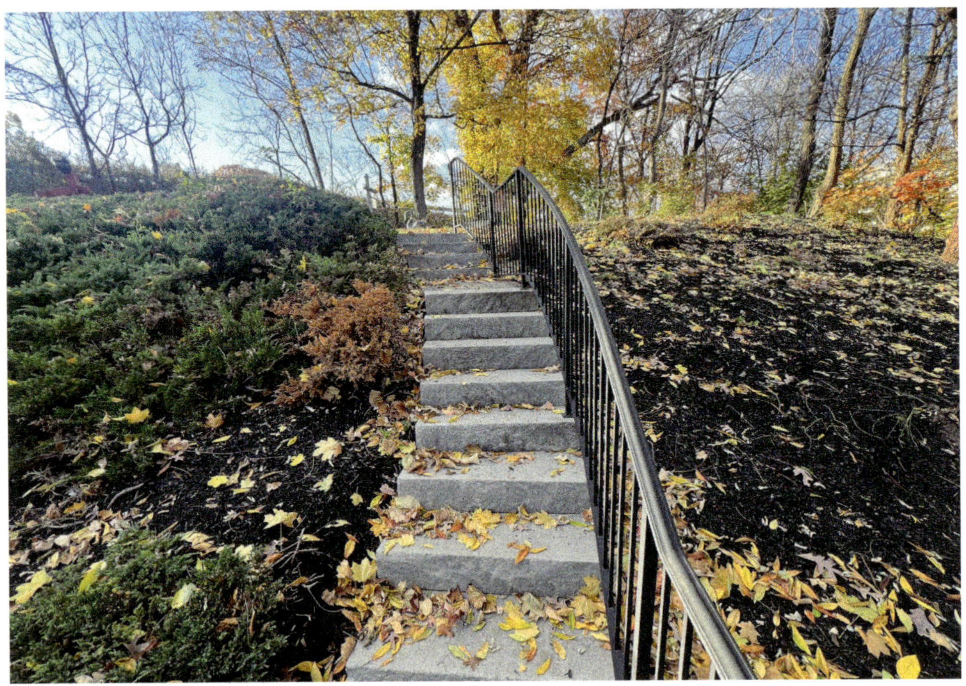

This is the staircase you take to get to the Little Lost Cemetery. It was donated by locals.

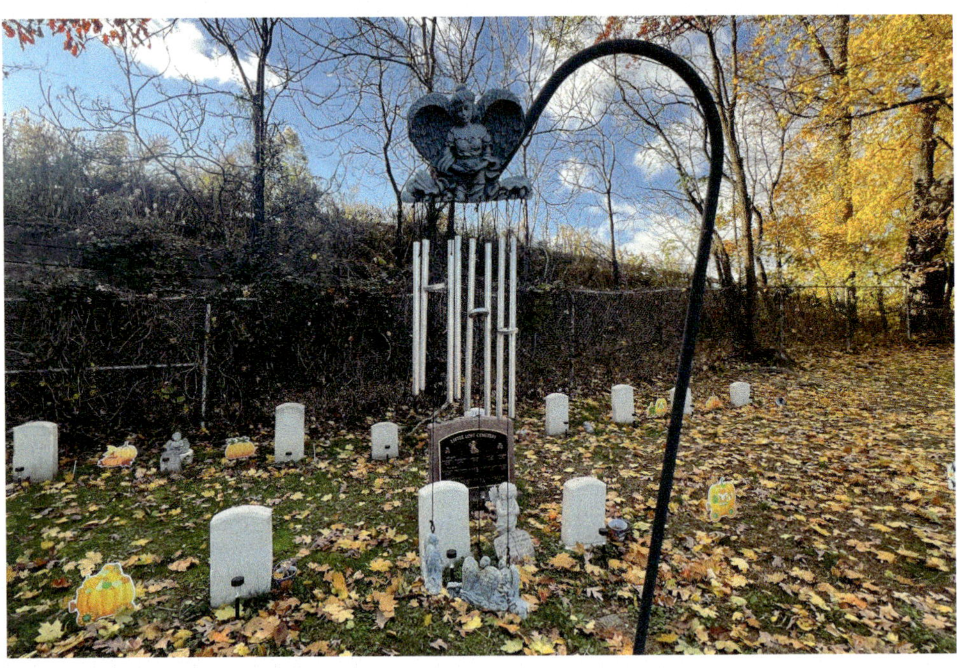

Little Lost Cemetery is very close to the wall separating it from Interstate 287.

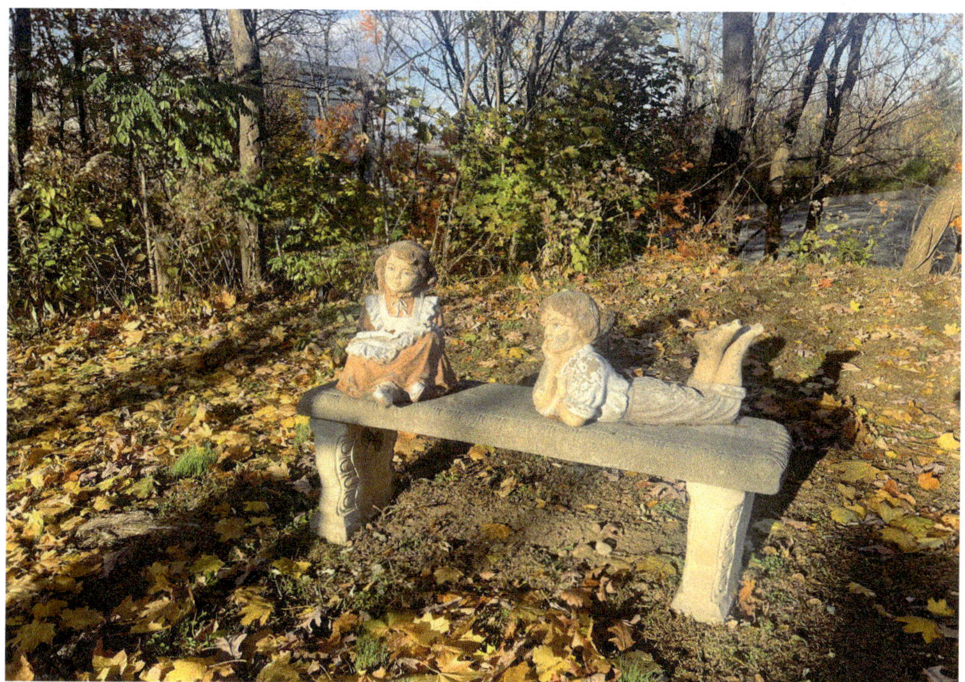

A bench with statues of children watches over Little Lost Cemetery.

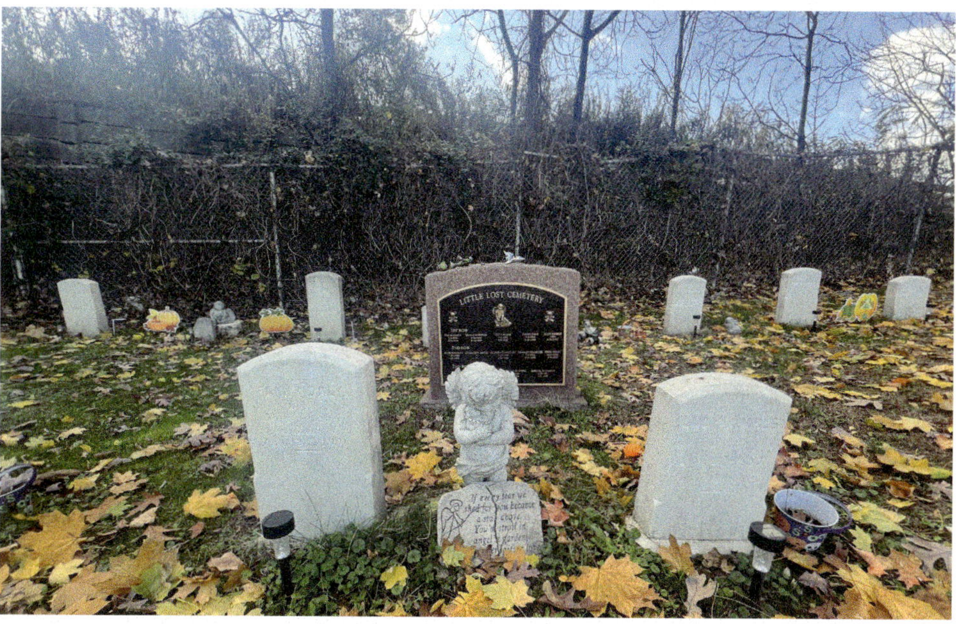

The angel statue is between the newest marked grave, for Fanny Daly who died in 1907, and the oldest marked grave, for Lucy Kimble who died in 1887. The stone behind them lists every known burial at Little Lost Cemetery.

The story of Little Lost Cemetery starts in 1881 when the Morris County Children's Home opened with funds from the State Charities Aid and Prison Reform Association.[2] It was established for orphans and children whose families arranged boarding, with the goal of moving indigent children out of the county almshouse.[3] The children housed at the county almshouse shared living space with adults including criminals.[4]

In 1882, twenty-two children were moved to their new home at Ailanthus Hall, a colonial mansion near the current cemetery.[5] Walking among the stones, I wondered what life was like for those children. Was there room for fun and playing, or was it a life of austerity and work?

The orphanage remained in operation for a little over forty years. Ailanthus Hall closed in 1929 due to the rise of foster home placement.[6] By 1933, any remaining children were sent to a residence on Mount Kemble Avenue.[7] Ailanthus Hall burned down in the 1950s, leaving only the cemetery behind.[8] The oldest marked grave is from January 20, 1887, for four-year-old Lucy Kimble. The newest marked grave is from June 24, 1906, for eleven-year-old Fanny Daly. The children died due to illness and their young age, even though there were doctors and nurses on call.[9] Any cemetery traveler will notice the abundance of children's graves in older cemeteries. They serve as a reminder of how often young people died of treatable or preventable diseases and accidents before the rise of modern medicine and safety standards. In this case, close quarters exacerbated the spread of disease.[10] It is rumored that victims of the Spanish flu epidemic were quickly buried without markers.[11]

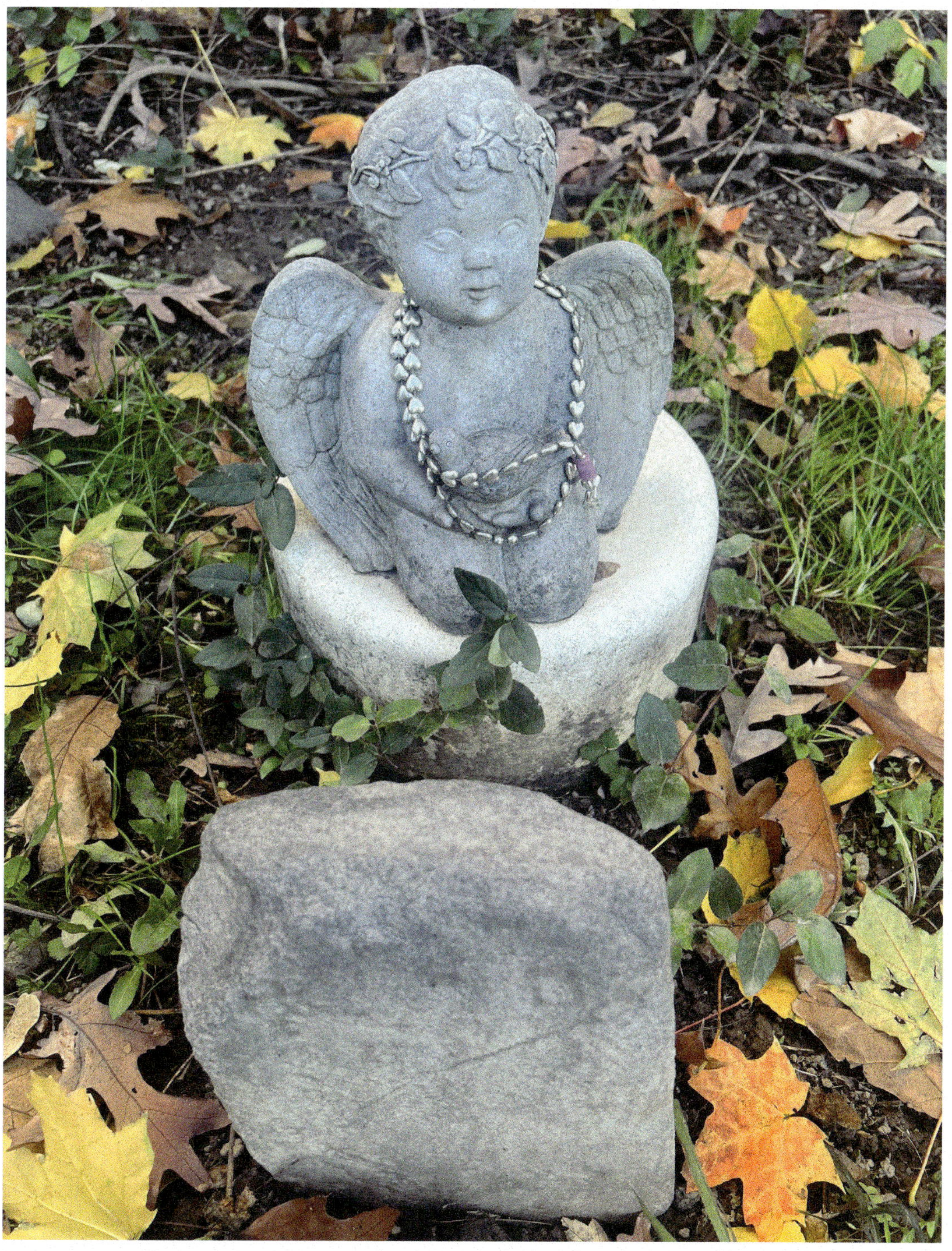

There are small decorations left in memory of the children buried at Little Lost Cemetery.

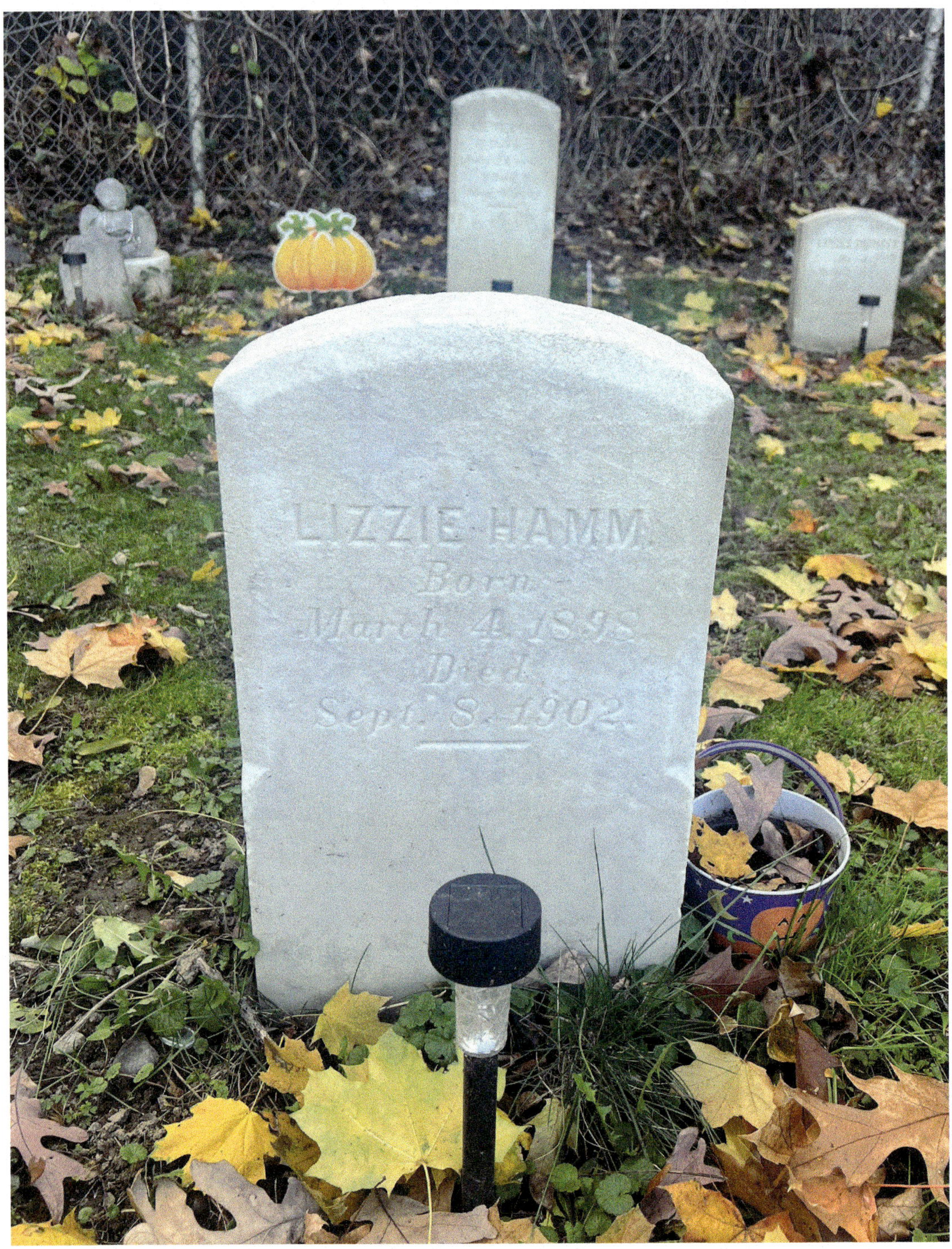

Almost every grave has some kind of decoration or memento left for the dead at Little Lost Cemetery.

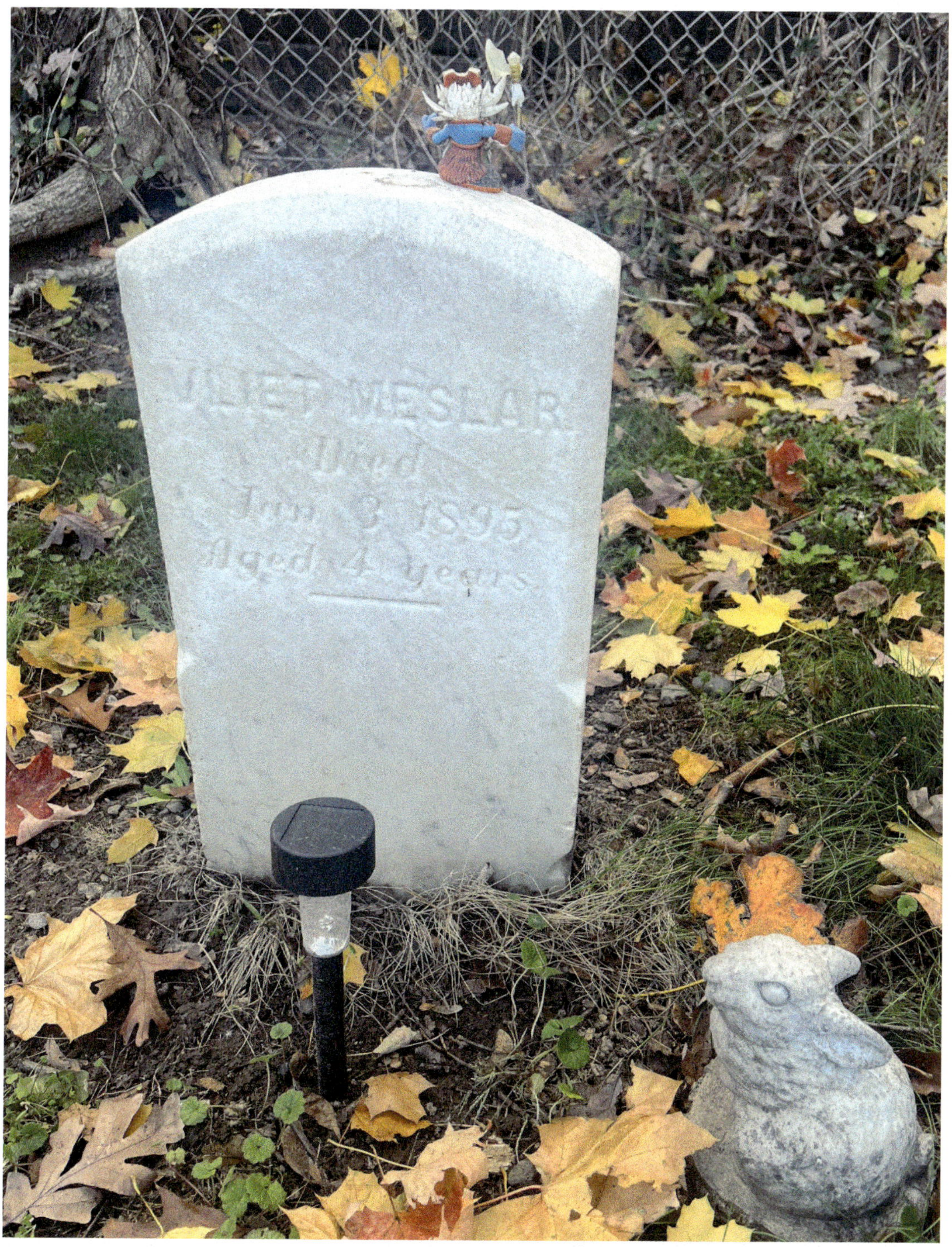

A grave for a four-year-old with a rabbit statue at Little Lost Cemetery.

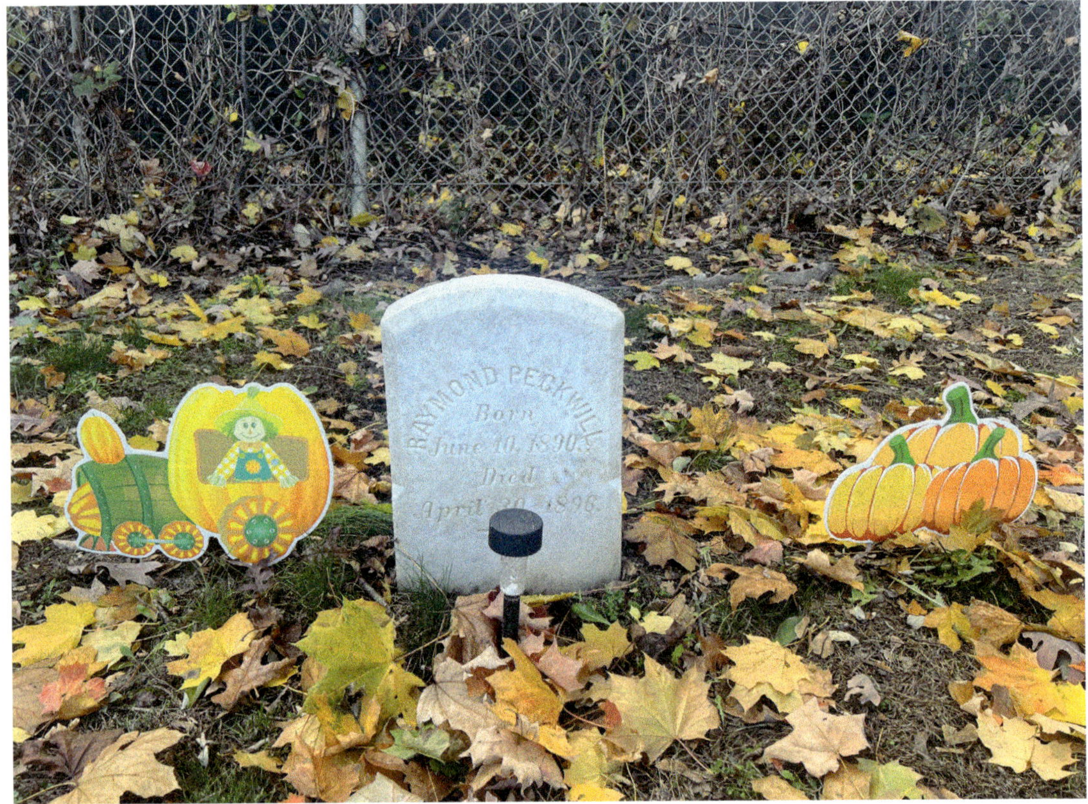

Halloween decorations adorn young Raymond Peckwill's grave.

By the 1970s, most residents of Parsippany-Troy Hills were unaware of the cemetery in their backyard, until the proposed addition of a ramp to expand Interstate Highway 287. The cemetery, which by then was in the backyard of the fire department, was directly in the path of the proposed on-ramp.[12]

The cemetery was revived through the efforts of locals. It is currently protected from northbound traffic by a concrete retaining wall, a guard rail, and a chain-link fence.[13] Fire District Six was instrumental in saving the cemetery.[14] It is currently maintained by private citizens and volunteer firefighters.[15] Local Boy Scout and Girl Scout troops have also helped to maintain the cemetery.[16] Charitable organizations installed new cement stairs and the new headstone listing the known children's names after the restoration efforts were publicized.[17] There have been attempts to record all of the children's names but some of the stones are too eroded to read.[18] The results are nice. It's a peaceful spot next to an incredibly busy highway.

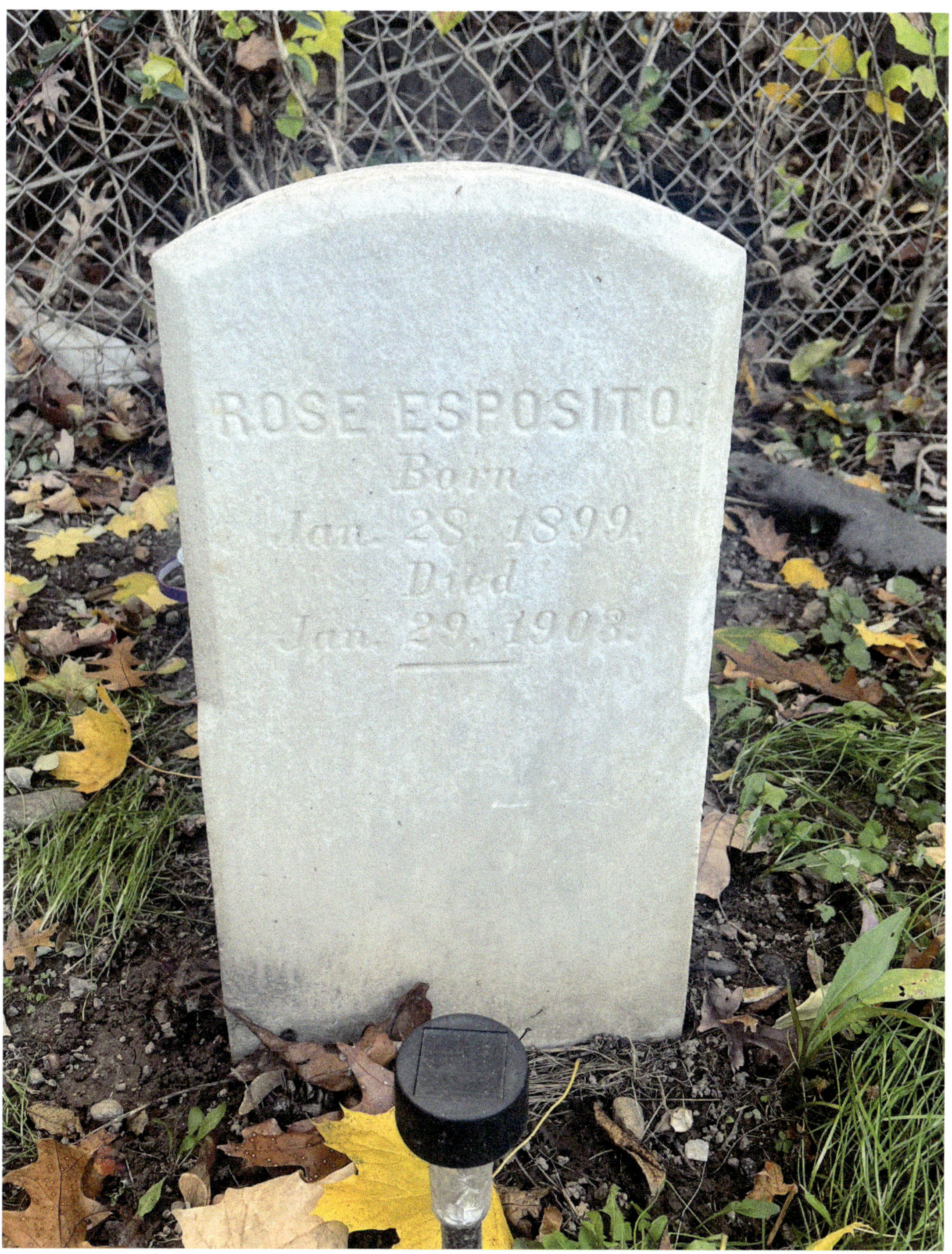

Rose Esposito's grave is close to the retaining wall dividing the cemetery from Interstate 287.

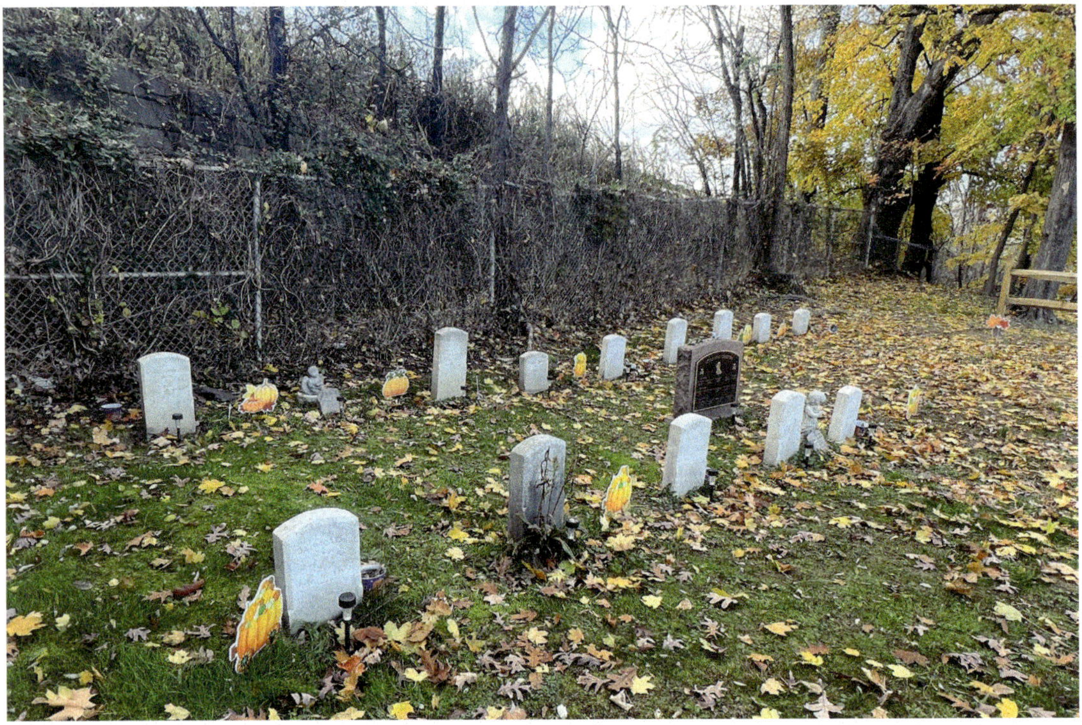

Little Lost Cemetery is very small with only two rows of marked graves.

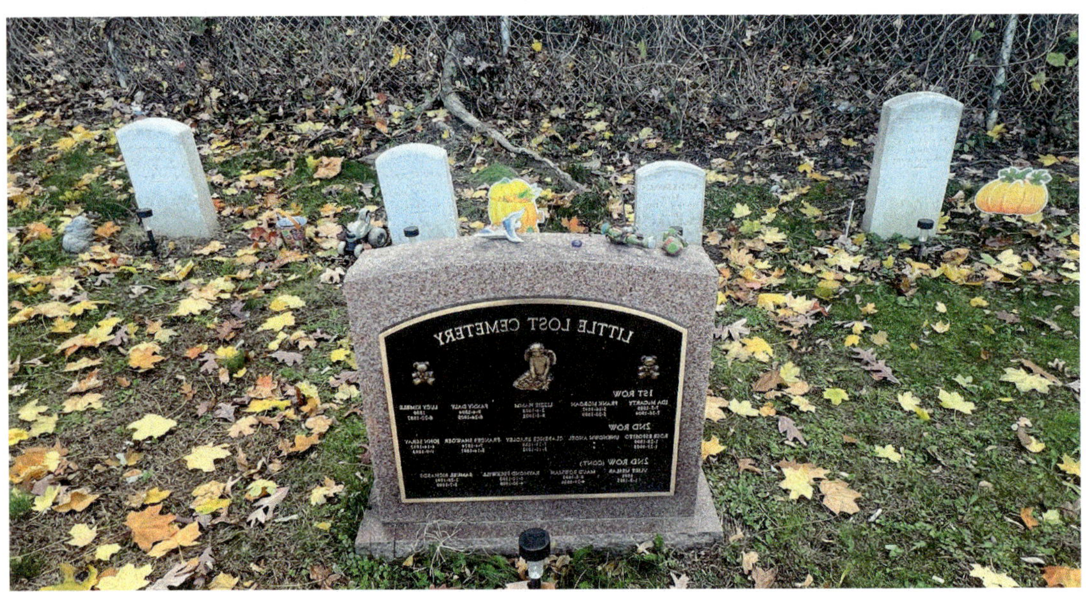

A stone donated by locals that lists all the known burials at Little Lost Cemetery.

This cemetery is straightforward to get to. The address is easy to find, and you don't have to hike or follow GPS coordinates to find it. I had no issue parking in the parking lot behind the firehouse. It's open to the public with the obvious caveat not to disturb the firefighters or firehouse. This would be an ideal destination for someone who is new to cemetery exploring.

2
Mary Ellis Grave

17 US-1, New Brunswick, NJ, 08901

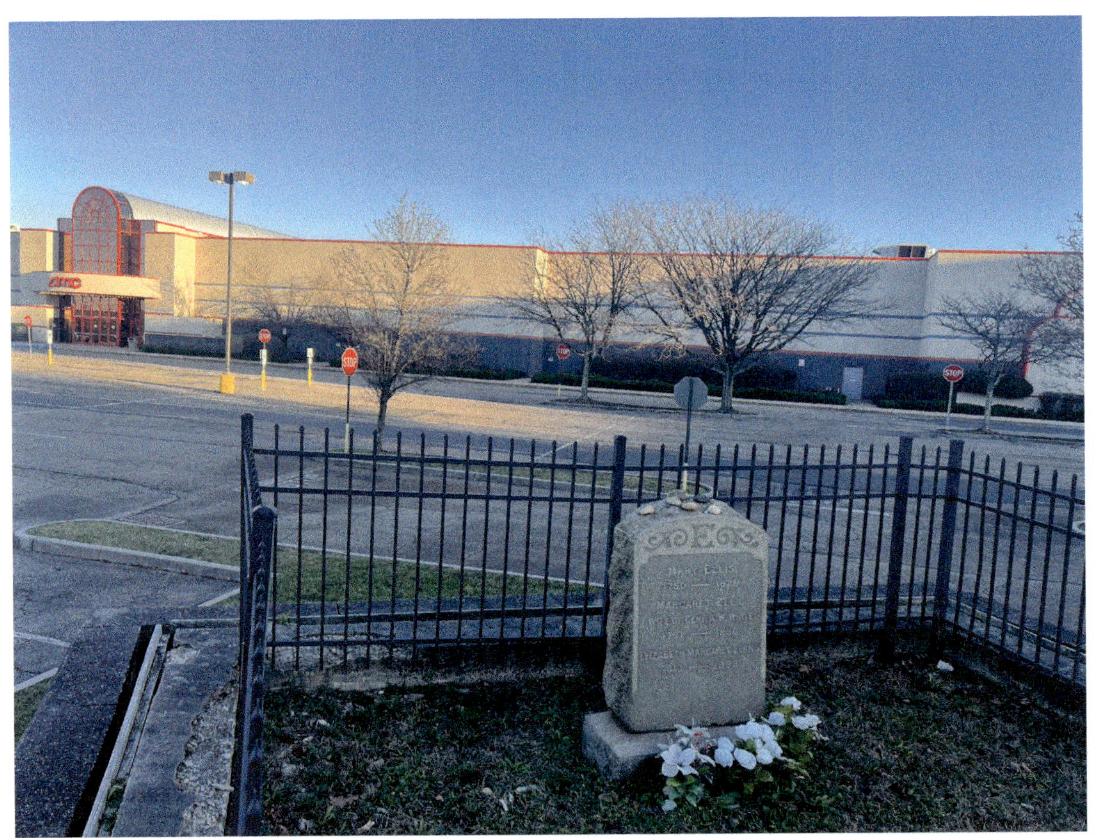

The view of the AMC Theater from the top of Mary Ellis's grave. It's not enough that I had to climb to the top of the retaining wall to get this photograph, it turns out the blocks on the top are also uneven and loose.

Mary Ellis is a New Jersey legend, and in her case, it can be difficult to distinguish fact from fiction. Her grave, which contains Mary Ellis and seven other people, is in the back parking lot of an AMC Theater in New Brunswick. I imagine most theater patrons wouldn't be aware that her grave was there. It's easy to miss unless you park at the very back of the lot. The grave looks like an odd landscaping choice when viewed from the theater. It's elevated over 6 feet above the ground and is surrounded by a retaining wall with an ornate iron fence on top that adds even more height. I climbed the wall to get better pictures of the grave. My boyfriend offered to take the pictures for me. I insisted on taking the pictures myself. I felt like I had to be the one to take the pictures since I would be the one telling Mary's story.

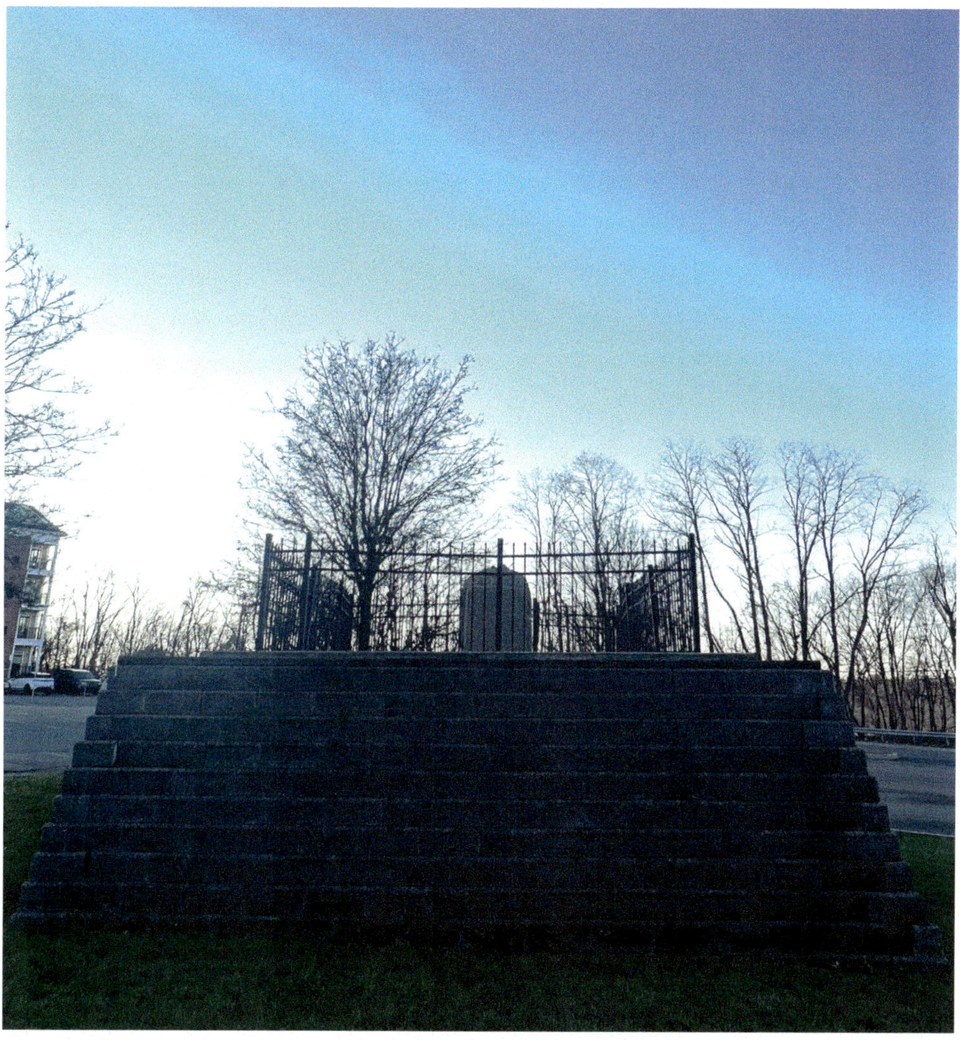

I had to fight the setting sun to get a reasonable picture to show exactly how elevated Mary's grave is. The top left shows a portion of the housing development that now exists on part of what was once the Ellis estate.

There are eight people known to be buried in Mary Ellis' grave, including Mary and possibly one unidentified servant.[1] The original marker is gone.[2] Instead, the grave is marked with a modern stone with seven names.[3] The current fence is a modern addition.[4]

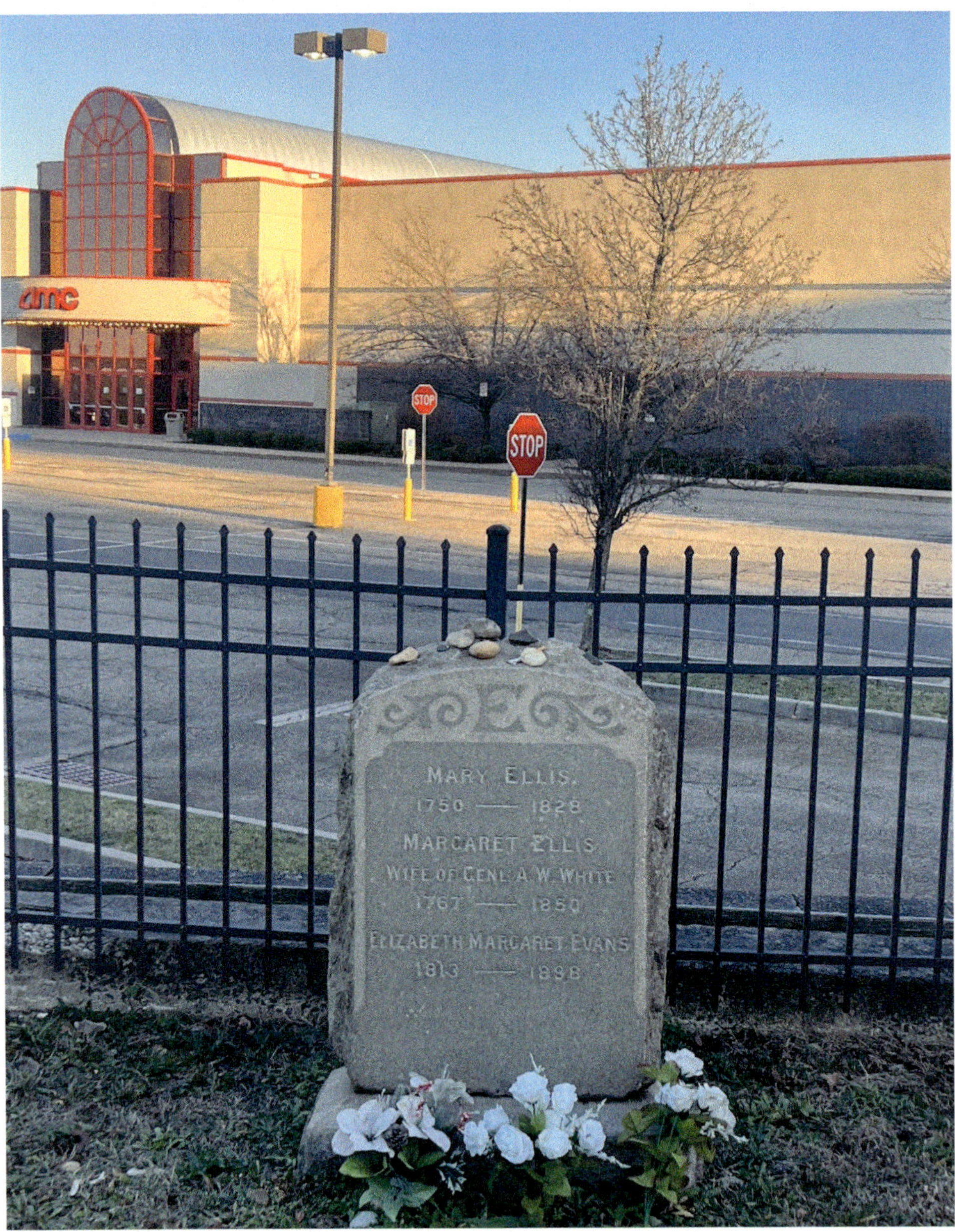

A front view of Mary's grave with three names listed. People are still visiting her grave, as evidenced by the flowers and stones left on top of her headstone.

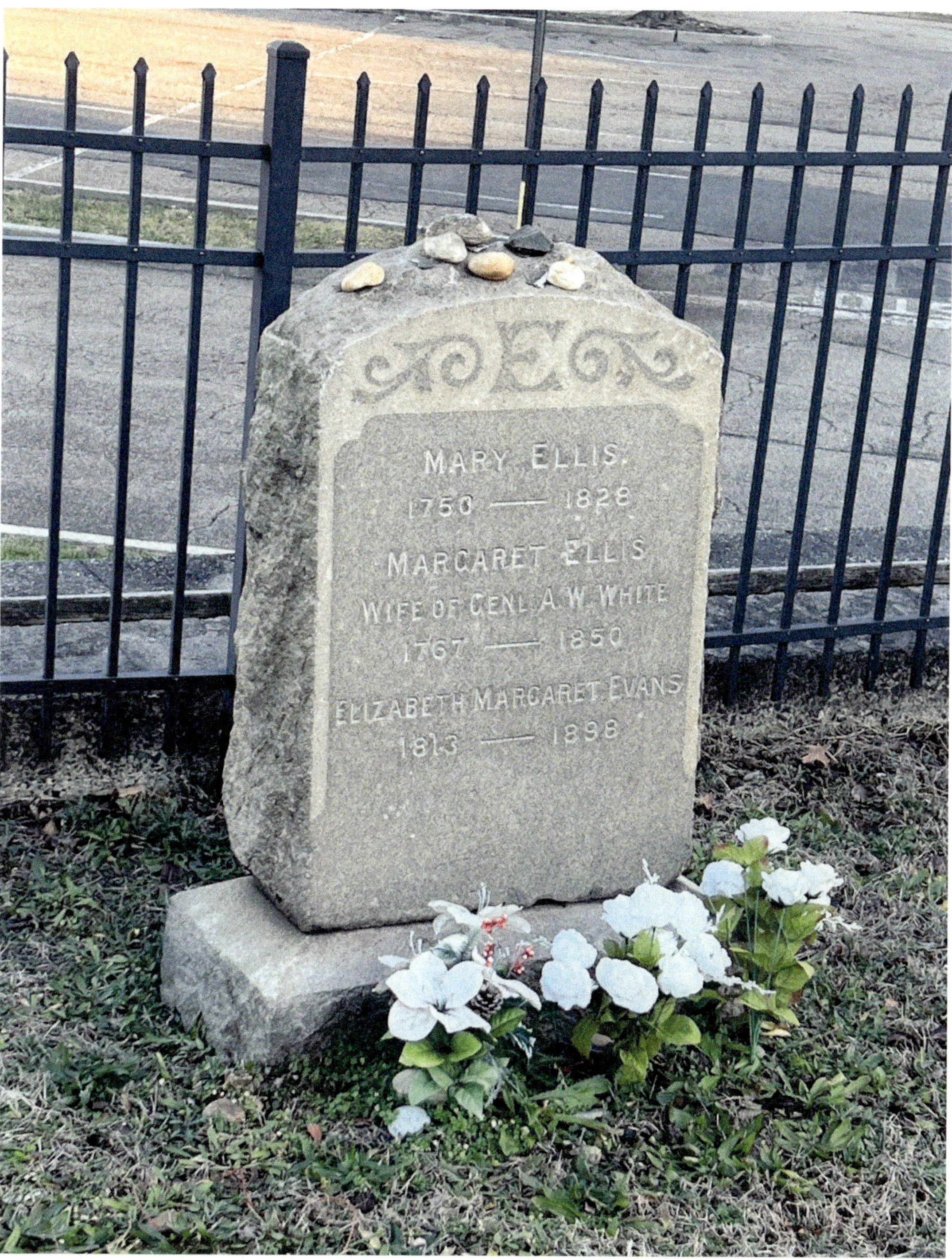

A close-up of the front of Mary's grave, with her sister, Margaret White, and niece, Elizabeth Mary White, engraved on the stone.

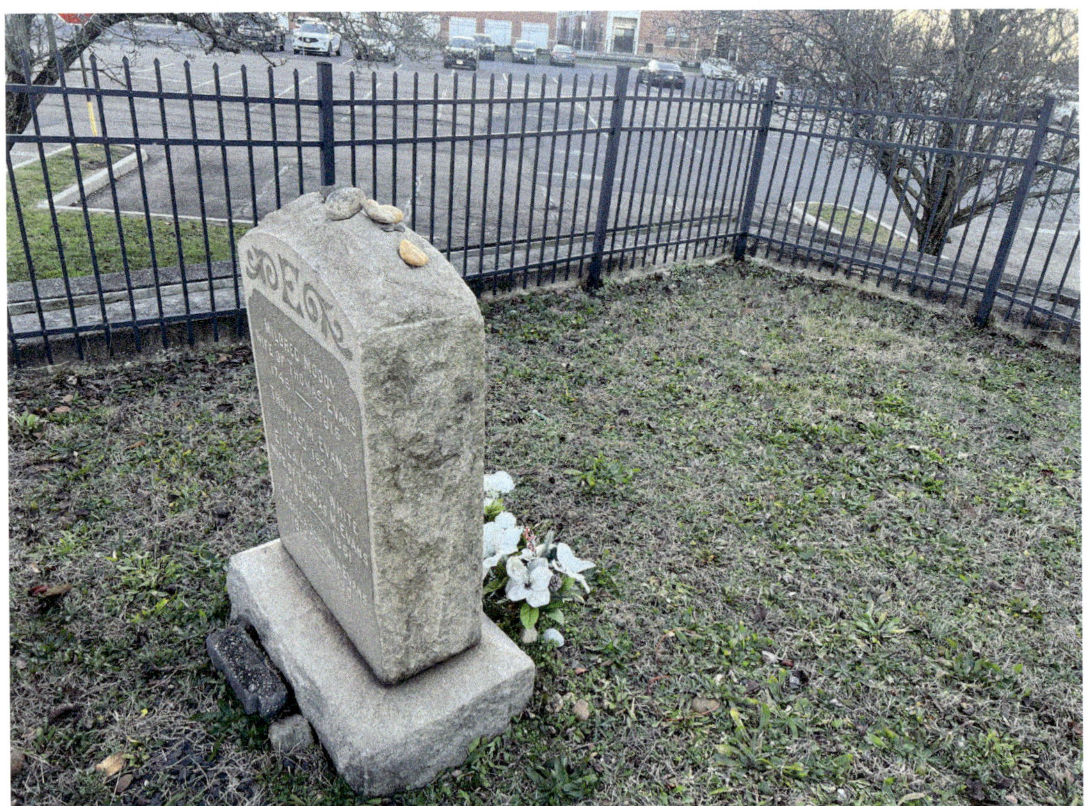

The back of Mary's headstone lists Mildred Moody (only known as a wife of Thomas Evans), Thomas M. Evans (Eliza Mary White's husband), Eliza Mary White, Isabella Johanna Evans (Elizabeth and Thomas's daughter). I had such a hard time getting this photo, as this corner of the wall was particularly treacherous.

Mary Ellis was born in South Carolina in 1750.[5] Mary's parents died when she was very young.[6] In 1784, Mary moved to New Brunswick and lived with her younger sister, Margaret, and her brother-in-law, General Anthony White, at Livingston Street and New Street.[7] General White met Margaret when he was stationed in South Carolina during the Revolutionary War.[8] Mary, who was not married, decided to move to New Brunswick with Margaret when Margaret married.[9] Their home, which was at what is now the site of the George Street Playhouse, was a popular society spot and they hosted George Washington, Alexander Hamilton, and Thaddeus Kosciuszko.[10]

Mary owned land in town and on its outskirts and actively participated in the real estate market by the early nineteenth century.[11] Mary wasn't just a successful businesswoman. Mary voted in almost every city election, over a century before women's suffrage was ratified in the United States, with the approval of local officials who ensured that she was allowed to vote unchallenged.[12, 13] Mary moved with her sister to 100 acres of land near the Raritan River in 1813.[14] This land would eventually become her final resting ground.[15]

Burial in a church graveyard would have been considered a standard practice when Mary died but Mary wasn't devout. Mary Ellis had an important, personal reason to choose burial on private property. The inviolate nature of the grave is a very recent concept. In the late eighteenth and early nineteenth century, there were growing concerns about overcrowding and the security of burial yards, especially in the growing cities of America's East Coast.[16] The possibility of burial grounds being moved, abandoned, or vandalized were legitimate concerns of the time.[17] Mary was upset when she happened to witness the disinterment of bodies from a cemetery that was being moved to make way for city construction, and wanted a burial spot that would never be disturbed.[18] Mary purposely chose an isolated burial ground where she was sure this could never happen.[19, 20] Mary's niece had her buried overlooking the Raritan River on her own property in accordance with these wishes.[21, 22] Mary's burial spot is allegedly on a Lenni Lenape burial mound.[23] *The New Brunswick City Directory 1855–1856* references the possibility of her burial site being on top of a Lenni Lenape burial mound: "Among the strange places in the vicinity, and one that has excited as much interest as any other, except the Mine Hole, in the Northern part of the city, is the Indian Mound, on the farm of Mrs. Evans, in the middle of which, by her own request, Miss Ellis was buried."[24]

The gravesite was described as wooded until the mid-twentieth century.[25] It is unclear exactly when Mary's gravesite became commercial property.[26] By 1943, John Burke Sr. had acquired the Evans's property which was the site of Raritan Playland Amusement Park until 1955.[27] In 1965, the Burke family built the Great Eastern Discount Center on the property.[28] Construction for the department store left a 20-foot-deep pit where Mary's grave was.[29] Burke Sr. wanted to move the eight graves but discovered that he needed written permission from all surviving heirs to move the graves.[30] All surviving heirs currently have the right to enter the property and tend the grave.[31]

The Burke family were the first people to enclose the grave with retaining walls.[32] Four concrete walls were built around the grave and monument when the 15-acre site was filled during the construction of the Great Eastern Discount Center.[33] By 1966, the grave remained in the center of the parking lot.[34] The grave was protected from public view by the cement walls with a wire fence on the top.[35]

The retaining walls were soon filled with garbage.[36] In 1975, the Route 1 Flea Market opened on the property.[37] The pit with Mary's grave was cleaned when the flea market first opened but the grave was overgrown and filled with garbage again within a year.[38] Burke said, "It was a garbage dump instead of a place of reverence for the dead."[39]

In July 1980, John Burke Jr. and Ray Travis, who was in charge of the Route 1 Flea Market, decided to fill the retaining walls with dirt.[40] According to Mickula's 2005 *Report for the Cultural Resource Consulting Group*, filling the pit with earth actually raised the grave 6 feet above the level of the parking lot, instead of just raising the grave to ground level. With the pit filled, Burke and Travis planned to landscape the dirt around the grave.[41]

The flea market was demolished by the early 1990s. The property eventually became a Loews Cineplex and is currently an AMC Theater. The parking lot was regraded, making the grave even taller than the surrounding parking lot. The current retaining wall and trees near the grave are new.[42]

There are the facts of Mary's life and death, and the facts about where her grave stands, but there's also a legend about her life and this is where the record becomes unclear. Mary was unmarried when she moved to New Jersey with her younger sister.

In the 1790s, Mary was rumored to have fallen in love with a sea captain and former Revolutionary War officer.[43] His identity is unknown. Mary never wed because she was waiting for the sea captain to return.[44] Mary's story is believed to be the inspiration for the song "Brandy (You're a Fine Girl)" by the band Looking Glass.[45] Looking Glass denies this, although the band was formed at Rutgers–New Brunswick and there's a good chance they heard the story of Mary Ellis.[46]

This grave is easy to find. It's very high (I would estimate over 6 feet above the parking lot) and is surrounded by landscaped grass. The wall surrounding it is almost vertical. I would urge against climbing it for your personal safety and to maintain the integrity of the retaining wall.

3
Mount Pleasant Cemetery

375 Broadway, Newark, N.J., 07104

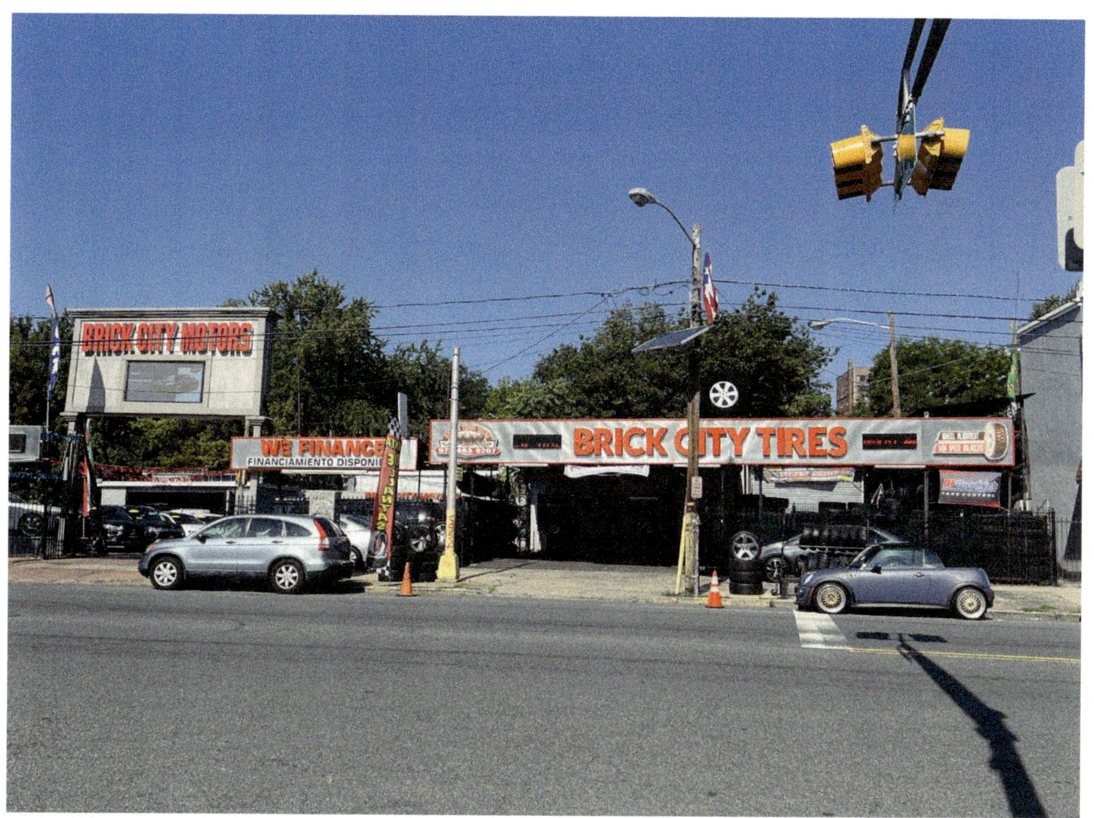

The view from across Mount Pleasant Cemetery. There's also an elementary school next to the cemetery. The neighborhood is very busy although it was remote when the cemetery was built.

Mount Pleasant Cemetery is a hidden gem located in the North Ward of Newark, N.J. It's next to an elementary school and has multiple used car dealerships and auto body shops across the street from it. When you step through the gates that are very similar in style to Green-Wood Cemetery in Brooklyn, it's like being transported into a park. There is a small spot to park inside the cemetery if you decide to drive here. I have a soft spot for Newark since I've lived here for the last twenty years. There's so much beautiful architecture and culture that most people don't know about, especially if you only pay attention to the sensationalist news about the city. This is worth a visit for any taphophile.

Mt. Pleasant Cemetery was originally built for the city's elites.[1] Burial at Mount Pleasant in the 1840s was a way to measure social status.[2] The cemetery consists of 36 acres of land extending from Broadway at its western boundary that extends almost to the Passaic River.[3] The cemetery was on the city's outskirts when it was originally built.[4]

On December 6, 1843, Horace E. Baldwin convened a small group of Newarkers regarding a proposal for a rural cemetery in Newark.[5] A committee was formed to purchase land, obtain subscriptions for the sale of lots, and seek incorporation.[6]

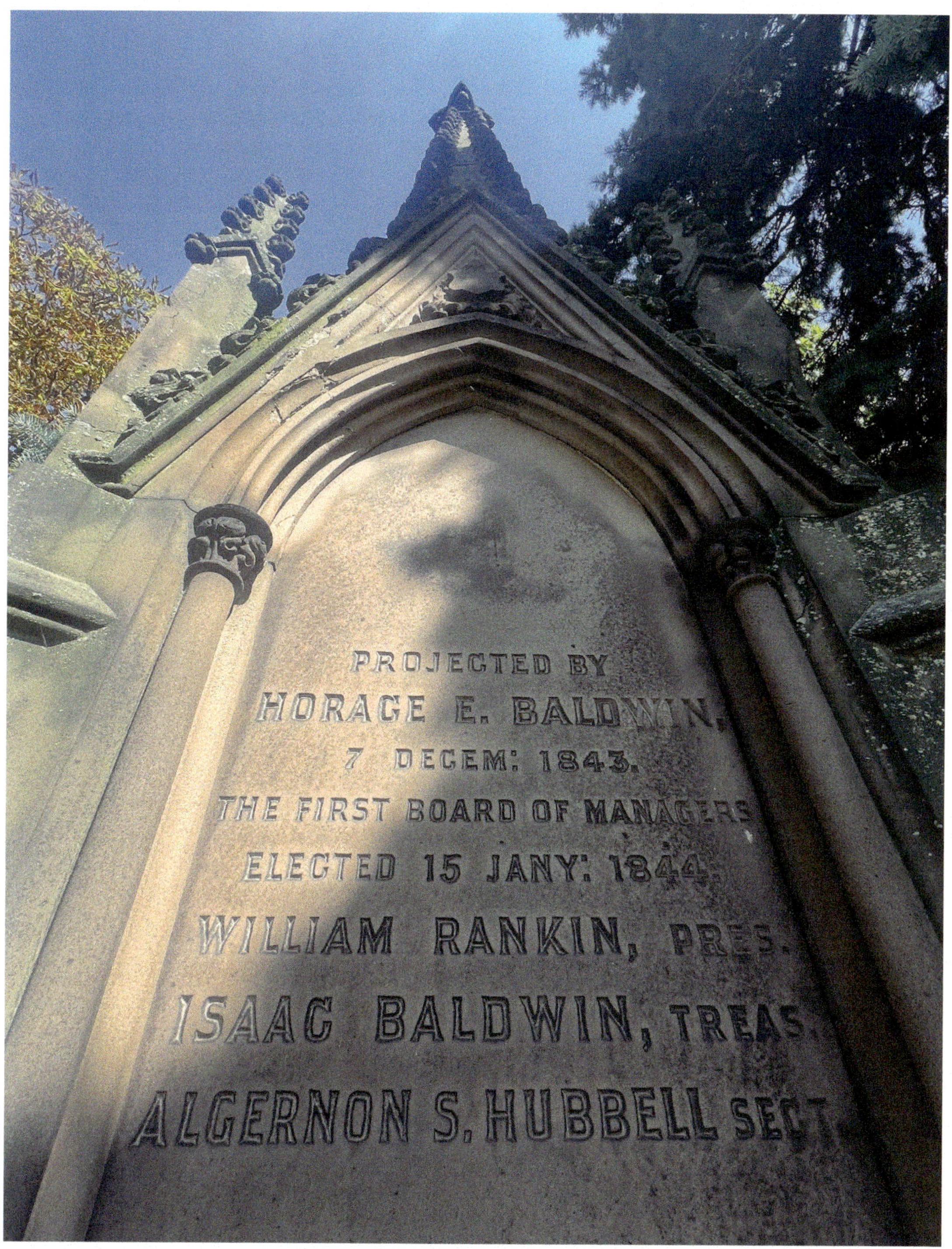

The plaque dedicated to the founders of Mount Pleasant Cemetery.

Mount Pleasant Cemetery was never meant to be just for the dead; Mount Pleasant was meant for the living to enjoy picnics, carriage rides, summer outings, and viewing the Passaic River Regatta.[7] In the nineteenth century, many progressive community members promoted the creation of large, well-landscaped cemeteries outside of city limits.[8] Mount Pleasant was inspired by Mount Auburn Cemetery in Boston (1831) and Green-Wood Cemetery in Brooklyn (1838), two early examples of rural cemeteries in America.[9]

It helps to understand the rural cemetery movement of the nineteenth century if you want to understand the history of Mount Pleasant Cemetery. City graveyards in the nineteenth century were unsightly, crowded, and a hazard to public health.[10] A rural cemetery is a burial ground on the outskirts of a city designed following conventions of a picturesque style of gardening.[11] Rural cemeteries differed from the traditional church burial grounds because they were planned, followed a grid system, had deliberate landscaping choices, and were larger than a church burial ground. Rural cemeteries began to replace urban graveyards and churchyards in the nineteenth century.[12]

The rural cemetery was meant to be a place for the dead to rest and the living to enjoy the beautiful setting.[13] One thing to remember is that the mortality rate was higher then and that death was viewed as a normal part of life. People died at home and had funeral services at home. There wasn't this disconnect between life and death that exists in the modern world. Many families came regularly for social outings at most rural cemeteries.[14]

The grouping of graves into family plots was an important feature of rural cemeteries that impacted monument design.[15] Colonial cemeteries tend to be very chaotic. Two people in a family could be buried together, but when the next death occurred years later, all the graves near their family could be occupied, which led to family burials being scattered around the cemetery based on whatever space was available at the time.

Mount Pleasant Cemetery was incorporated on January 24, 1844, and officially dedicated on June 18, 1844.[16] In 1877, a new entrance gateway was designed and constructed by architect Thomas Slent.[17] This gate is the current one standing.[18] The north wing of the gate had the keeper's residence and the south wing had offices and a reception room.[19] A Victorian gothic receiving vault was also constructed.[20] A receiving vault is a temporary vault meant to held casketed remains, usually in wintertime when the ground was frozen back when graves were dug by hand.

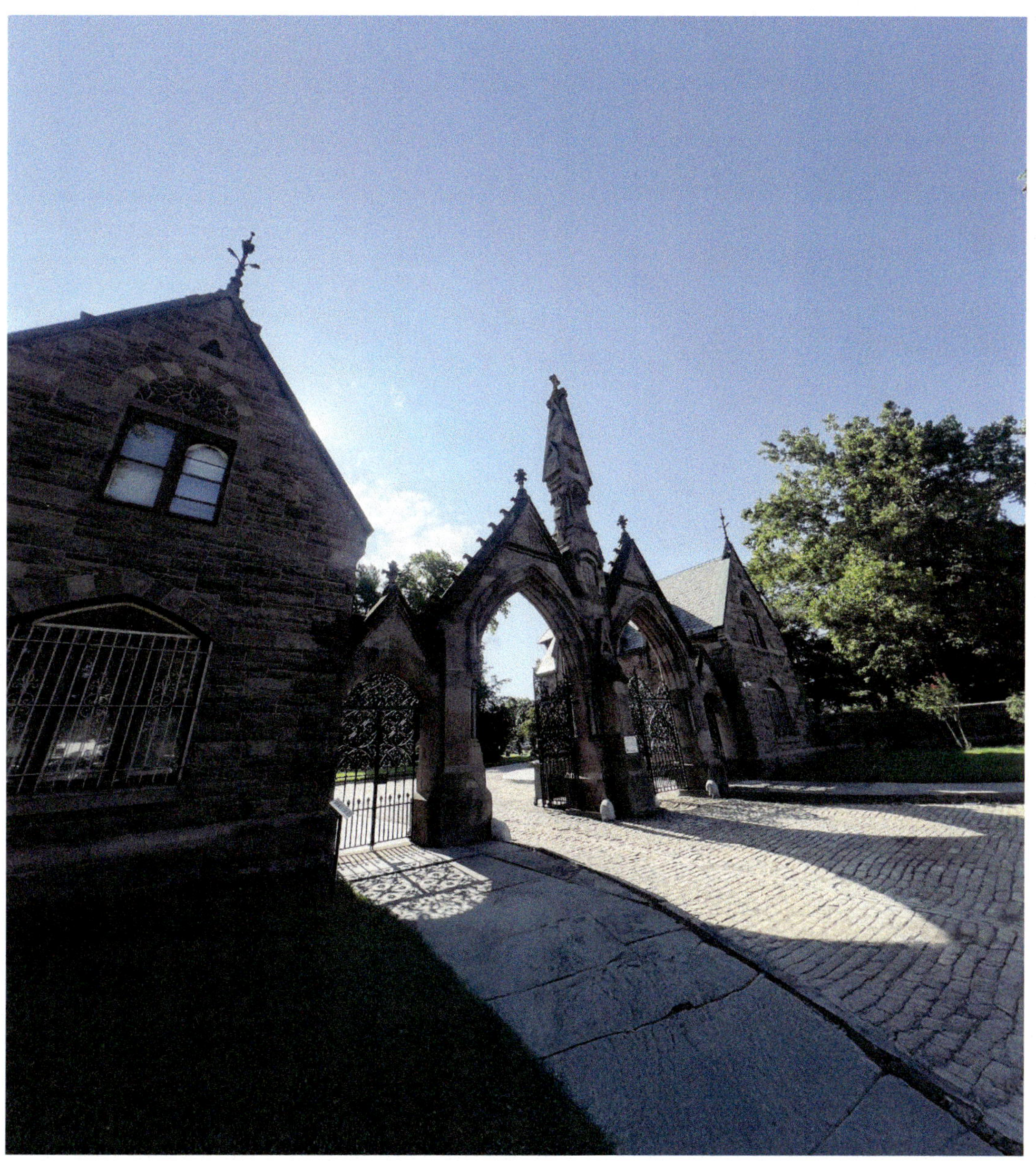

The gates to Mount Pleasant Cemetery. They resemble a smaller version of the gates at Green-Wood.

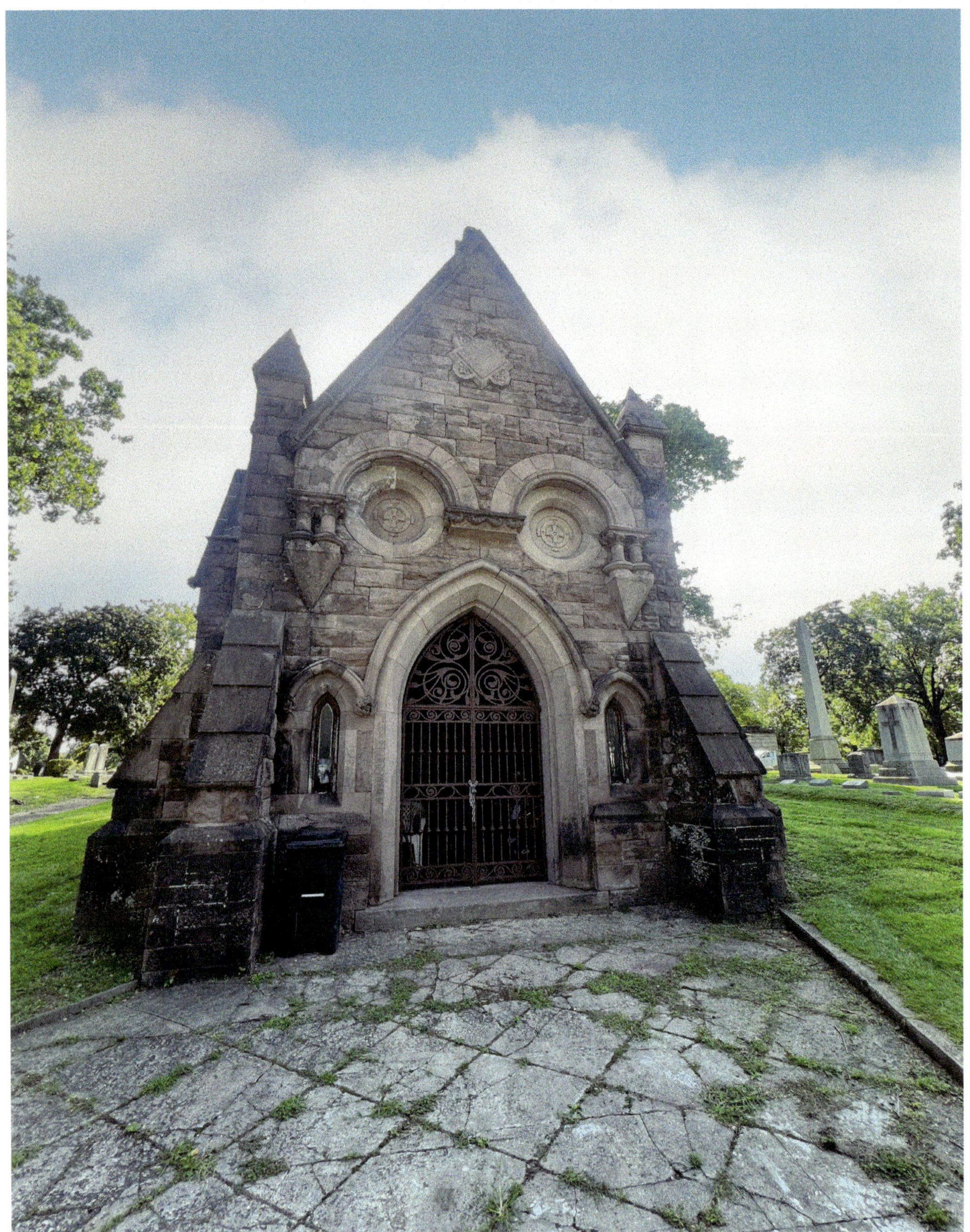

The Victorian Gothic receiving vault at Mount Pleasant Cemetery. I peeked inside and it looked like it's currently being used for storage.

The oldest graves at Mount Pleasant Cemetery are for those who died before Mount Pleasant opened.[21] As older graveyards in downtown Newark closed due to urban expansion, bodies and stones were moved to Mount Pleasant.[22] Mary Ellis was right to be concerned. In 1959, the Old First Presbyterian Church burial ground was converted to a parking lot and bones that were recovered from there that were thought to be from the Kinney family vault were reinterred in the Kinney plot.[23]

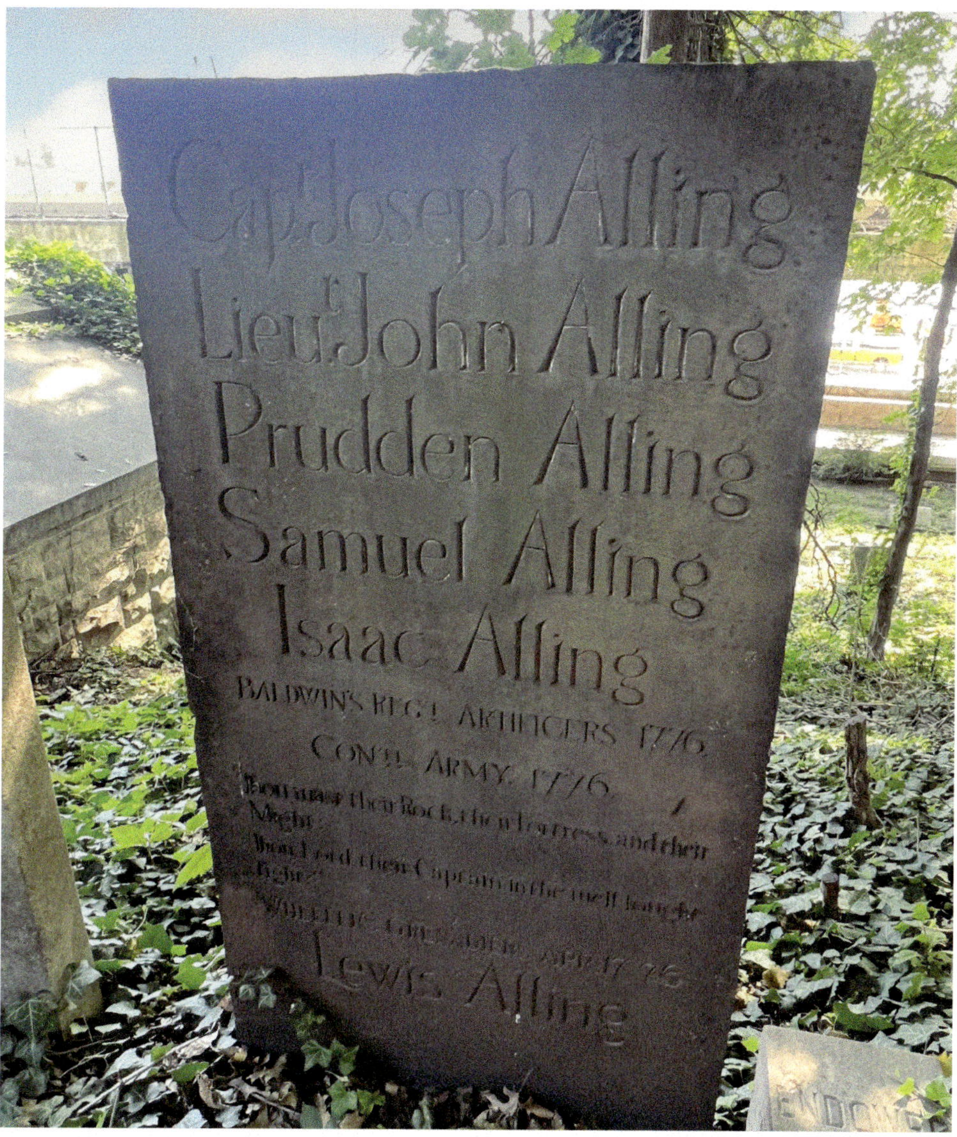

One of the oldest stones in the cemetery is for Captain Joseph Alling, Lieutenant John Alling, and Prudden, Samuel, and Isaac Alling. They weren't originally buried at Mount Pleasant Cemetery.

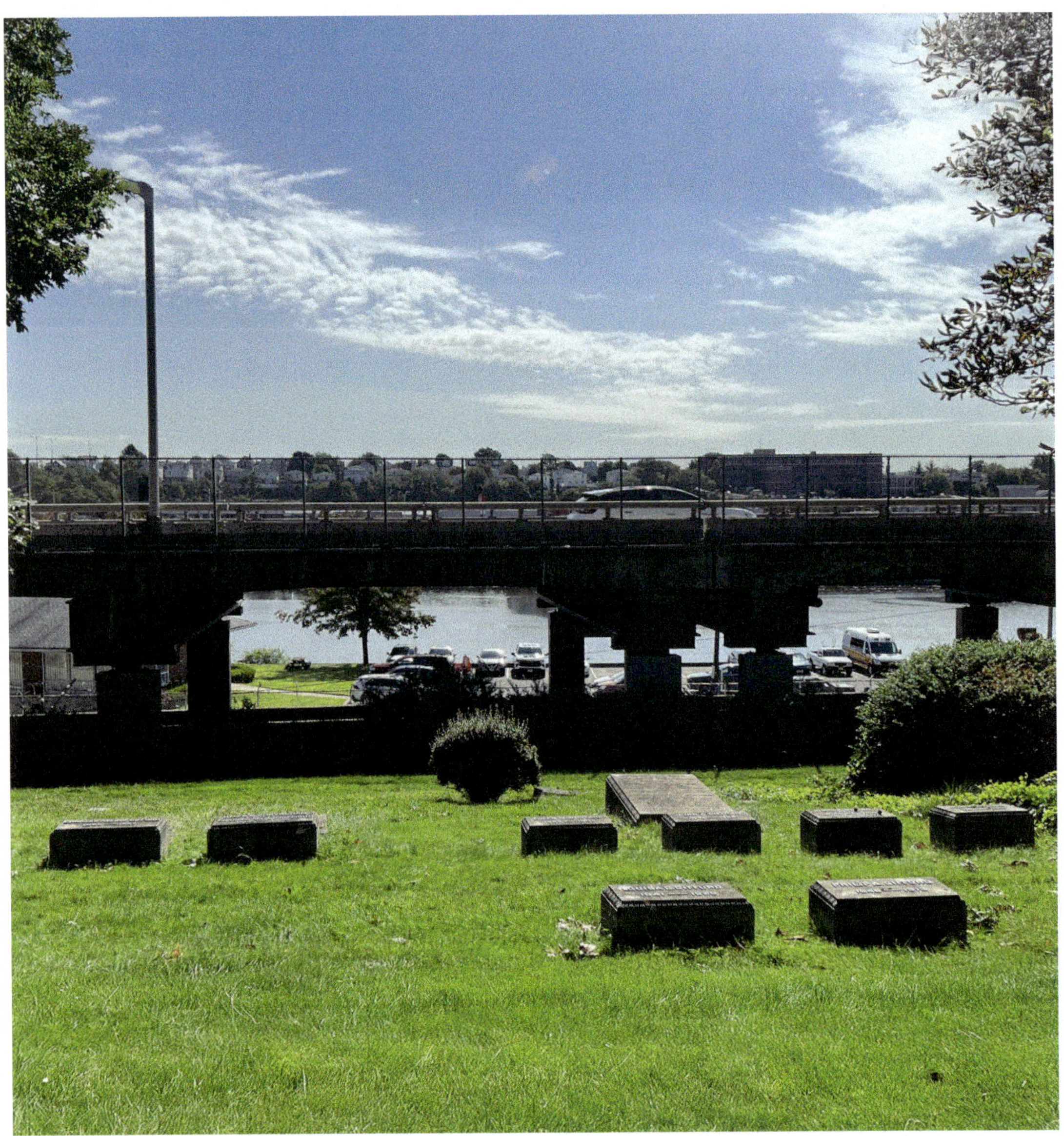

The view from Mount Pleasant Cemetery facing the Passaic River, with McCarter Highway. I never paid attention to how close the cemetery was to the Passaic River until I visited it for this project. It's easy to see why it was such a choice spot for people to watch the Passaic River Regatta.

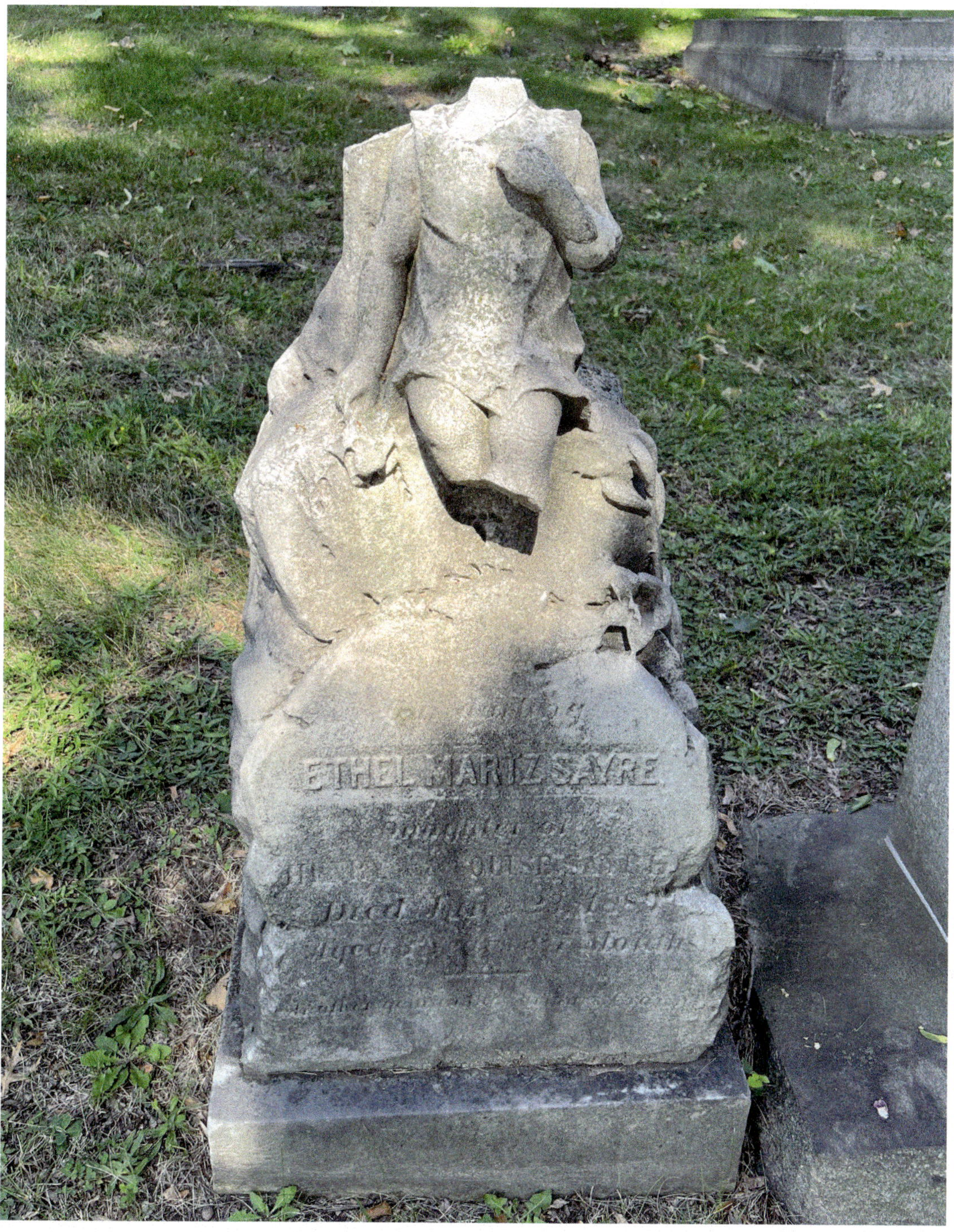

Many urban cemeteries reflect the economic upturns and downturns of their cities and Mount Pleasant Cemetery is no exception. It's unclear if this monument was purposely vandalized or succumbed to time and the elements.

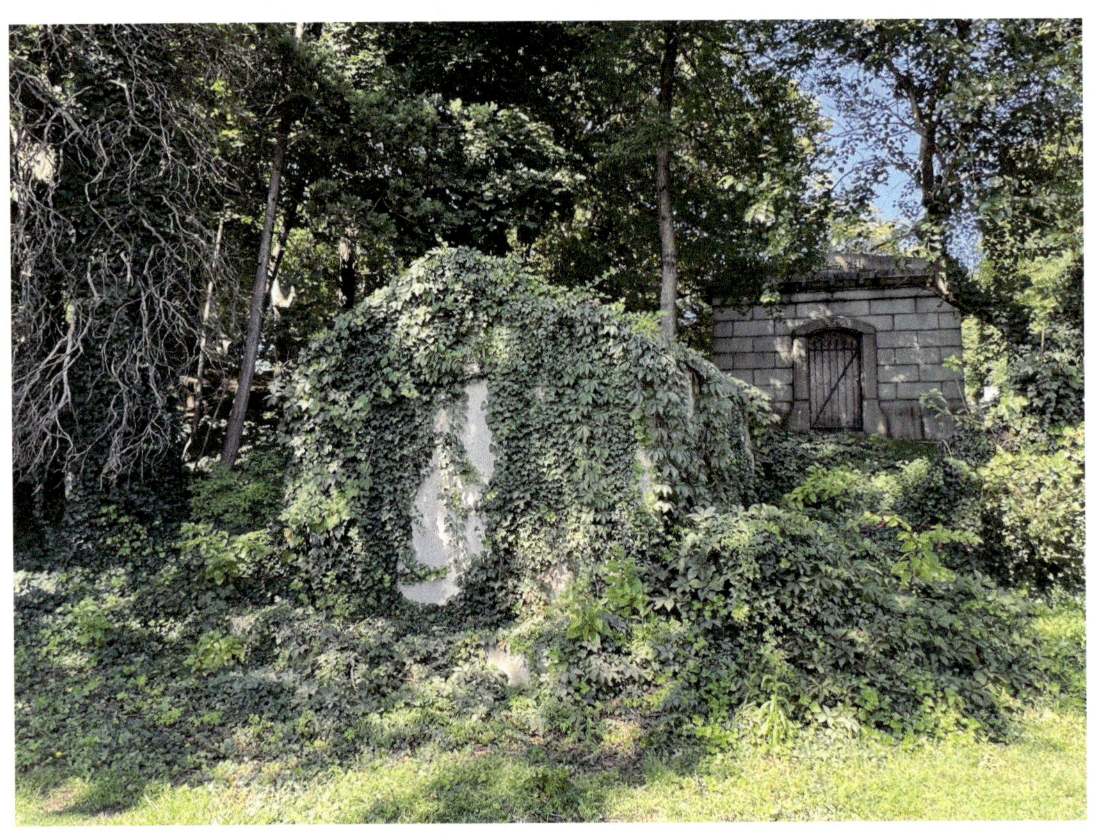

A mausoleum at Mount Pleasant Cemetery being overtaken by nature.

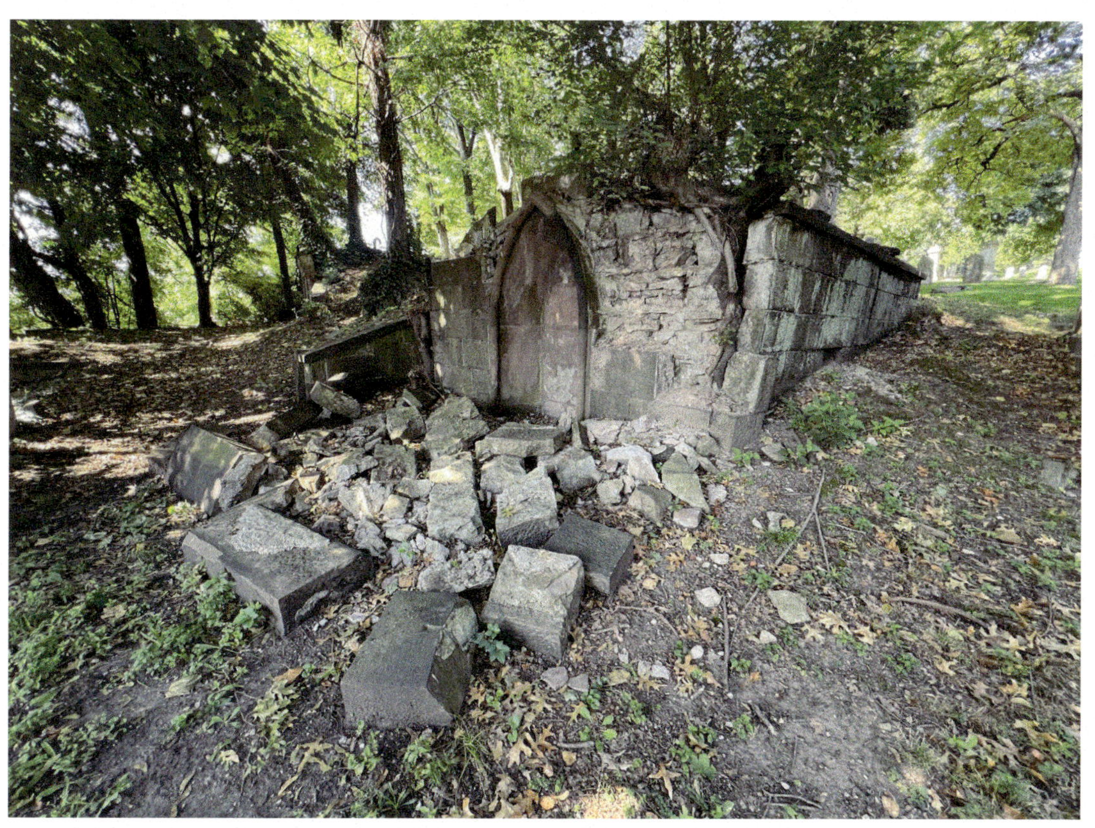

Another crumbling mausoleum at Mount Pleasant Cemetery.

The large amounts of space in rural cemeteries led to monument styles that would be impossible in crowded churchyards.[24] Monument styles at Mount Pleasant range from Gothic, Romanesque, Egyptian, Renaissance, Baroque, and Neoclassical revivals.[25] The obelisk was prominent in Egyptian and Roman times and was revived in the eighteenth century.[26]

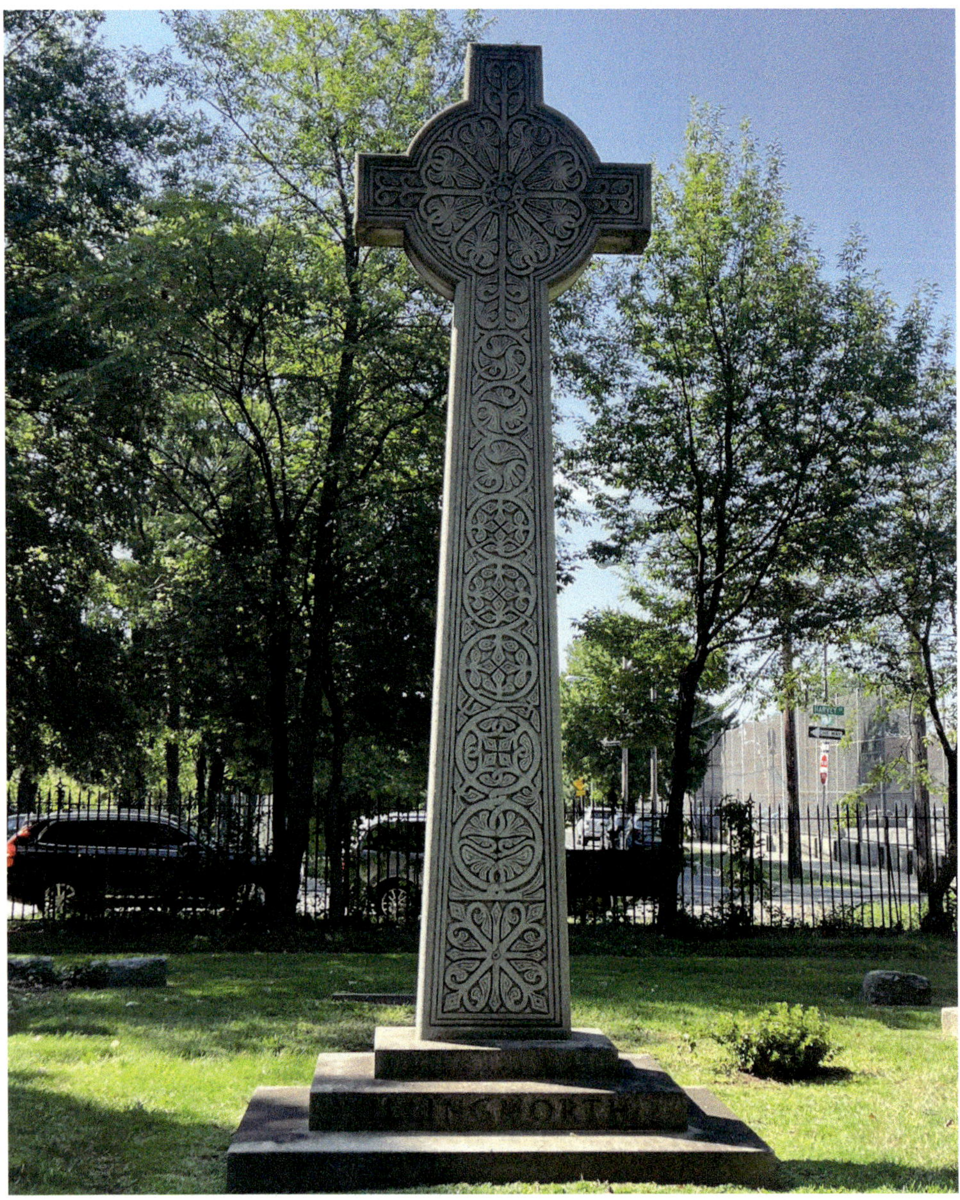

A cross-style monument for the Illingworth family.

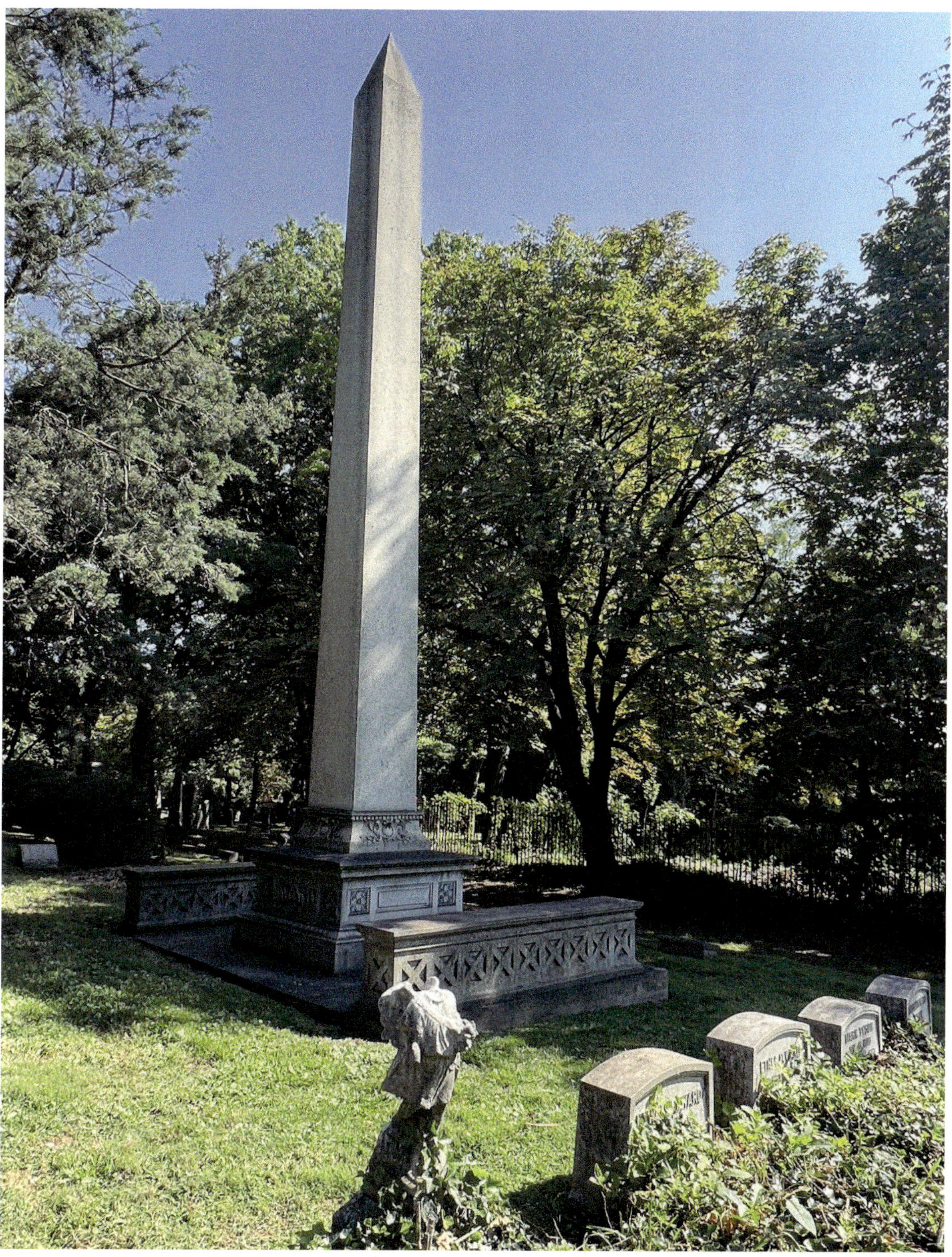

An obelisk for the Ward family features a mixture of ancient Egyptian and Greek elements.

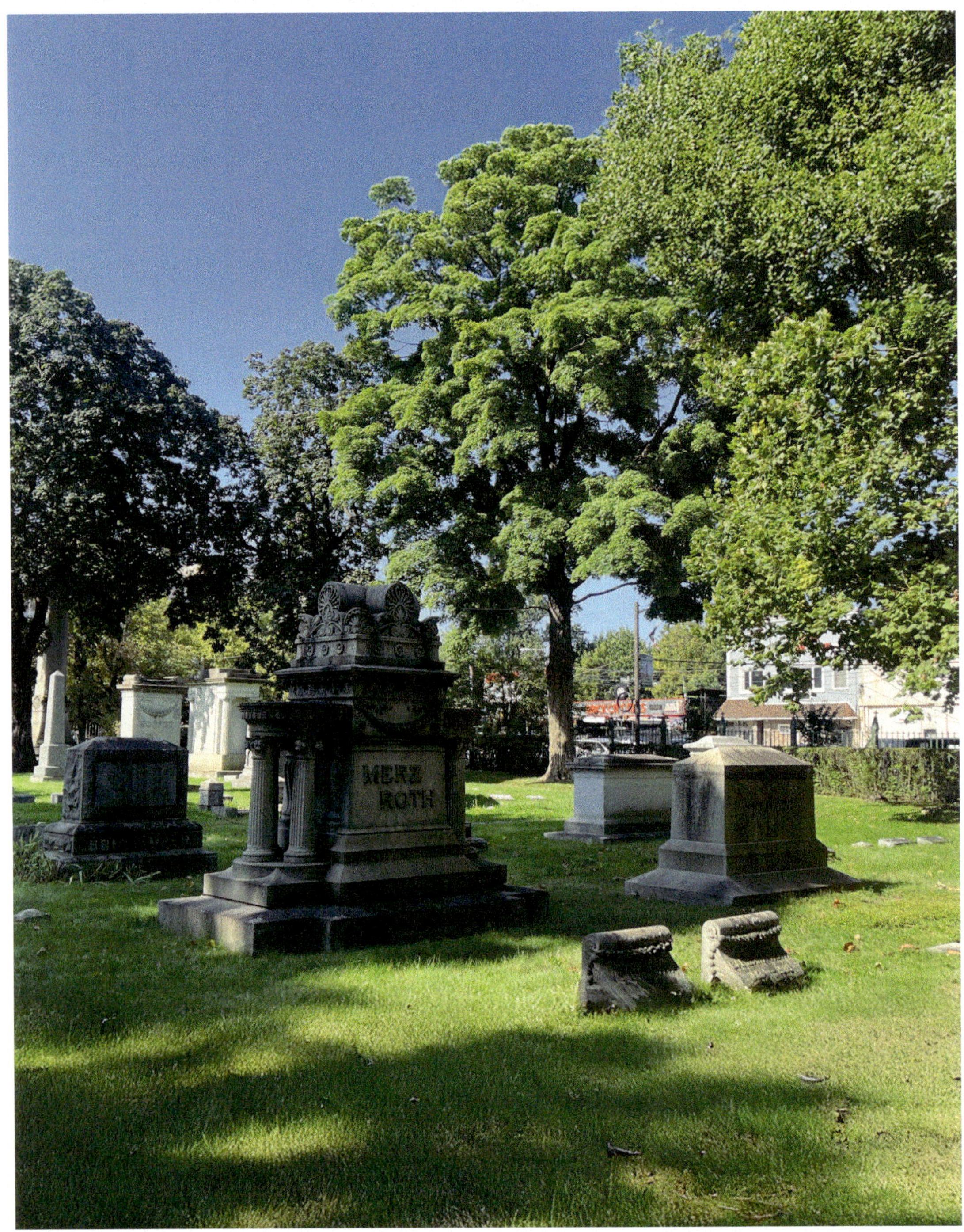

The Merz Roth monument is an example of a family monument that identifies which family is buried there. It's possible that there are multiple burials in that plot without each burial having an individual stone. The monument reflects the popular Victorian Neoclassical revival.

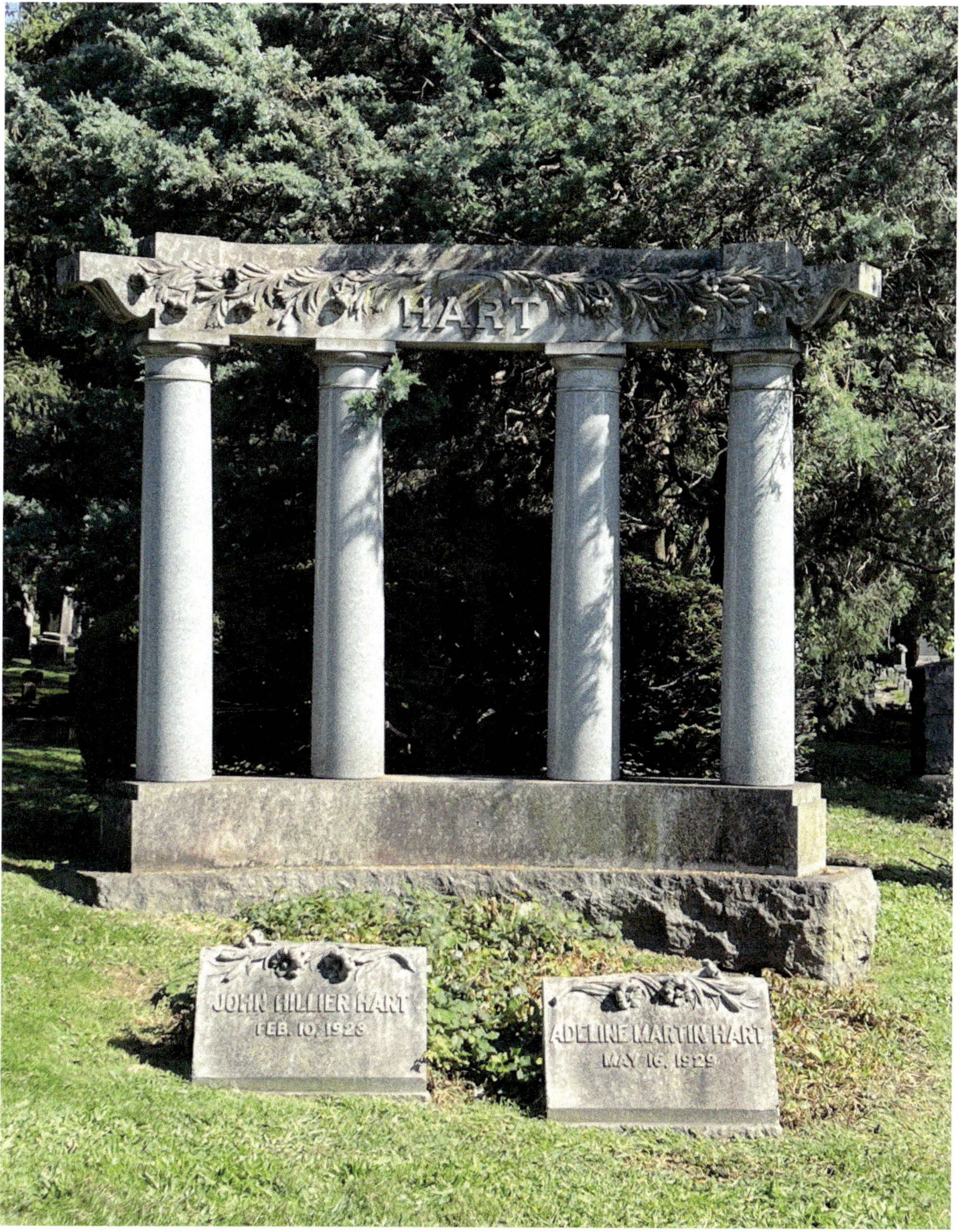

The Hart monument is an example of the Greek Neoclassical revival at Mount Pleasant Cemetery. One main monument displays the family name, while leaving room for multiple members of the family to be buried in the same plot. This would have been impossible in a colonial churchyard.

The mausoleum reemerged in popularity as part of the Neoclassical revival.[27] The very wealthy had mausoleums with bronze doors and stained-glass windows built in mausoleum row.[28] John Dryden, the first president of Prudential Insurance Company, has the largest mausoleum in the cemetery.[29]

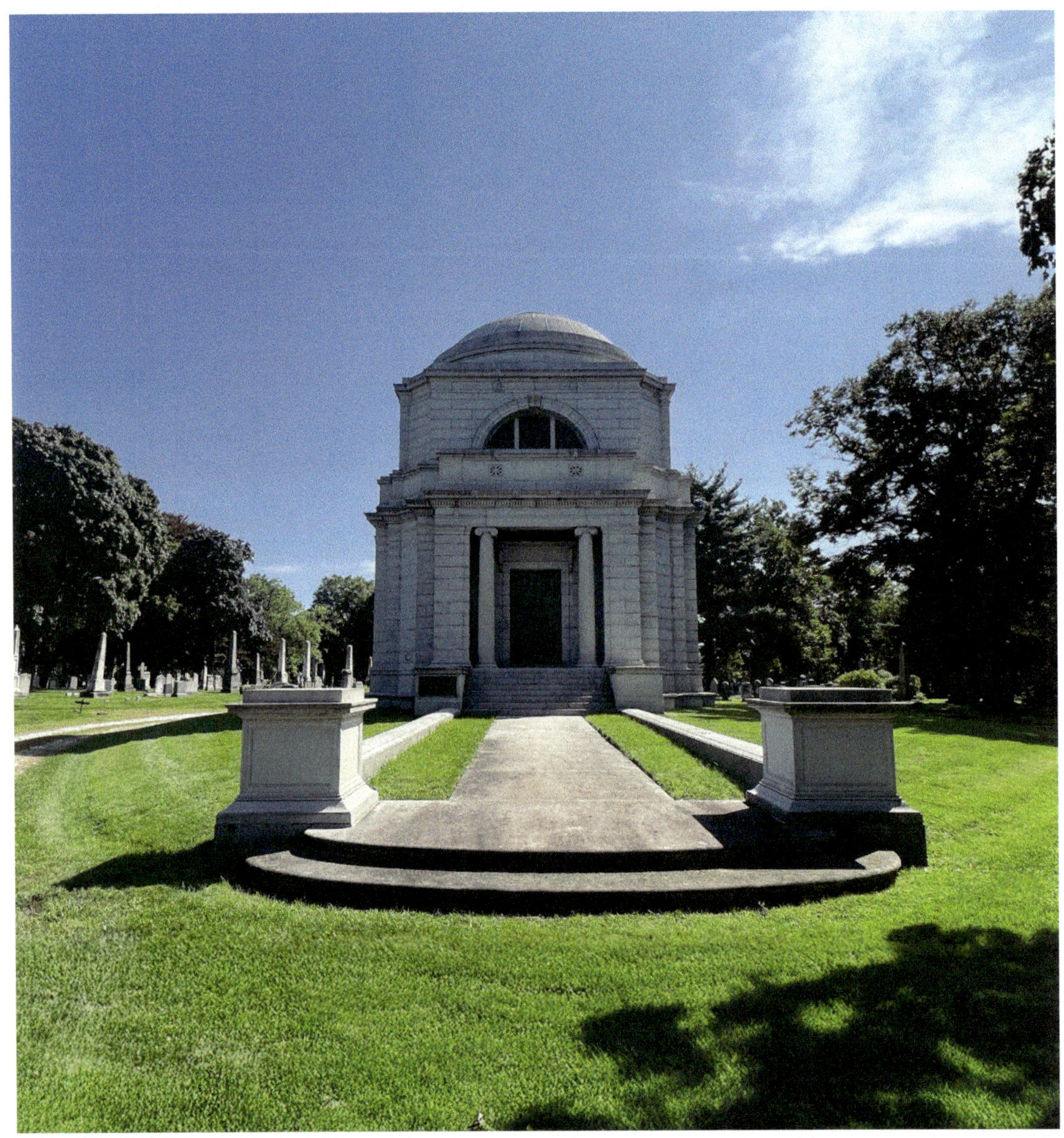

The Dryden mausoleum, built for John F. Dryden (1839–1911), former U.S. senator and the founder of Prudential Insurance Company. This is the largest mausoleum in Mount Pleasant Cemetery.

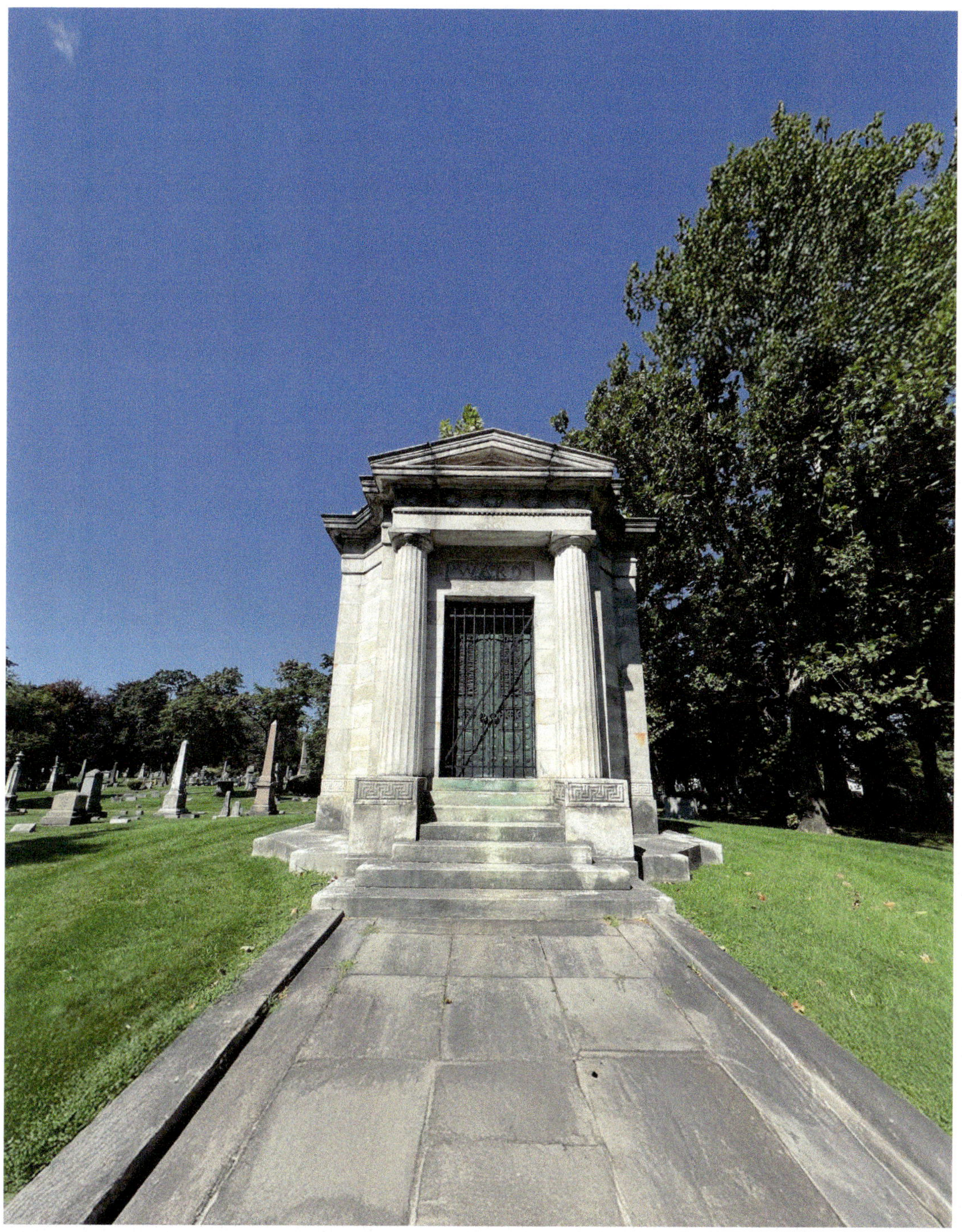

The Ward mausoleum was built for Dr. Leslie D. Ward (1845–1910), who built the first hospital in Newark.

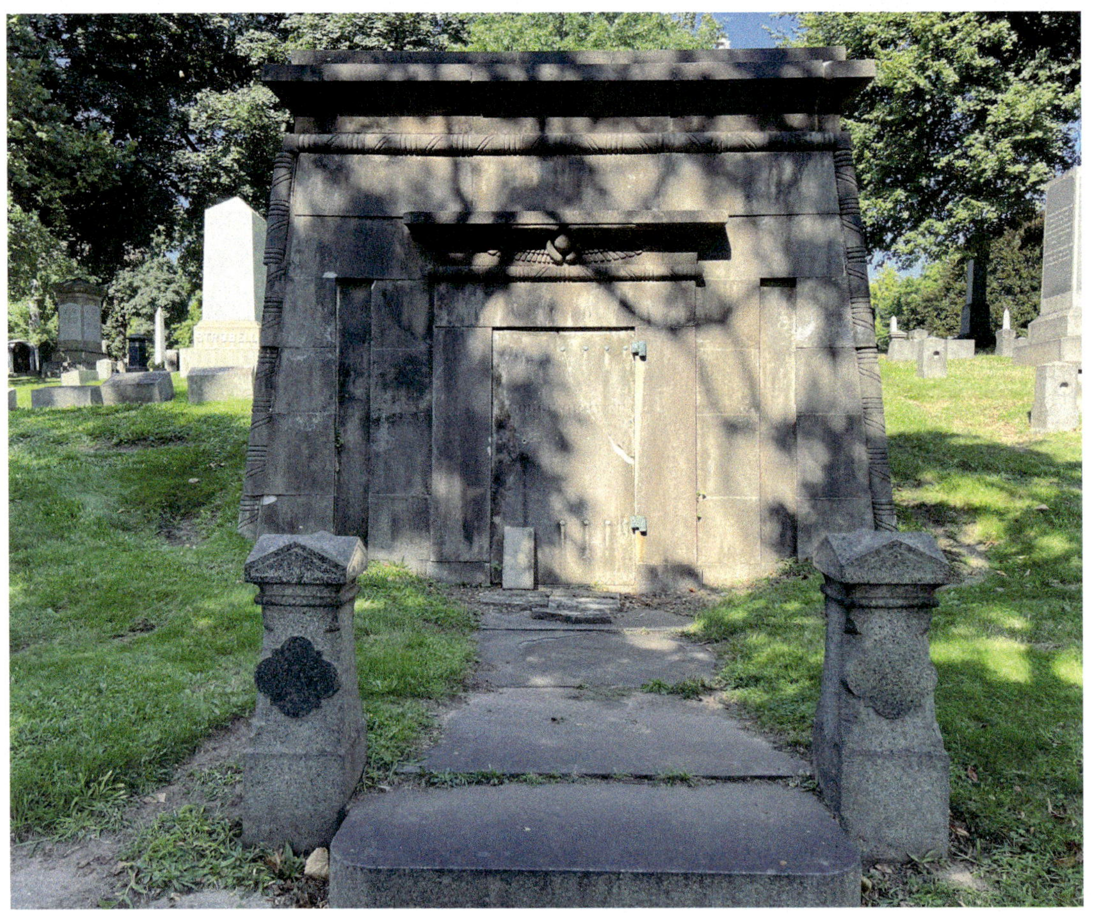

The Opdyke mausoleum is an example of the Egyptian revival style in Mount Pleasant. I love the Victorian's obsession with Egypt. This is one of my favorite mausoleums.

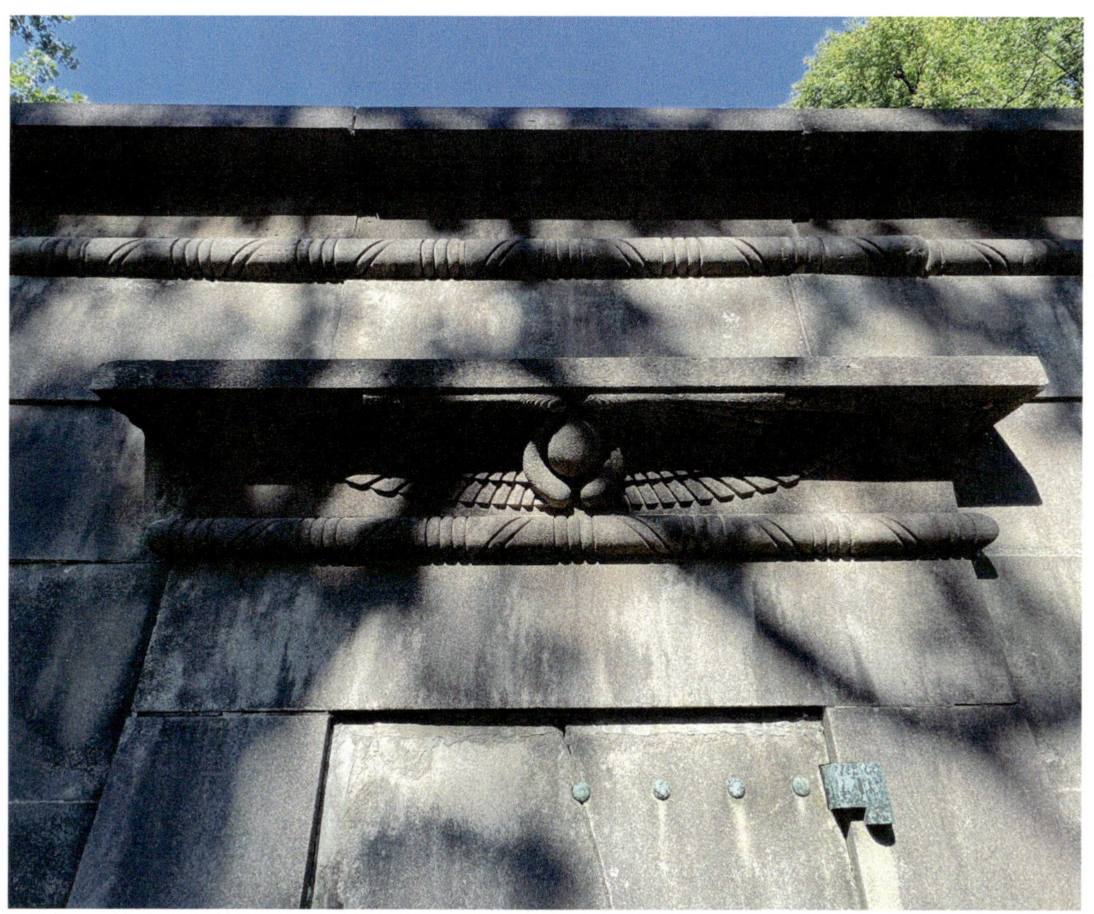

A close-up of the winged sun, called "Behdety," on Opdyke's tomb. This represented Horus of Edfu in ancient Egypt.

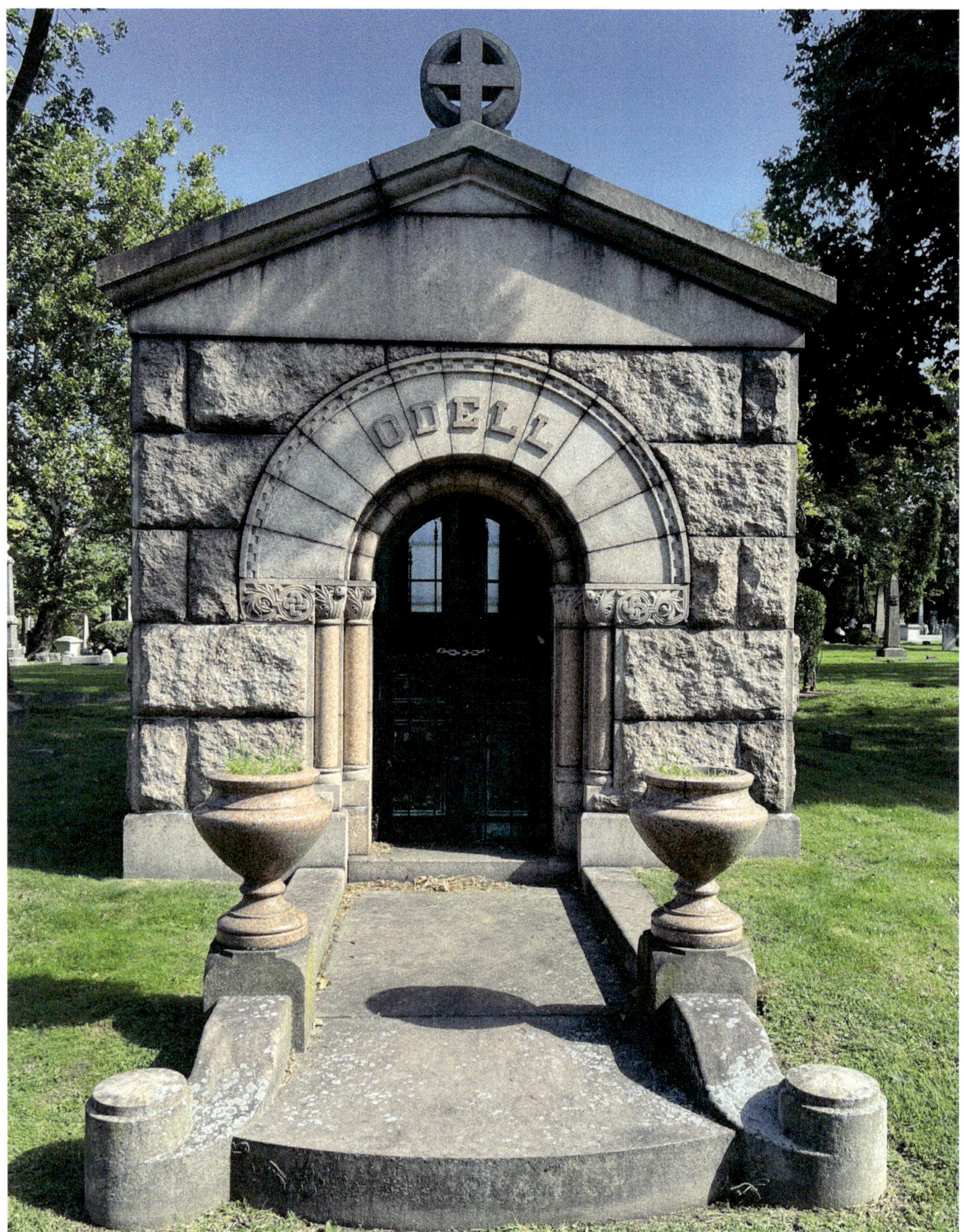

The Odell mausoleum is made of granite and brownstone in a Romanesque revival style.

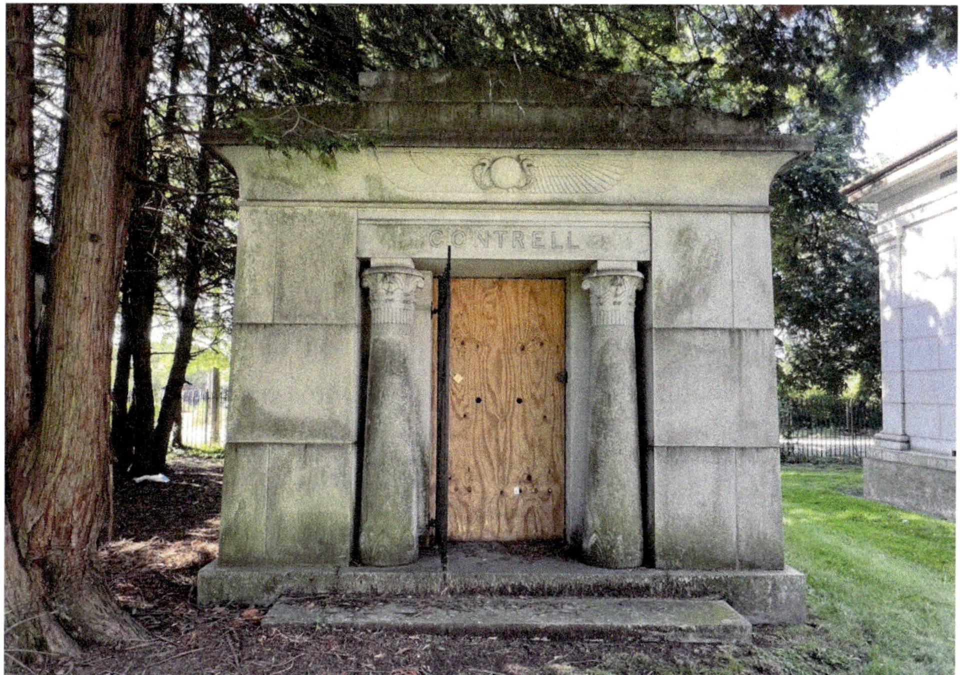

Above: The Contrell mausoleum is another example of the Egyptian influence on Victorian design. The Contrell mausoleum features Behdety and Egyptian-style columns.

Below: A close-up of the Contrell mausoleum shows the cobras adorning the winged sun.

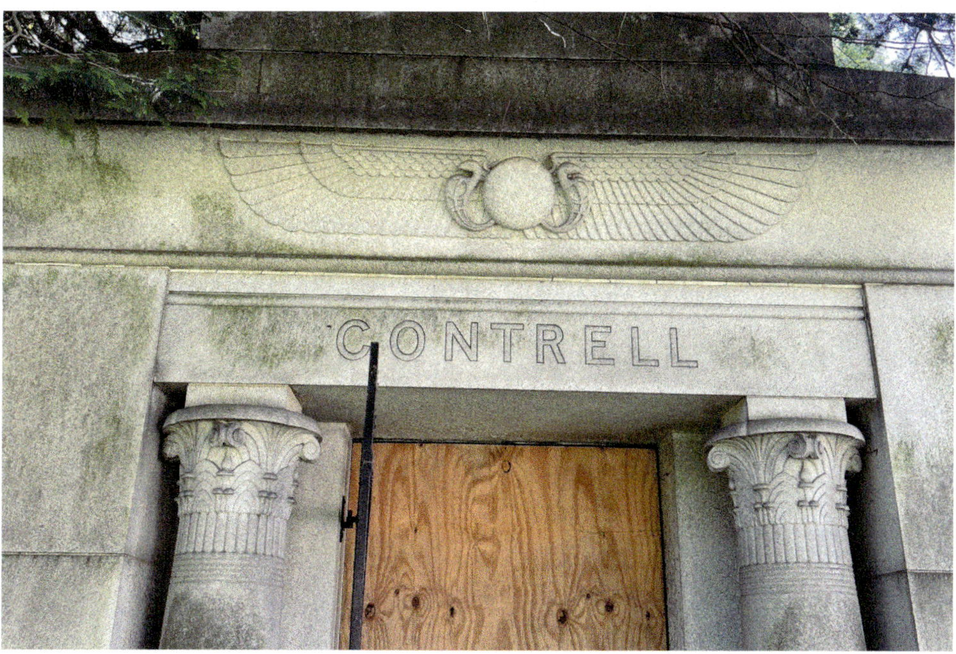

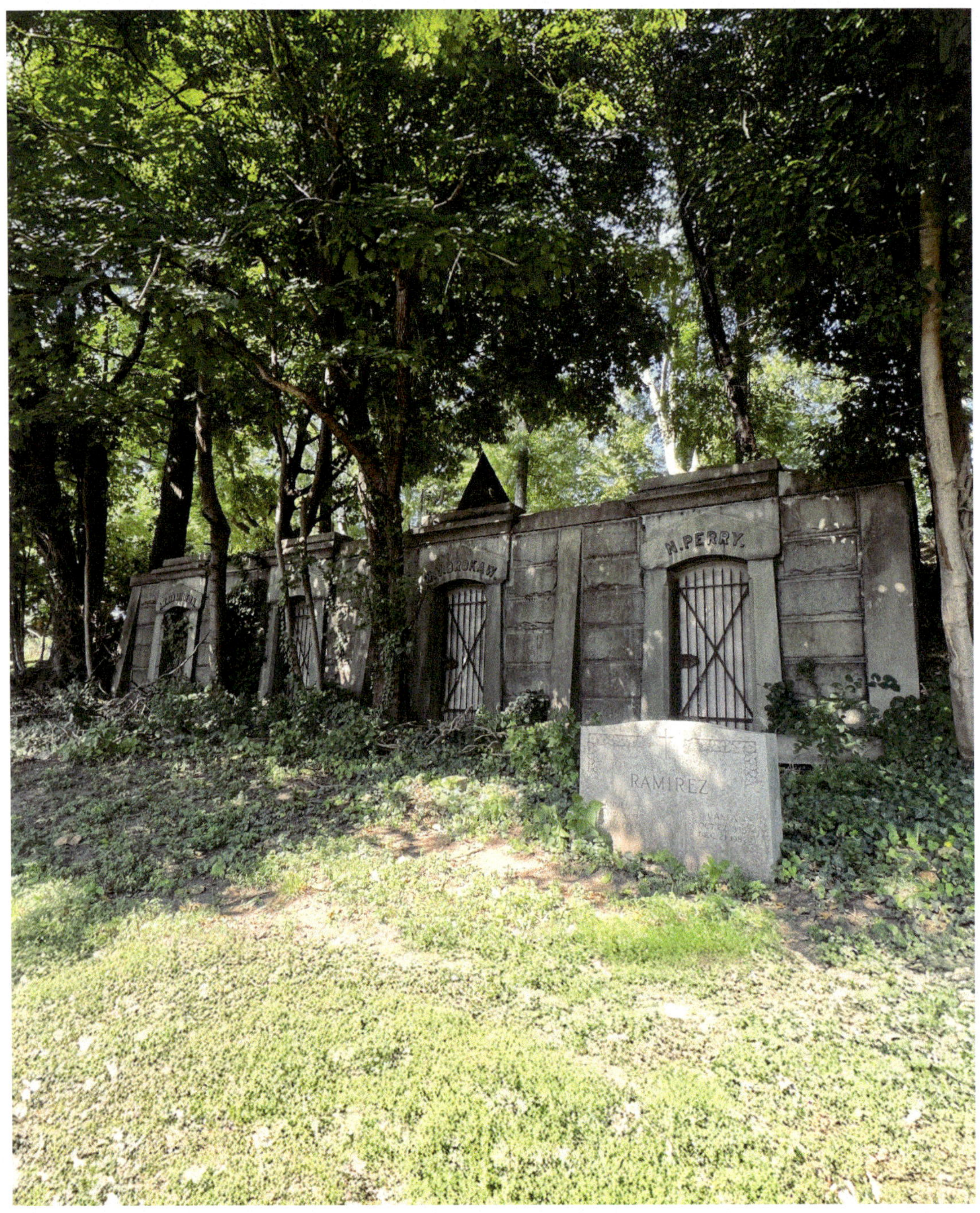

A row of mausoleums at Mount Pleasant close to the Passaic River side of the cemetery loom behind a modern headstone.

Mount Pleasant is beautiful to walk through. There's a wide variety of monuments ranging from the eighteenth-century headstones that were moved here when they were reinterred from other cemeteries to elaborate Gilded Age mausoleums. It's like a park in a city that's desperate for green spaces.

One of the exceptional monuments is the Firemen's Monument which was unveiled on June 3, 1888.[30] It was designed for Newark's unmarried firemen.[31] The centerpiece is a 35-foot-high column with a statue of a fireman on the top.[32] The column is surrounded by rows of graves and the entire section is enclosed with a fence made of hooks, ladders, and firehoses.

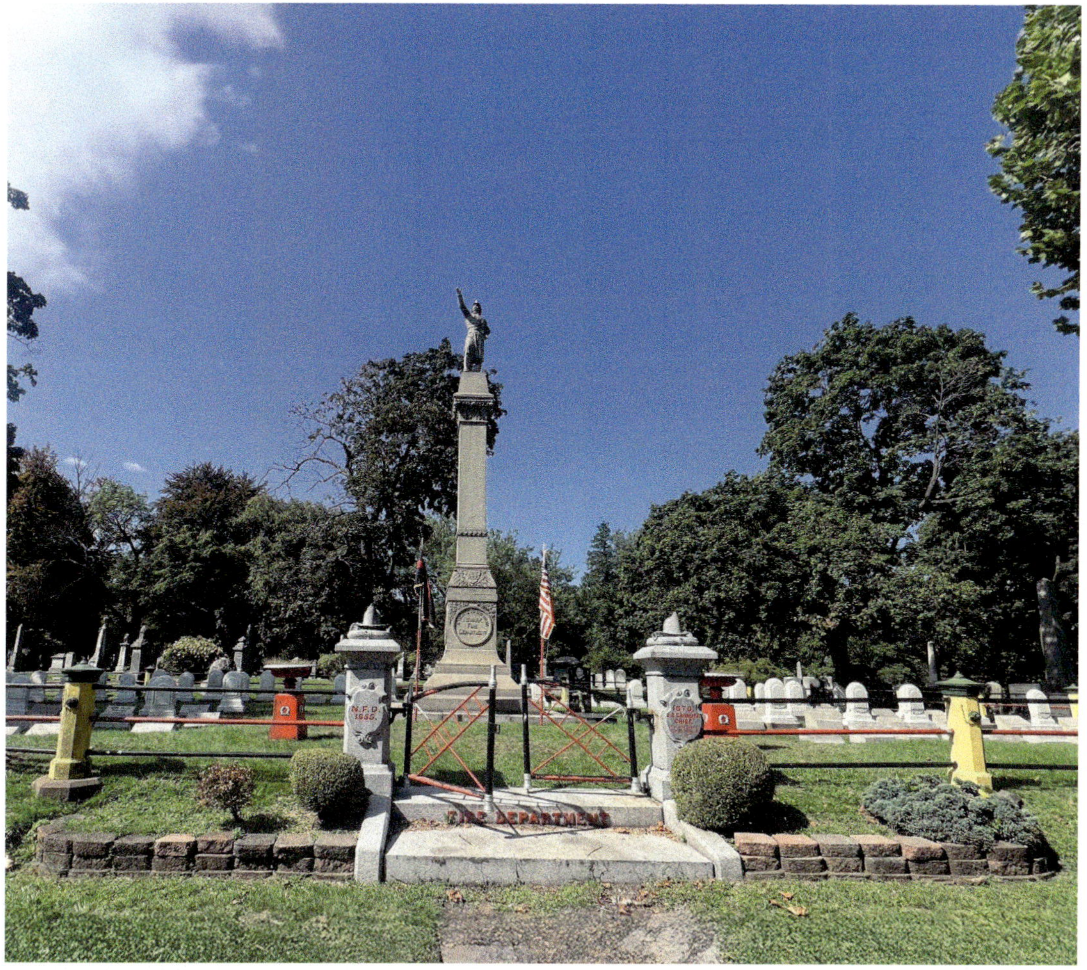

The firemen's monument commands attention even from a distance. The fence is designed to look like the tools a fireman would use.

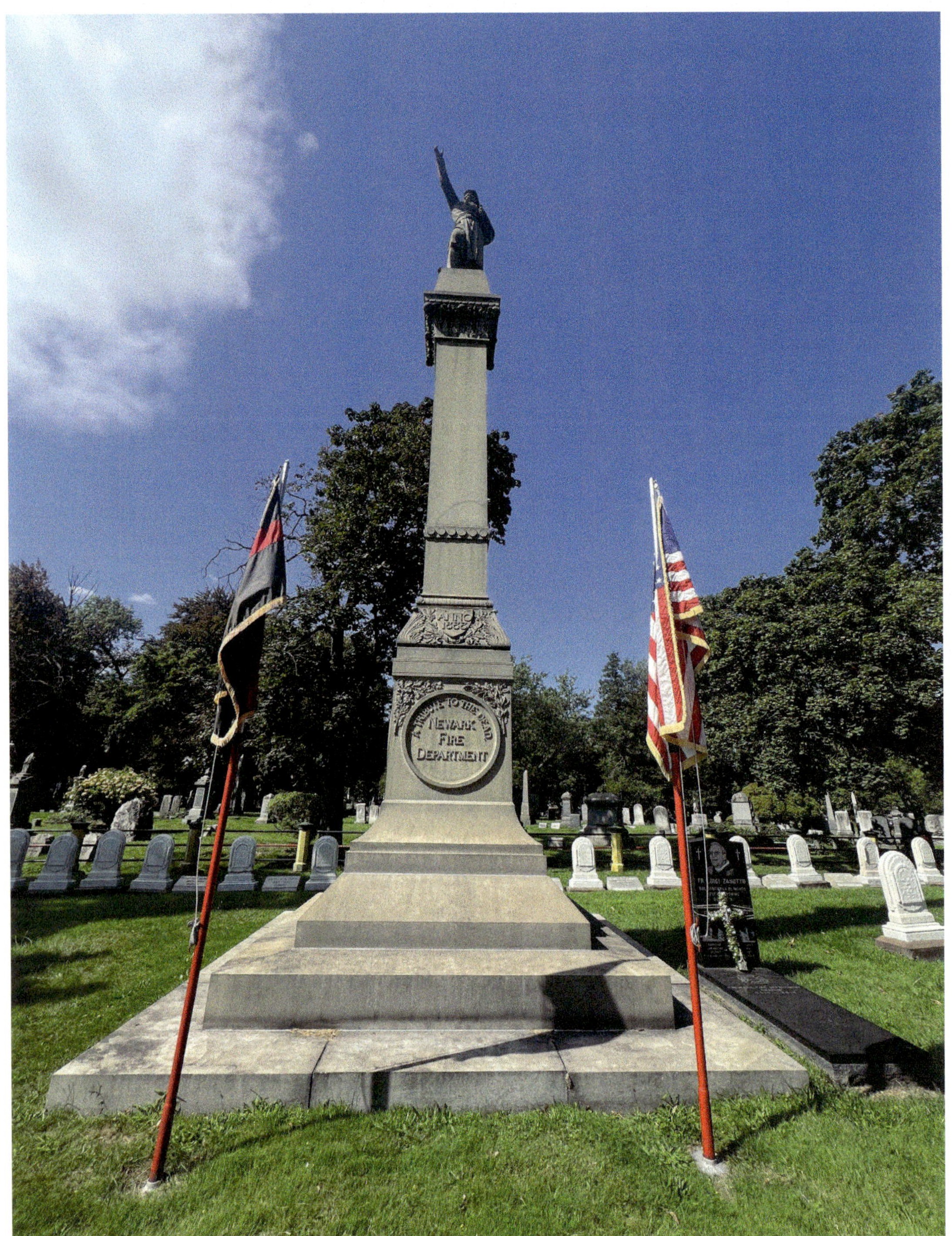

The column of the firemen's monument flanked by flags.

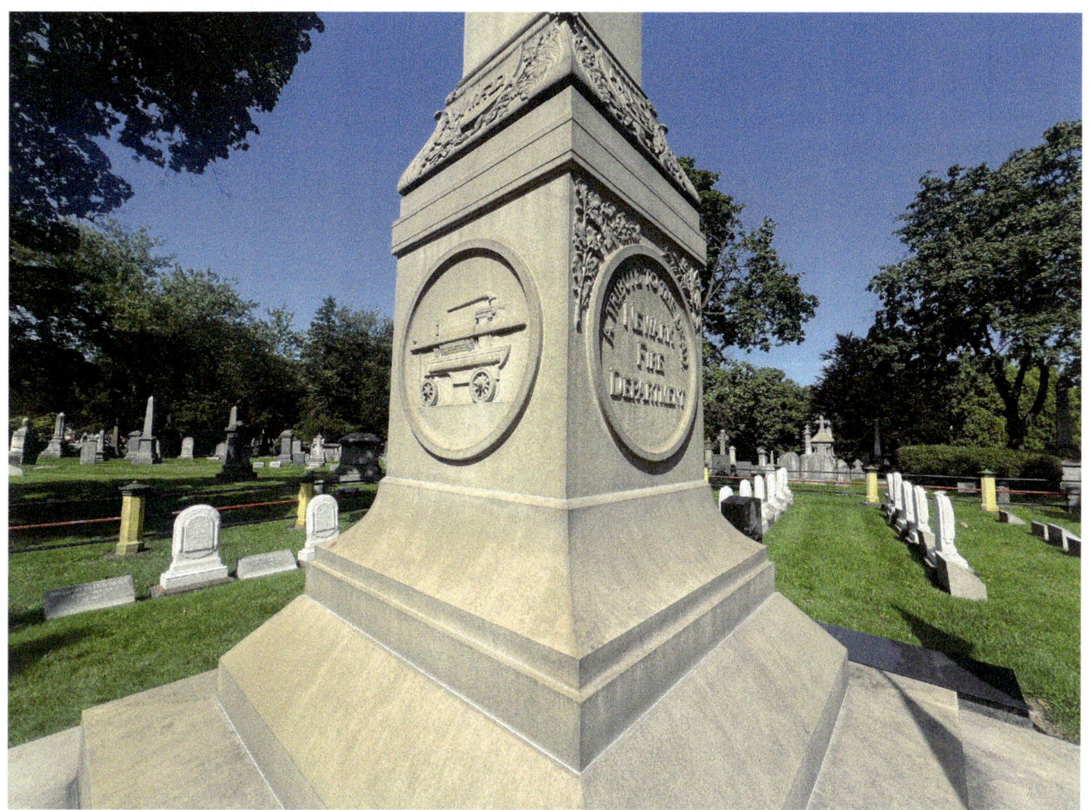

The base of the column of the firemen's monument is decorated with fire engines.

My favorite monument is for Maud Munn. It features a statue of a young girl in a dress. The statue was made in 1892 for an eleven-year-old dance student.[33] Maud loved to dance so she's wearing her dance dress in the statue commissioned by her father.[34] Maud was the only child of Albert G. Munn and Mary Munn.[35] Maud died on New Year's Day in 1892 of scarlet fever.[36] Maud's statue is one of the most famous monuments in the cemetery. I've read that at one point it was enclosed with a glass cloche for protection but that's long gone.

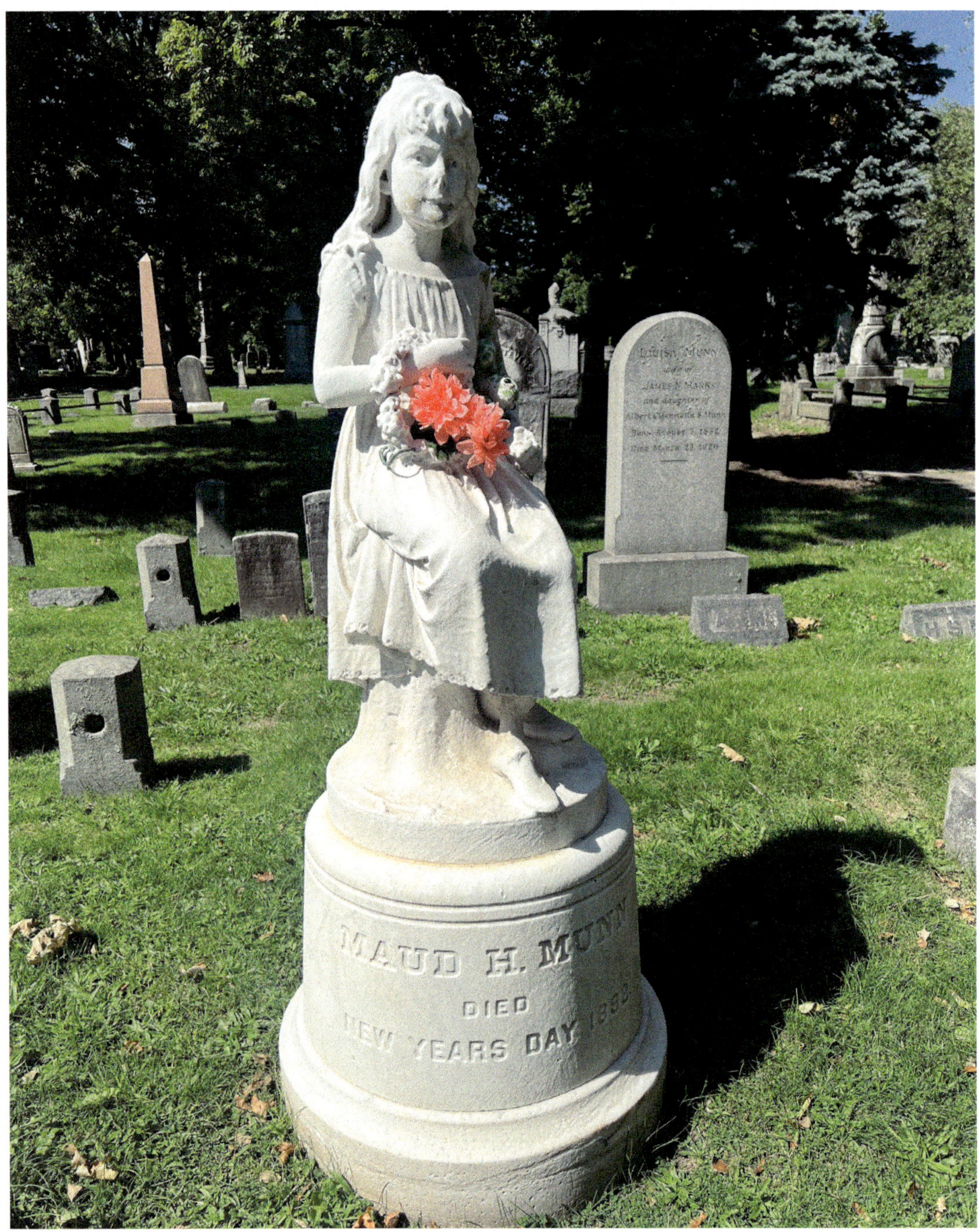

People still leave flowers and gifts for Maud Munn, who died at the age of eleven.

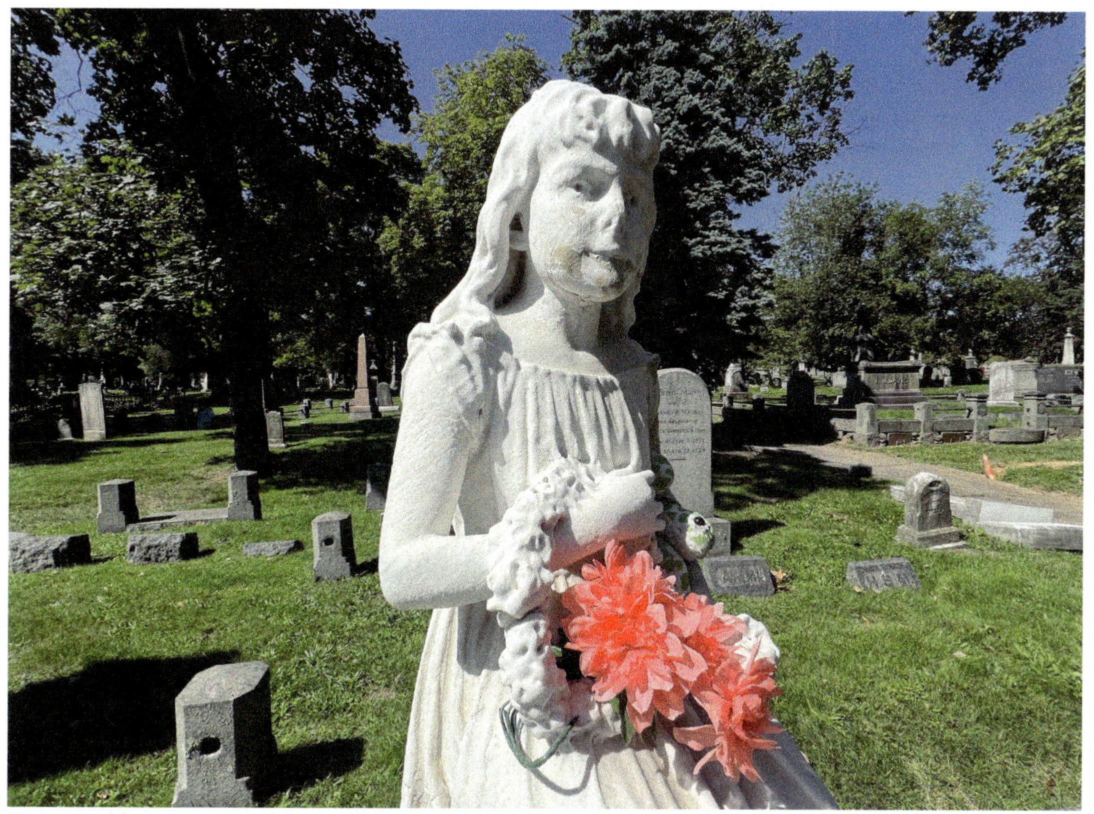

Maud's statue has suffered from the elements and time but is still striking.

Mount Pleasant is a beautiful place to visit and offers an interesting glimpse into Newark history. Is it safe? That's the number one, most annoying question that I get when people find out that I live in Newark. People will frequently ask me if a venue or restaurant is safe and I always wonder if they ask that when they're visiting towns whose populations are mostly white. I've been to Mount Pleasant Cemetery multiple times as a solo woman with no issues. I would remind anyone that they're in a city and to have basic situational awareness. Pay attention and turn off your music. I did see evidence of homeless encampments at the Passaic River side, where it's easy to access the cemetery by walking on the side of McCarter Highway. I would urge anyone to leave the homeless alone if they're not hurting anyone. The cemetery is well taken care of and has staff on the grounds. The superintendent and a groundskeeper saw me as I was taking notes and photographs for this section. They were very friendly and had a wealth of knowledge about the cemetery.

4
Harsimus Cemetery

435 Newark Ave., Jersey City, NJ 07302

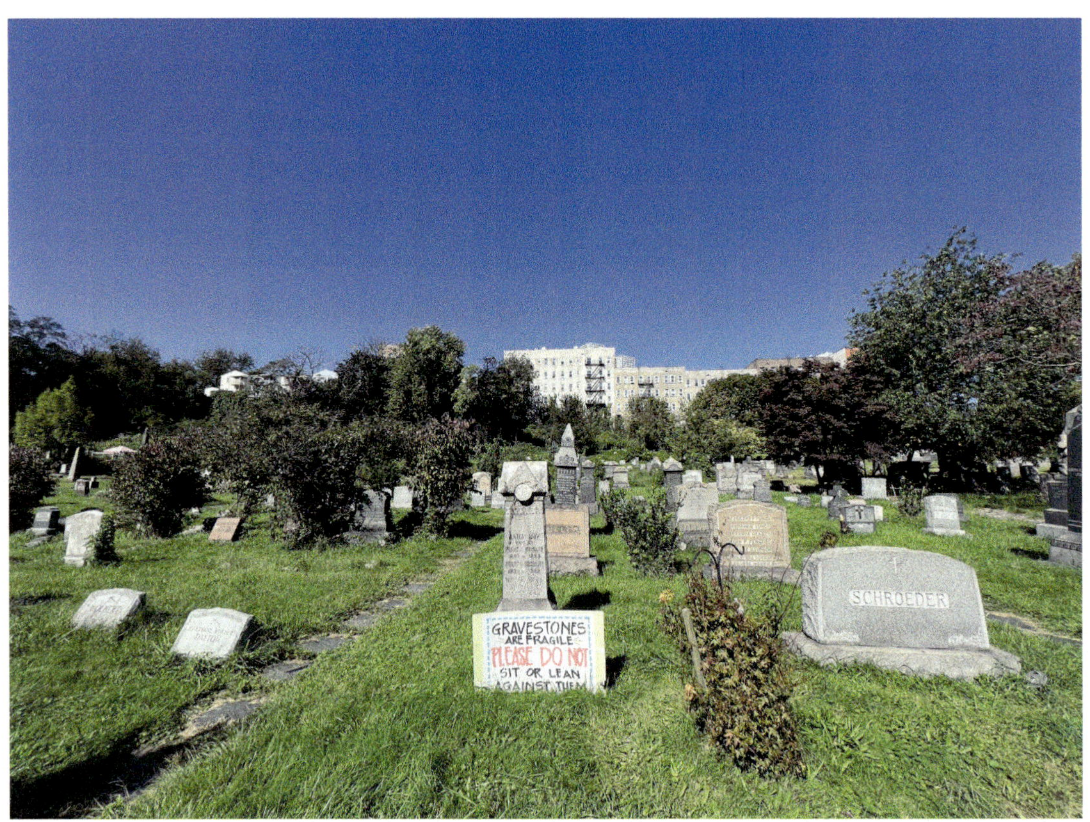

A view of Harsimus Cemetery from the main path. You can see apartment buildings in the background. There are burial vaults built into the hill near the apartment building.

Harsimus Cemetery is right in the middle of New Jersey's second most populous city, Jersey City. Located about a ten-minute walk from the Journal Square train station, it's possible that the thousands of daily commuters who travel through that transit center are unaware that there's a heavily forested cemetery full of animals so close to them. I am biased towards Harsimus Cemetery. I shouldn't have a favorite cemetery, but it's my favorite cemetery in this book. I love the variety of monuments from a wide variety of cultures. The story of Harsimus Cemetery is a story of rebellion, immigration, urbanization, mismanagement, and resilience.

Deaths caused by yellow fever outbreaks in the eighteenth century and cholera outbreaks in the early nineteenth century led to overcrowding in cemeteries in New Jersey.[1] Fear of cholera and miasmas led to restrictive legislation regarding where cemeteries could be built in the northeast in the 1820s, particularly in New York City.[2] This was a response to the failures of government and medicine to alleviate these epidemics.[3] At the time yellow fever was a national issue whose origin and transmission were completely unknown.[4]

By 1829, the church graveyards in Jersey City were overcrowded.[5] This issue wasn't unique to Jersey City but was common throughout the northeast.[6] One solution was to move cemeteries from central locations in cities to the outskirts.[7] As communities became less isolated and the population grew, it became prudent to establish burial grounds not associated with the church and away from city centers.[8] The motives for American burial reform were the insecurity of private burial and concerns about epidemics.[9] Rural cemeteries were supposed to replace the crowded city cemeteries.[10]

Harsimus Cemetery is a transitional style cemetery that falls somewhere between the colonial churchyard and rural cemetery.[11] The colonial churchyard is characterized by its small size, lack of a grid layout, and adjacency to a church, while a rural cemetery lacks a church, is bigger, is preplanned, and has winding roads and more plantings.

The story of Harsimus Cemetery starts with a body. In the fall of 1829, the body of an unidentified man washed up on the banks of Harsimus Cove.[12] The John Doe's body attracted a group of people who decided to bury him with a marker in case friends or family were looking for him.[13] They pooled what they thought would be enough money for a burial.[14] This was the nineteenth-century version of a GoFundMe. The residents tried to bury him at the local churchyard but couldn't afford the fee.[15] The sexton at Bergen Cemetery reportedly charged $12.00 just to open a grave.[16] The citizens were outraged by the high price and decided that something had to be done.[17] A public meeting was held and it was decided to open a new cemetery that was independent of Bergen Cemetery.[18] David C. Colden, who was the son of the mayor of New York City at the time, was elected the first president of Harsimus Cemetery and subscriptions were taken for funding.[19] Colden was elected while his father was passing laws restricting burial locations in New York City and I have no doubt that influenced David's official involvement with Harsimus Cemetery.[20]

Work on the cemetery started in 1830, and the cemetery was incorporated on February 8, 1831.[21] Harsimus Cemetery was a pioneer in successful cemetery incorporation. The right to create private corporations was a new concept in America that the British had never granted to its colonies.[22] By the 1790s, the use of a charter was extended from municipalities to private groups and associations.[23] Private cemetery corporations ensured that families could protect their graves.[24] Lot-holders were considered proprietors under incorporation and were allowed to select board members and be involved with management of the cemetery, a right denied to families with church burial.[25] Incorporation allowed the separation of the dead from church and state with the family at the forefront.[26]

About 3 acres of land on the eastern downward slope of Bergen Hill were set aside for the cemetery.[27] A seven-member board was elected with four trustees being enough to conduct business.[28] The oldest surviving grave marker is dated 1830 for a man named Andrew Gammel.[29] I've seen Andrew Gammel's last name spelled multiple ways in my sources but I'm going to defer to how his name is spelled on his stone and hope that the carver knew how to spell.

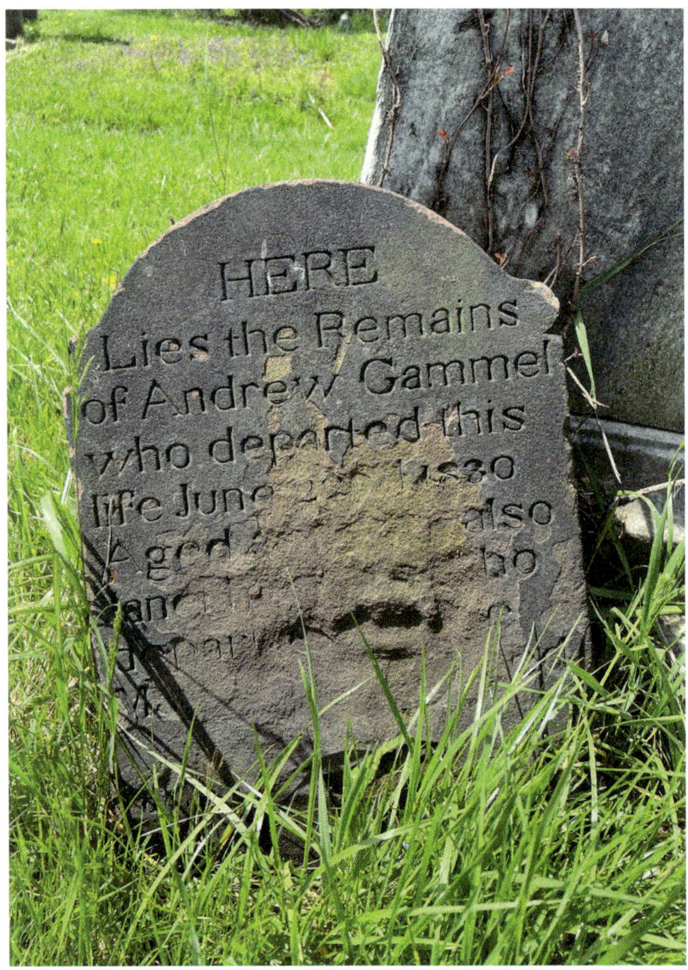

A close-up of Andrew Gammel's stone. I was unable to find it during my first visit to photograph Harsimus Cemetery. Mandy Edgecombe, the cemetery's historian, pointed it out to me when I interviewed her. You can see where the stone is exfoliating and much of the inscription is lost. It's unclear if it was damaged due to being moved or occurred naturally over time.

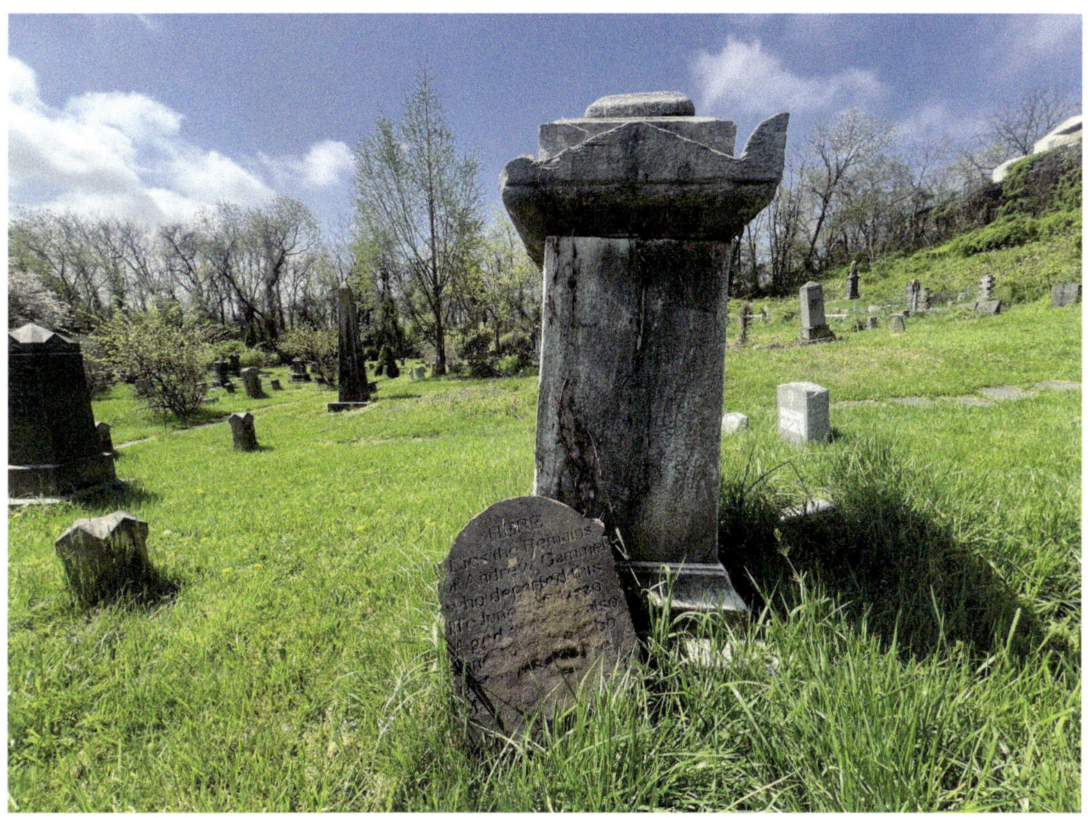

A wide view of Andrew Gammel's stone. It's lying next to another monument. It's unclear if he's actually buried there or near there. There is a base for a headstone without a stone on top of it a couple of feet from where Andrew's stone is resting, but it seems too big for his stone.

The oldest graves were buried two by two, either one person on top of the other, or one person in front of the headstone and one person behind it, with names on both sides.[30] The oldest stones are brownstone, which is interesting because it inscribes well but it exfoliates in sheets so the inscriptions could flake off.[31] In the late 1700s, it was unknown where limestone deposits were.[32] Jersey freestone (the name for brownstone) was easy to get and cheap.[33]

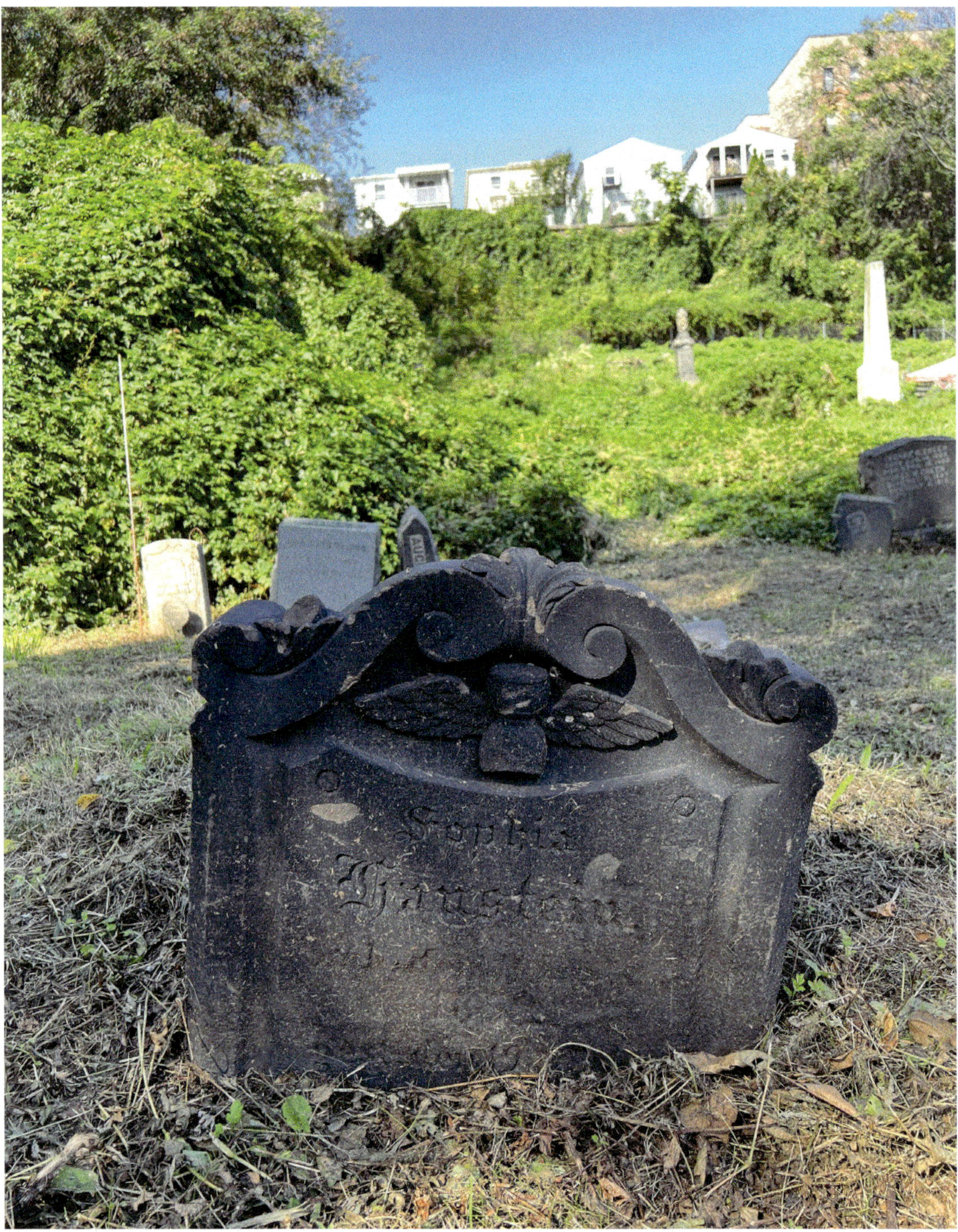

This little brown headstone is one of my favorites in Harsimus Cemetery. I like it because it is half buried, and I wonder how that happened. Most of it is illegible or buried, but I love that the mortality image of the winged hourglass remains.

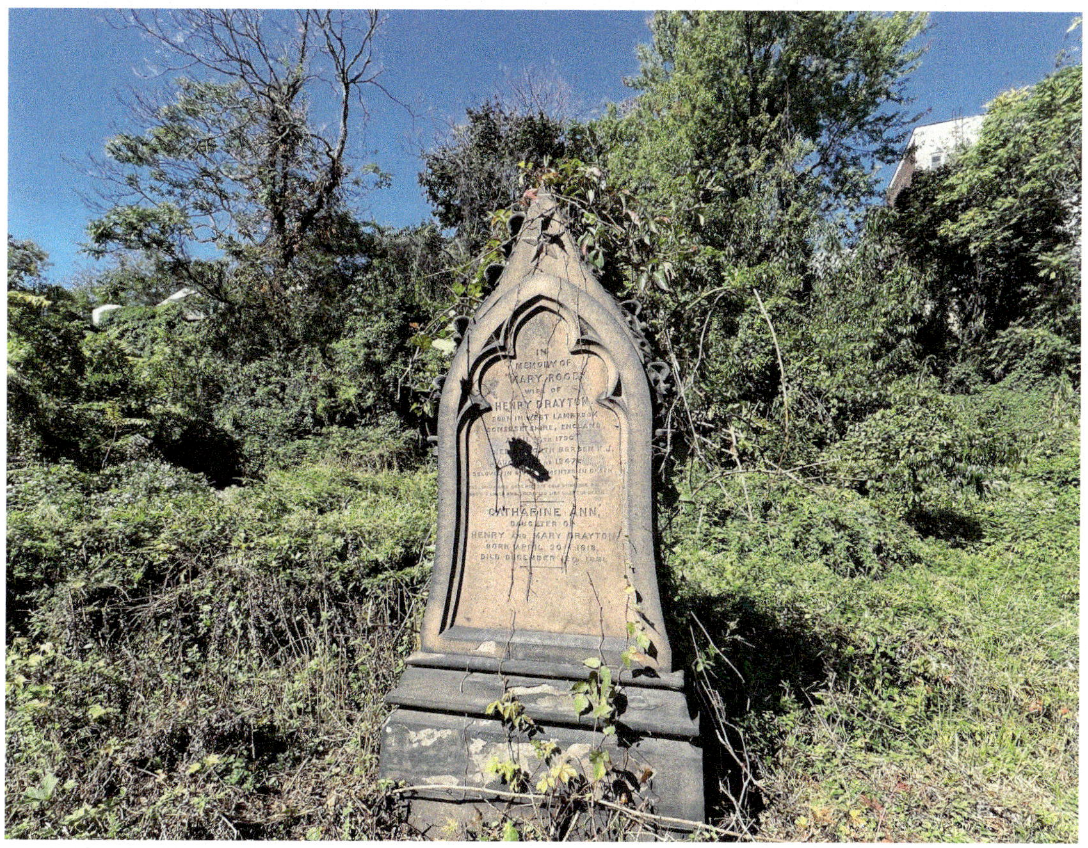

Mary Rood's headstone is my favorite headstone in Harsimus Cemetery. It immediately commands attention when you enter the cemetery. The shape reminds me of something you would see in a church and I think the inscription is really beautiful: "The spoiler hath come with his cold withering breath, And the loved and cherished lies silent in death."

The cemetery was in a quiet part of the city when it was first constructed.[34] Many prominent families of Jersey City were buried in Harsimus Cemetery.[35] The cemetery became so popular to visit and so crowded that tickets were soon required for admission.[36] I've attended events held at Harsimus Cemetery and it's very entertaining to me when I see outraged comments online about how disrespectful it is to charge tickets for an event at a cemetery, when Harsimus Cemetery required tickets for admission at one point because there were so many people going there to picnic and canoodle.

Growth in Jersey City in the early nineteenth century led to land by the cemetery quickly becoming expensive.[37] It was known as early as 1831 that the railroads were speculating on land near the cemetery.[38] In 1853, the trustees tried to purchase more land, but the available land was already developed or too expensive.[39] New York Bay Cemetery overtook Harsimus in popularity after the Civil War.[40] By 1899, there were city streets nearby and a railroad at the foot of the hill.[41] The cemetery was never bigger than 6 acres.[42]

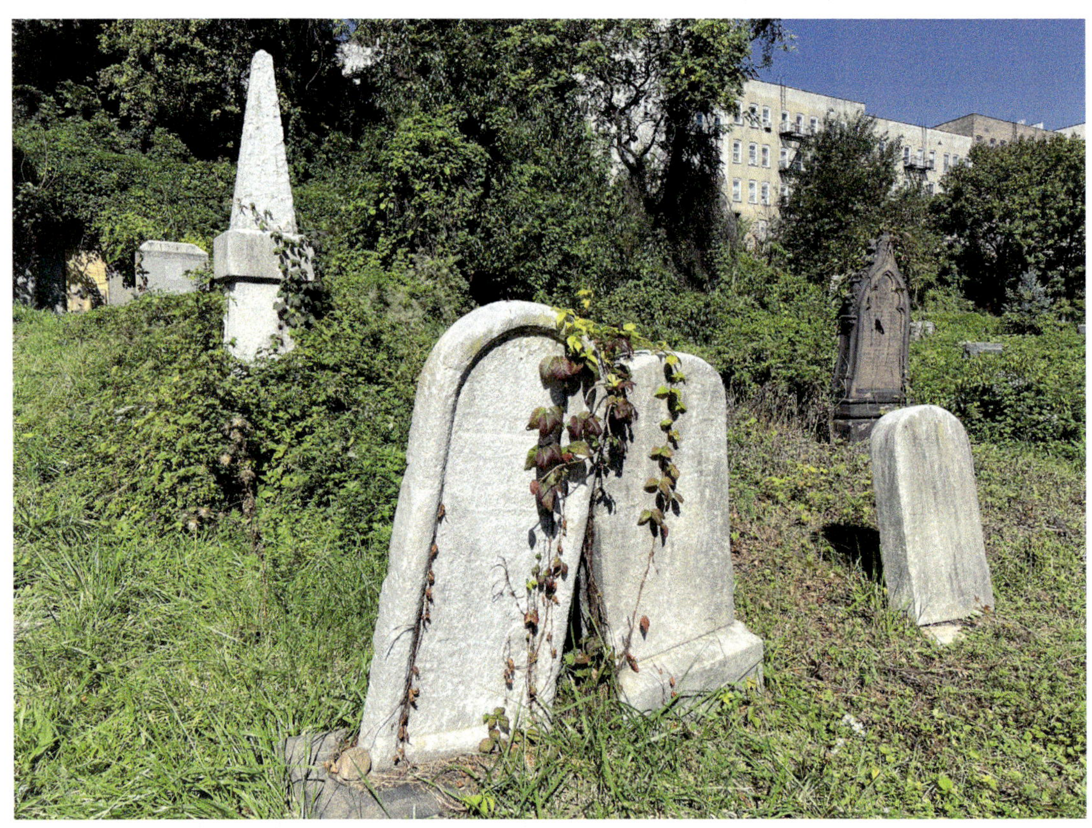

This picture of two stones with buildings in the background shows just how close the buildings come to Harsimus Cemetery.

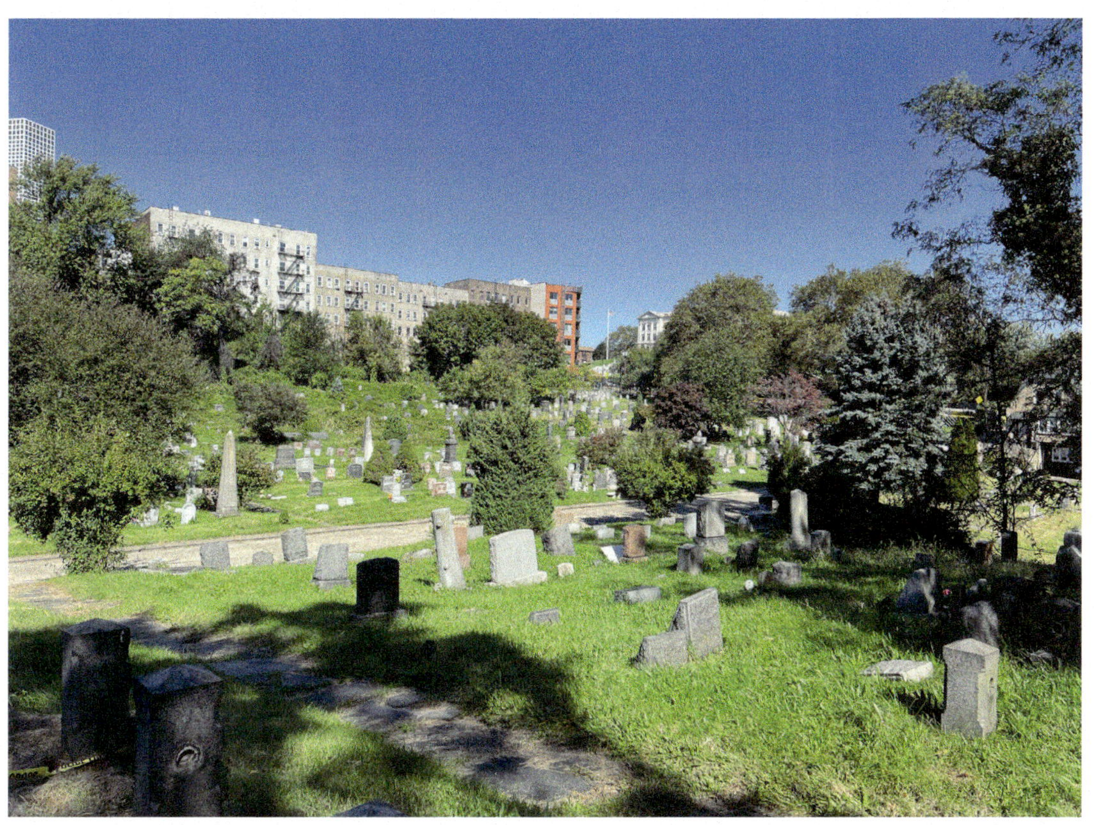

The view of Harsimus Cemetery looking north and west from the New Jersey Turnpike side. The photo was taken on one of the many small side paths throughout the cemetery.

Harsimus Cemetery continued to reflect the immigrant demographics of the neighborhood despite its lack of popularity among the elite. In the 1880s, it served Germans; in the 1890s–1900s, it served Russians and eastern Europeans; and in the 1910s–1920s, it served Italians.[43]

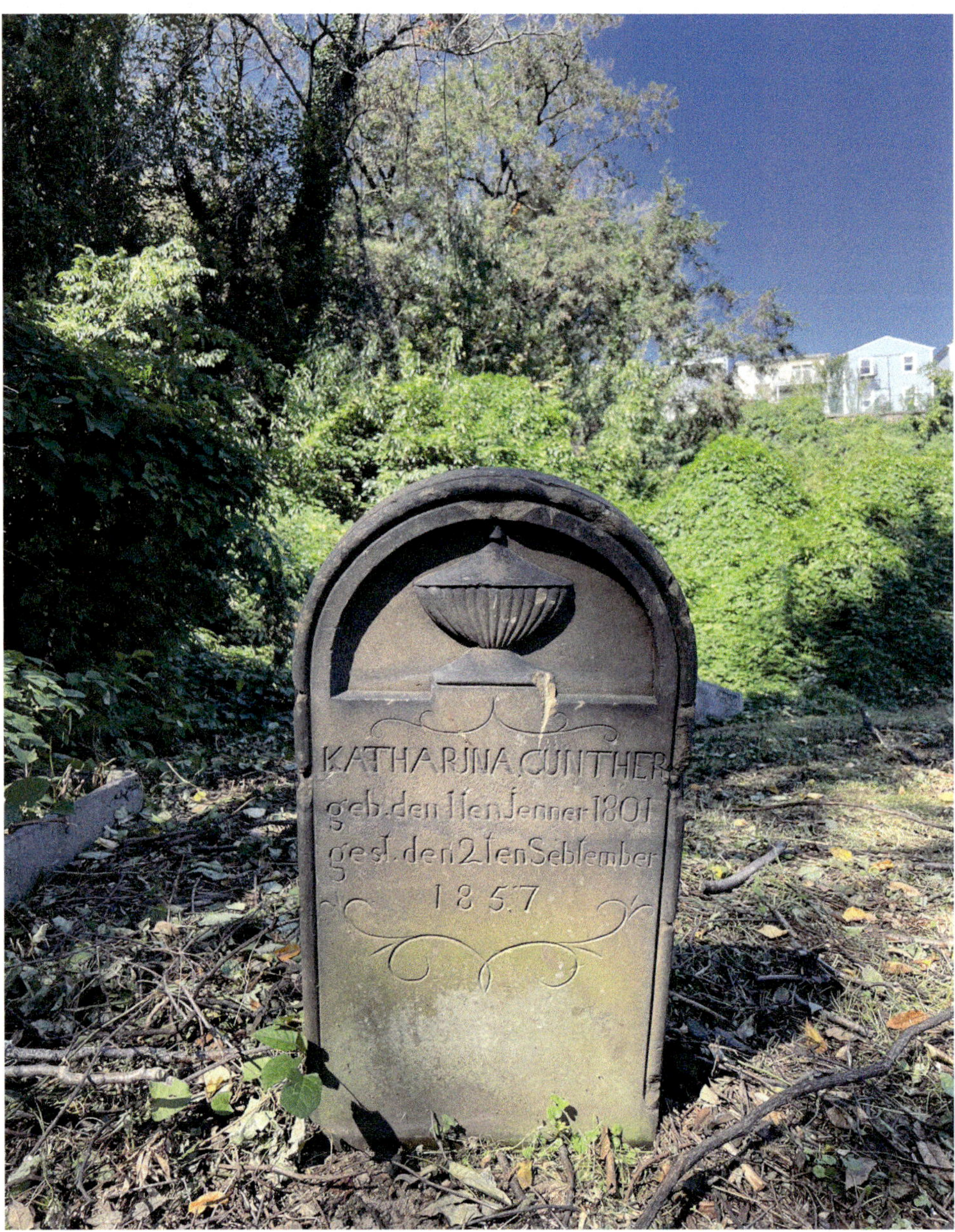

A headstone inscribed in German in one of the emptier corners of Harsimus Cemetery. The apartments of Jersey City are ever present in the background.

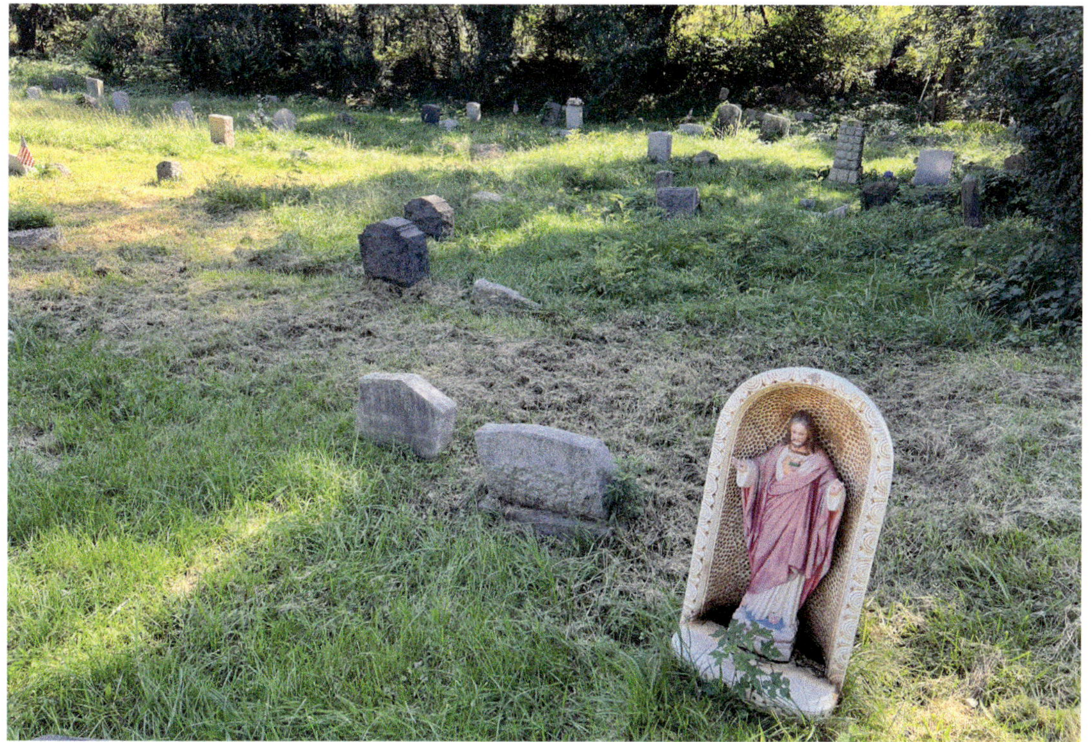

A Jesus statue watches over Harsimus Cemetery.

Space quickly became an issue for Harsimus Cemetery. In 1876, the grounds were resurveyed, and all unsold family plots were converted to single plots to have more room for burials.[44] The cemetery was at capacity by the twentieth century.[45] This has led to some of the issues the cemetery faced in the early twenty-first century. In 2001, the former groundskeeper, Louis Sandomenico Jr., was disciplined for charging excessive burial and upkeep fees.[46] Some graves were also improperly sold twice, meaning that plots that were already owned by one family were sold to another family.[47]

The cemetery was effectively abandoned when the president of the board of trustees died in 2007, after decades of neglect.[48] In January 2007, there were five board members listed in the cemetery's annual report: Maureen Burgess, Rita Goscinski, Olga Mistarila, William DeNoble, and Pauline Markowicz.[49] Maureen Burgess, who was the president of the board of directors, died in December 2007.[50] Goscinski and DeNoble, who were related to each other, also died in 2007.[51] Mistarila said that she was elderly and couldn't run the cemetery while Markowicz was unreachable.[52] This led to the cemetery workers leaving after being unpaid after the board disbanded.[53]

By May 2008, no one was running the cemetery and $100,000.00 was unaccounted for.[54] The burial records were also missing in the absence of a board.[55] Jorge and Flor Peralta were the caretakers who lived in the gatehouse with their two sons and kept the cemetery records locked in a safe.[56] The Peraltas moved because they were unpaid and told Hector Sullivan, a maintenance man who also served as a gravedigger, that they no longer wanted to run the cemetery, and moved to the Jersey Shore.[57] The original maps were saved and have been restored.[58] The caretaker's son originally took the books but they were recovered and given to the genealogical society to scan.[59] Michele LaMonica Egar, the current director of Harsimus Cemetery, described the situation to me at the cemetery's 2024 Earth Day Event:

> He took them … I don't think he took them for the money. I think he took them more for safekeeping. His mother called Eileen and said, "Hey, my son took these books," and we immediately picked them up. … she (Flor) called immediately, and we picked them up. But there are still some books that are missing from the original burials 'till about 1890.[60]

In June 2008, a new board of seven trustees was elected, with Eileen Markenstein serving as the president and treasurer.[61] Eileen Markenstein had worked for Morgan Stanley and took care of the cemetery's finances.[62] Thirty-five plot owners voted in the election at the Hudson County Improvement Authority in Jersey City.[63] Markenstein herself had four generations of family buried at Harsimus Cemetery.[64] Markenstein and the new board organized community clean-ups and fundraisers to benefit the cemetery.[65] Eileen Markenstein died suddenly in 2020 and is buried in the cemetery that she worked so hard to save.

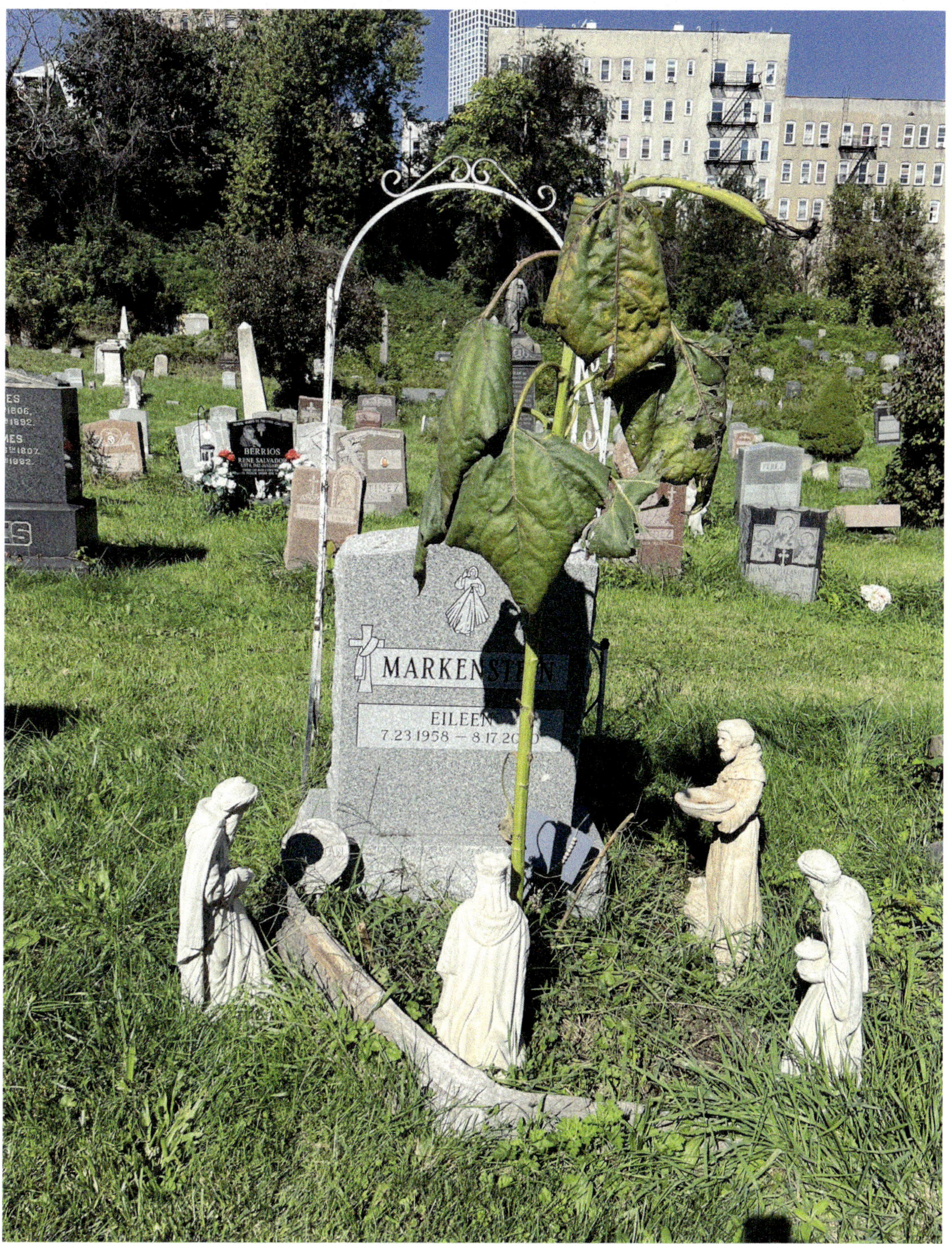

Eileen Markenstein's stone at Harsimus Cemetery is well-tended and loved.

Harsimus Cemetery has a legacy as part of the community that extends beyond being a cemetery. Burial scenes from *The Sopranos* were filmed at Harsimus Cemetery.[66] In 2017, the Jersey City Alternative Art Market partnered with the cemetery to host events to fundraise for restoration and maintenance costs.[67]

Burials only happen a few times a year in plots that were previously sold.[68] No new graves are being sold.[69] The cemetery has to test the graves before burials to ensure no one is already there and to see how deep to bury.[70] Money now comes from events, fundraisers, and donations.[71] Goats are brought in during the warm months to tame the landscape.[72] I went to visit in October 2023 and the landscape was still shockingly wild and green. Eileen Markenstein said, "Before the goats, we'd have fifty volunteers out here hacking down weeds with machetes and, two weeks later, it would all be back … the vegetation can grow up to seven feet."[73]

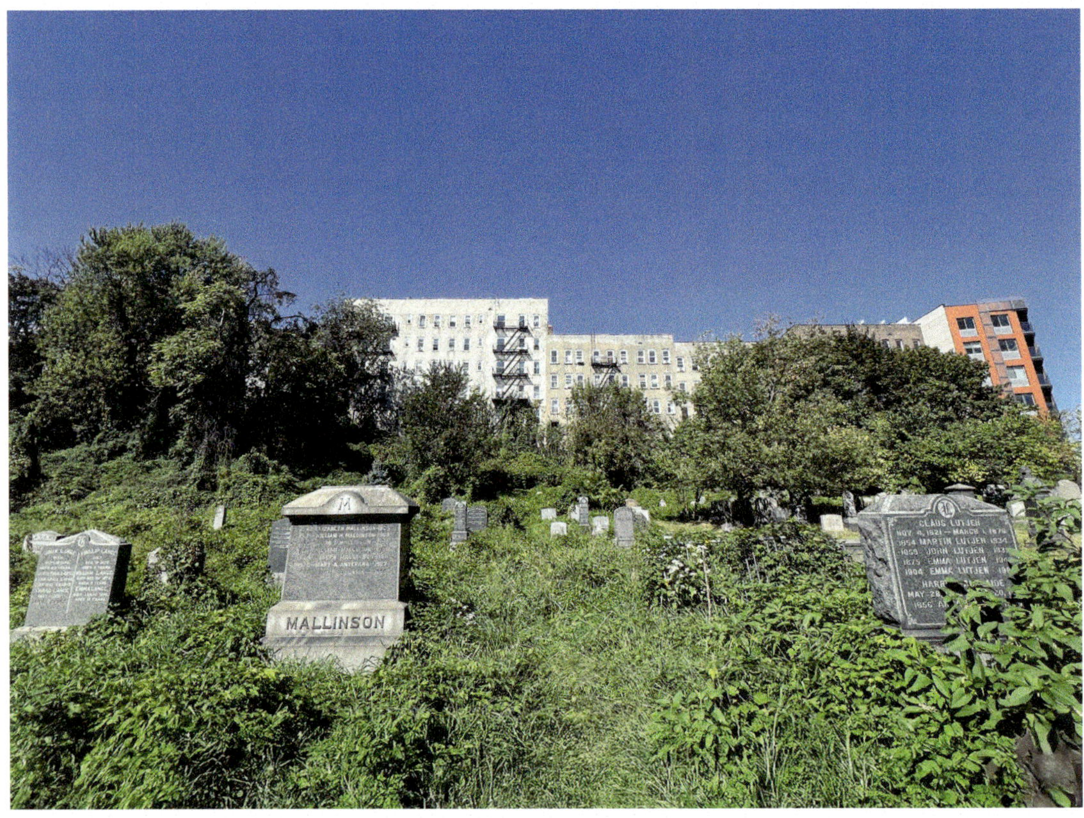

Most of the photographs of Harsimus Cemetery were taken in October 2023. This should give an idea of exactly how thick the vegetation can grow here.

Michele LaMonica Egar became involved in the care of Harsimus Cemetery with Eileen Markenstein in 2008. Eileen worked on the finances, while Michele took over the landscaping. Michele's goals for the future, besides maintenance and groundskeeping, are to build a scattering garden for cremated remains with a gate and a plaque, as a source of revenue.[74]

Maybe it's because of its tumultuous history, but Harsimus Cemetery has multiple ghost stories associated with it. John Wilson, a groundskeeper, reportedly saw a man smoking a cigar who vanished.[75] Michele has also witnessed an apparition of a woman in a beautiful white dress who smelled like roses.[76] "Eileen and I used to come up here to talk, and we both experienced it where we used to just come up here.... And she walks right through you.... And she said, 'Did you feel that?' And I was like, 'I felt it and I seen it.'"[77] There's also the story of a little boy who died while at his sister's funeral who has been seen playing with a ball on the steps at the cemetery.[78]

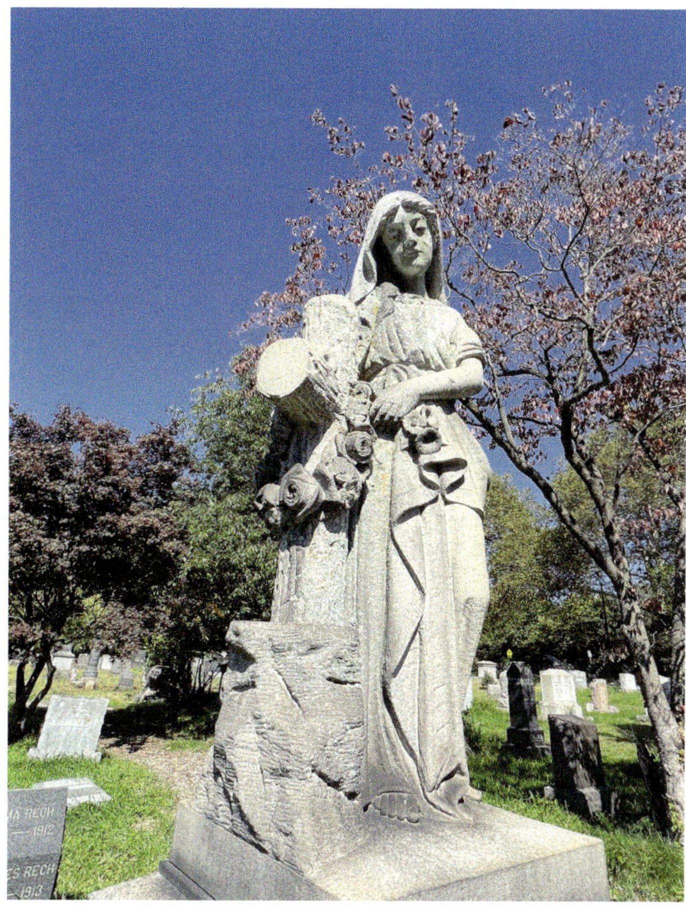

I always visit this statue whenever I visit Harsimus Cemetery. I couldn't resist using her as my cover image, I'm always struck by the beauty of the statue and surrounding trees.

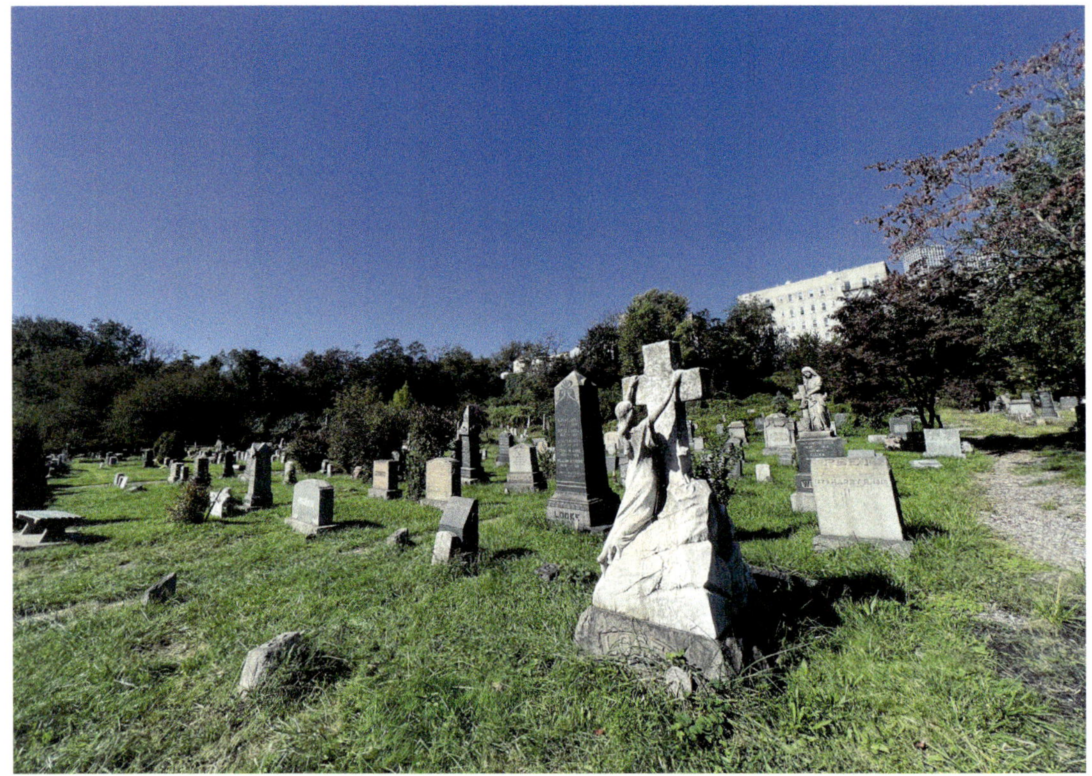

This is another beautiful statue that I always make a point to visit when I stop at Harsimus Cemetery. You can see another one of the side paths that takes you up Bergen Hill.

Harsimus Cemetery combines my love of city life and my love of hiking. You can see apartment buildings rising up Bergen Hill and the New Jersey Turnpike binds the cemetery on the opposite side. But, once you're in the cemetery, it's like you're in an oasis within a city. Here you'll see tombstone iconography ranging from the early nineteenth century through the twenty-first century. The stones are lovely, and the wildlife is so abundant that it's easy to forget that you're in the middle of a city. The walk to the cemetery from the Journal Square PATH station is easy and takes about fifteen minutes. The cemetery itself has one main path with many small paths branching off of it. The small paths can be treacherous due to loose stepping stones. Be cautious if you go off the trail, there are holes from grave collapses and burrowing animals. I would advise visitors to wear sturdy shoes and be careful where they step. Harsimus Cemetery hosts many events throughout the year that are worth attending.

5
Piscatawaytown Burial Ground/ St. James Episcopal Church Cemetery

2136 Woodbridge Ave., Edison, N.J. 08818

I initially visited this cemetery with the intent of only writing about the Hoopar Brothers. Their stone is one of the oldest surviving stones in New Jersey. Any readers from Europe are probably laughing but a seventeenth-century gravestone in New Jersey is a big deal. What I found at this cemetery is a unique part of New Jersey history that predates the Revolutionary War, and includes tornados, poisoning, and a legendary witch. I absolutely had to write about the entire cemetery.

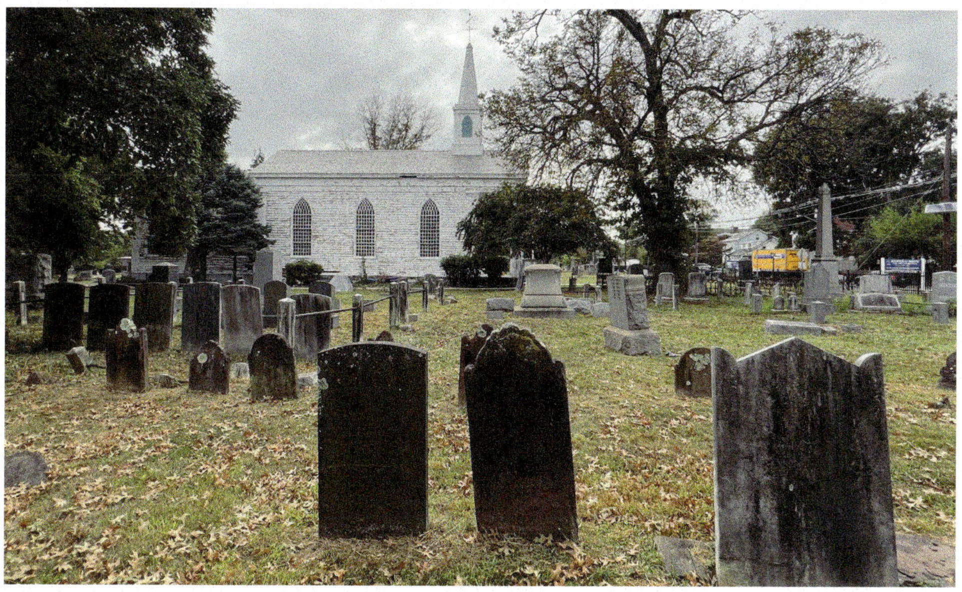

The view of Piscatawaytown Burial Ground standing in the older east side facing St. James Episcopal Church, which divides the older side of the cemetery from the newer west side.

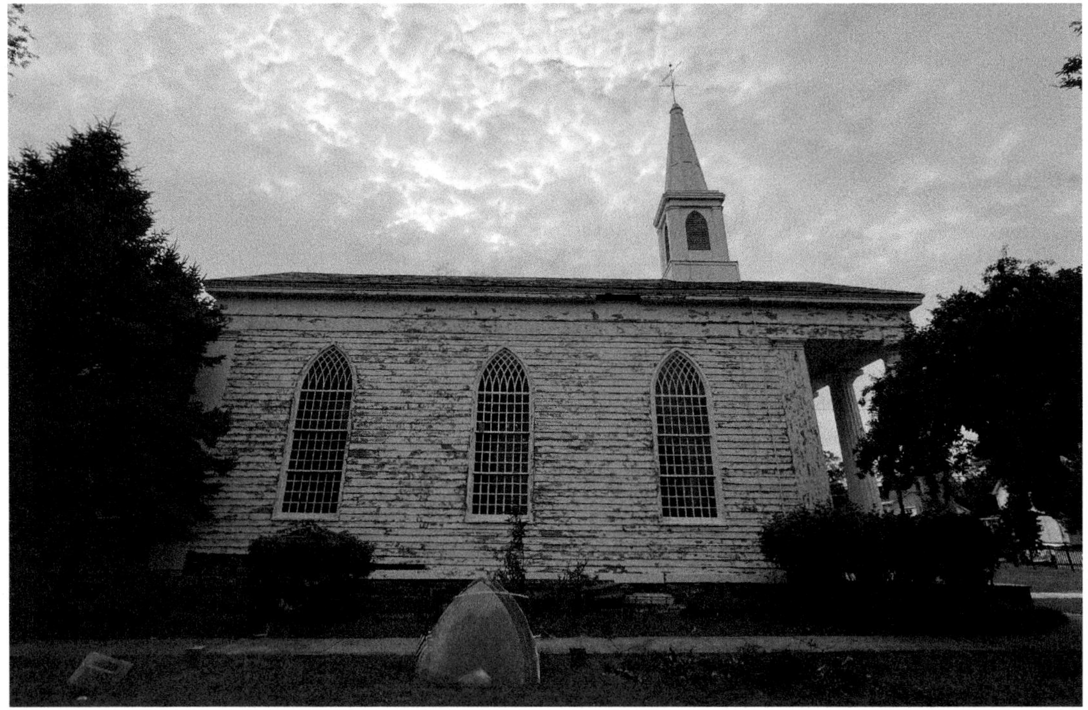

A close-up of St. James Episcopal Church at Piscatawaytown Burial Ground.

Piscatawaytown Burial Ground is one of the oldest cemeteries in Middlesex County. Burials include the original colonist families who settled in the area, possibly British soldiers who died during the Revolutionary War, and legendary witch Mary Moore.[1] On a personal note, I aspire to live my life so that after I die, I'm described as "legendary witch" and I'll be deeply disappointed if this isn't etched on my headstone.

The burial ground is only 3.09 acres of land.[2] It's divided into east and west sides with St. James Episcopal Church in the middle.[3] The burial ground is currently owned and maintained by Edison Township.[4] The oldest burials tend to be on the east side and the west side started being used around 1790.[5] There's a marked change in iconography as you walk from east to west, with the east side having predominantly soul effigies, that evolve into monograms, Victorian iconography, and more modern monuments.

The grave for the Hoopar Brothers predates the official 1695 date the cemetery was established.[6] Their monument is the oldest legible stone in the cemetery.[7] The stone is very weathered and hard to read and was damp from a recent rain when I visited, making it even more illegible. The transcription reads: "Spataters vnderneath this tomb lies 2 boys that lay in one womb the eldest was full 13 years old the youngest was twice told by eating mushrooms for food rare in a days time they poyseond were Richard and Charles Hoopar deceased Avgvst anno dom 1693." There are no other Hoopars in the cemetery.[8] I've read rumors that they were Lenni Lenape boys and the names listed on the stone were English names given to them, but I can't find any source that verifies this. I couldn't find any death record from that long ago.

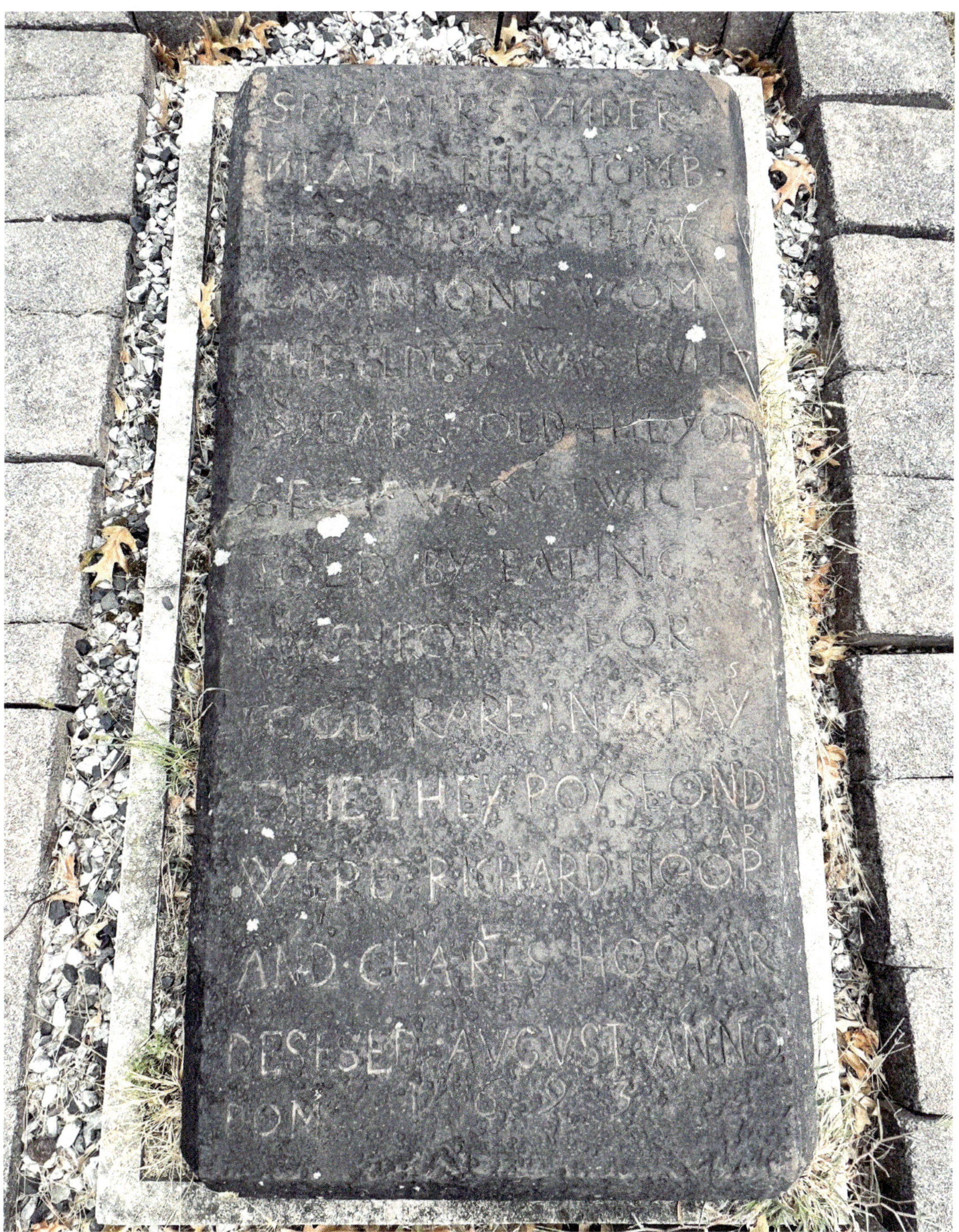

The stone for the Hoopar Brothers at Piscatawaytown Burial Ground. It's substantially bigger than the other stones in the cemetery. It was a damp, dreary day when I visited. I think the rain made the inscription harder to read.

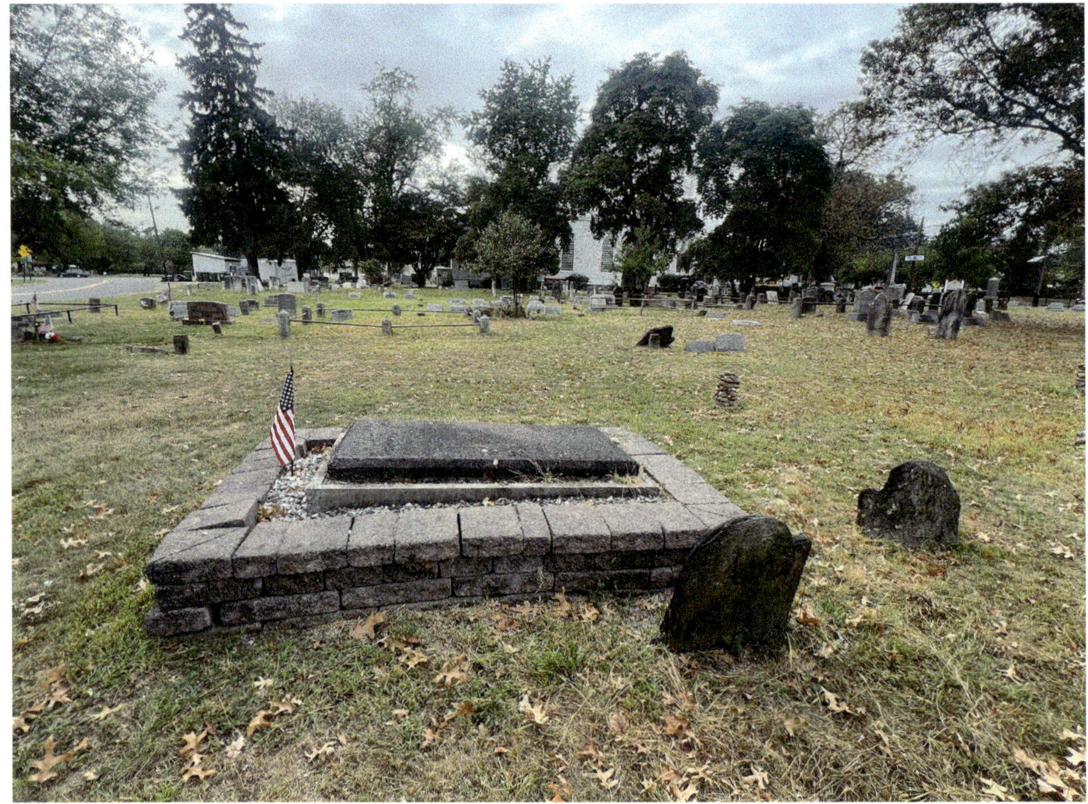

The view of the Hoopar Brothers's stone in the older section of Piscatawaytown Burial Ground with the church in the background.

The area was occupied by the British Army during the Revolutionary War from December 1776 through June 1777.[9] Legend says that thirty British soldiers were buried in front of church.[10] A ground penetrating radar study in 2021 showed that there was a trench along the fence line, but no evidence of British burials.[11, 12] That doesn't necessarily mean that there aren't British burials at the burial ground, they're just not at that location. There are multiple unmarked graves. This part of the cemetery currently has twentieth-century graves.[13] The same location was leveled when the cemetery was cleaned up in 1910.[14]

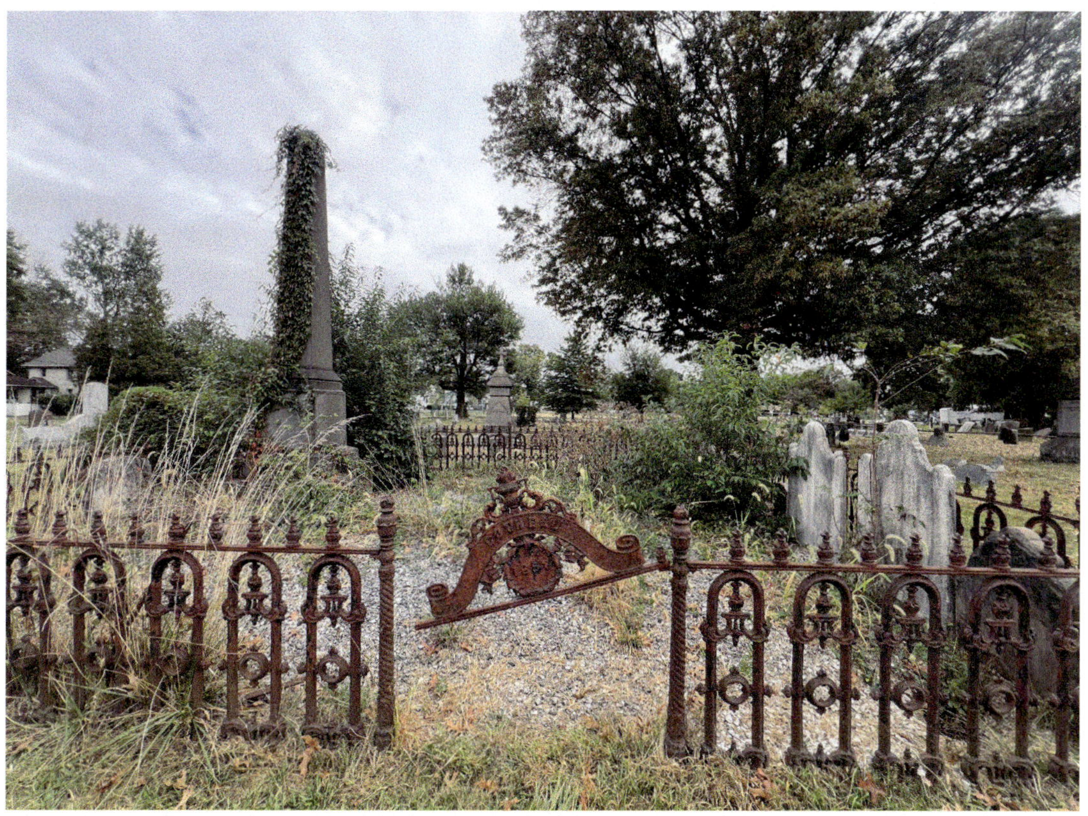

A trench built by the British Army during the Revolutionary War is said to be near the railing of the Cotheal family plot at Piscatawaytown Burial Ground. The fence is still beautiful even as it decays.

I couldn't resist writing about this cemetery after I read some of the legends associated with it. First is the story of Thomas W. Harper who died in the tornado of 1835. Legend says that he was standing outside in the storm and someone told him to enter the inn across the street from the church. Harper responded that he wouldn't fear God until he felt his power. Mr. Harper was then struck with a timber from the church, died four days later, and was buried in the burial ground.[15]

My personal favorite story is the story of Mary Moore. Her legend is a fairly standard "Colonial woman accused of witchery" story. What's interesting is what I discovered while researching Mary Moore. Mary Moore was accused of being a witch by her neighbors.[16] They said that she made animals do strange things, grew strange plants, and dressed like a witch.[17] I don't want to incriminate myself, but I have been known to dress cats in hats, I cultivate Venus fly traps, and I dress like a Victorian hag. I'm just saying that I meet the standard for being a witch if that's the only criteria given. Mary was allegedly hanged for her witchcraft and buried in the cemetery.[18] This raises my first question. Why would a witch be buried in consecrated ground? People who committed suicide weren't even allowed to be buried in consecrated ground, I can't imagine an honest-to-goodness, trafficking-with-the-Devil, bewitching-farm-animals, riding-a-broom witch would be allowed to be buried there. Unless Mary Moore was innocent and just died of her trials.

There is a Mary Moore listed on Dr. Ezra Mundy Hunt's original list of burials which was transcribed by the Metuchen-Edison Historical Society.[19] Mary Moore was real. According to Dr. Hunt's list, Mary Moore died in 1731 at the age of forty-one. But there's more to her legend. A teenage boy in the 1960s, 1970s, or 1980s allegedly stole her headstone and hid it in his closet.[20] This teenage boy was later killed crossing Route 1 and his brother smashed the headstone as retribution.[21] I don't see why that wouldn't just further enrage Mary Moore's vengeful spirit. I don't believe that Mary Moore was a witch or was ever even accused of being a witch.

What I discovered while researching this cemetery is that the colonial province of New Jersey never tried anyone for witchcraft.[22] The only legal record of witchcraft is the lawsuit brought by Abigail Sharp of Woodbridge against Abraham Shotwell.[23] I'm not saying that there weren't individual lynchings, but there aren't any recorded instances of any witch trials in New Jersey. This means that there was no recorded witch trial for Mary Moore.

On May 13, 1727, Abigail Sharp sued Abraham Shotwell in Middlesex County for £500 for trespassing. Shotwell had previously accused Abigail of witchcraft, saying that he saw her turn into a cat on the roof of his house, and that she bewitched his horse which later died. Abraham claimed to have seen Abigail flying early one morning. In the lawsuit, Abigail accused Abraham of maliciously contriving stories to purposely injure her reputation and to force her to face the penalties of being found guilty of witchcraft. Abigail also accused Abraham of ruining her business, her social life, and putting her in physical danger of a witchcraft trial. Shotwell pled not guilty.[24]

Nothing is known of Abigail's origins or the outcome of her case.[25] The three handwritten pages of Abigail's lawsuit are the only existing record remaining.[26] Abigail brought the lawsuit herself, which could indicate that she was either widowed or unmarried.[27] New Jersey's only recorded witchcraft trial is actually a lawsuit brought by the accused witch.

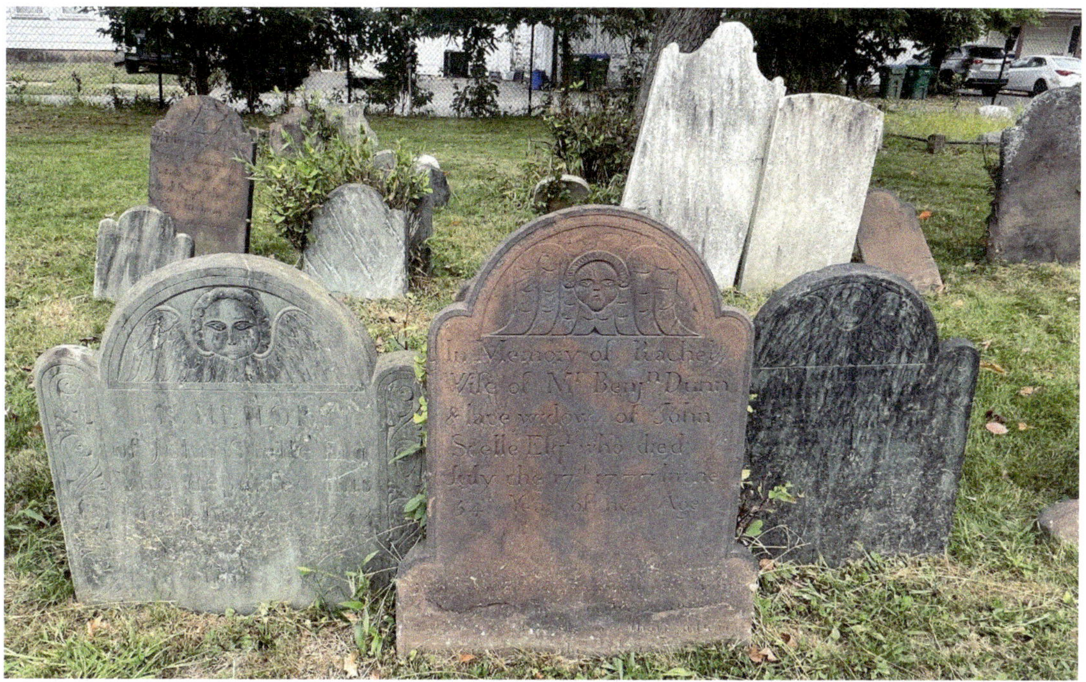

A grouping of three headstones at Piscatawaytown Burial Ground featuring three varieties of soul effigies. I couldn't help but be charmed by the varying styles and levels of grumpiness of these carvings.

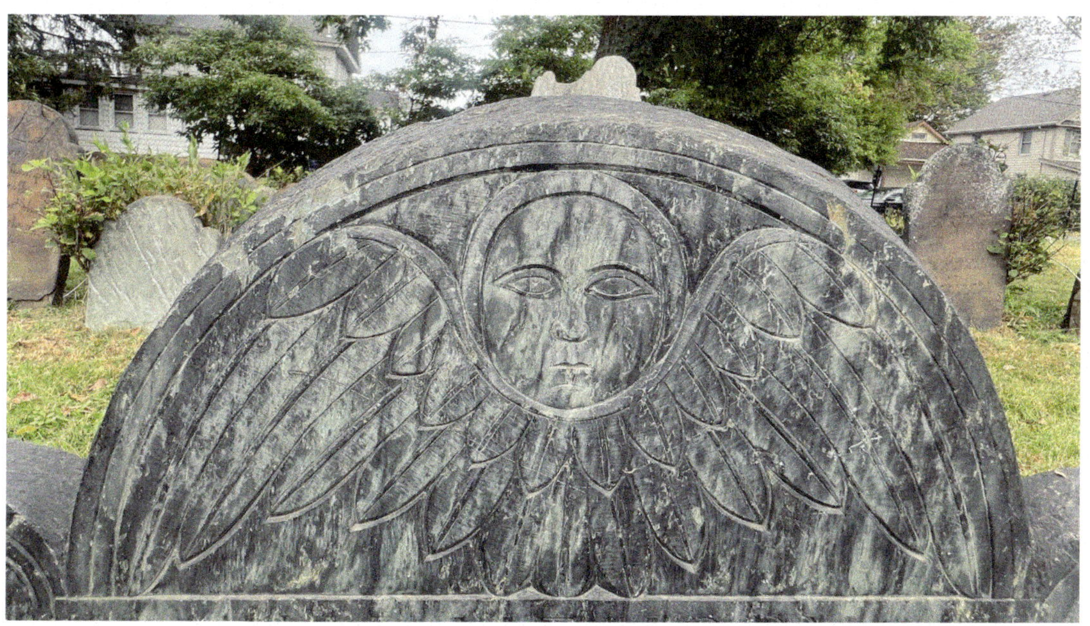

A close-up of one of the soul effigies at Piscatawaytown Burial Ground.

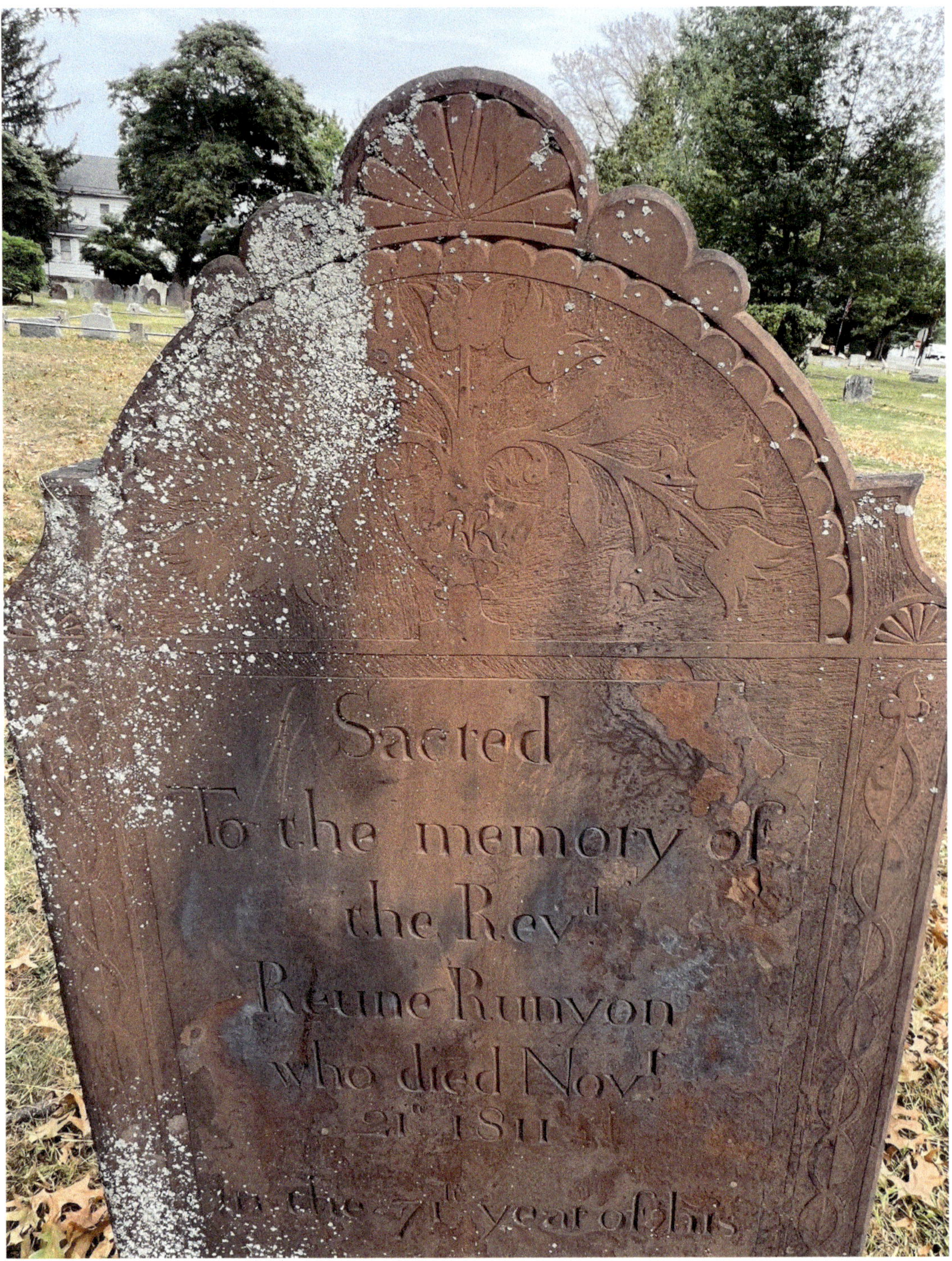

This headstone made of brownstone at Piscatawaytown Burial Ground features a floral motif that would become popular in the Victorian era.

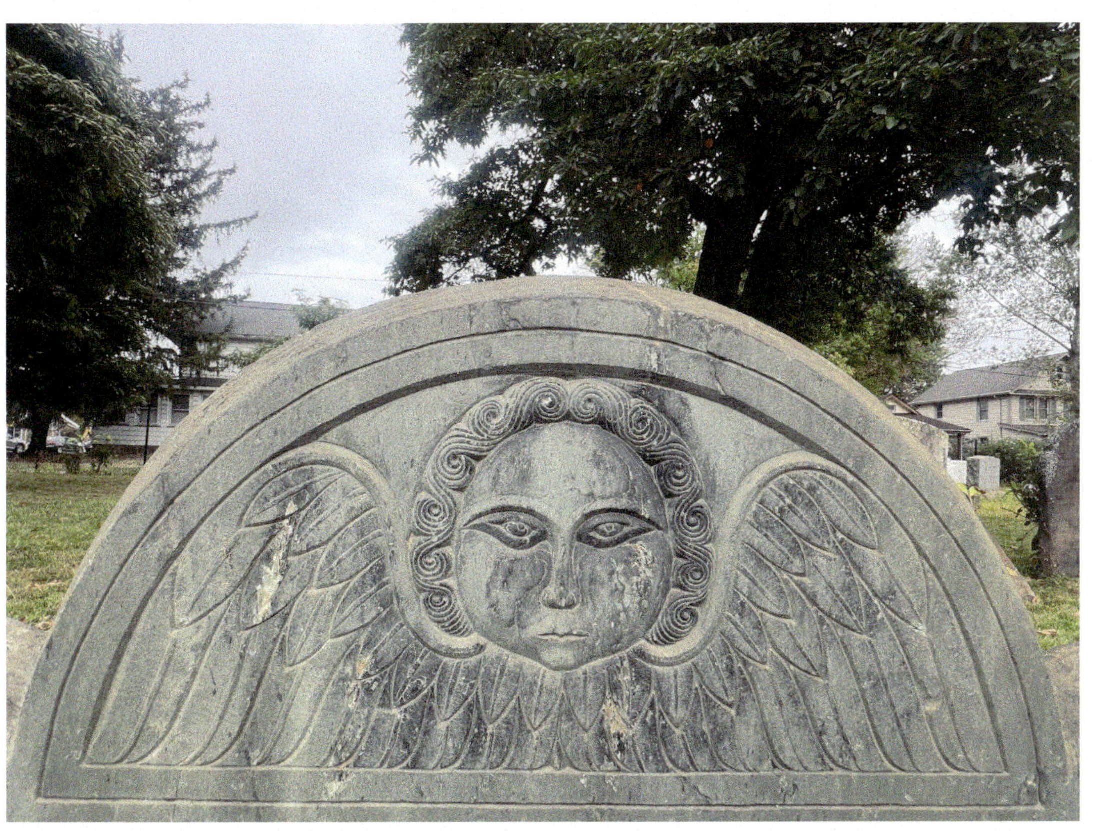

Piscatawaytown Burial Ground has a treasure trove of soul effigies. This is one of my favorites.

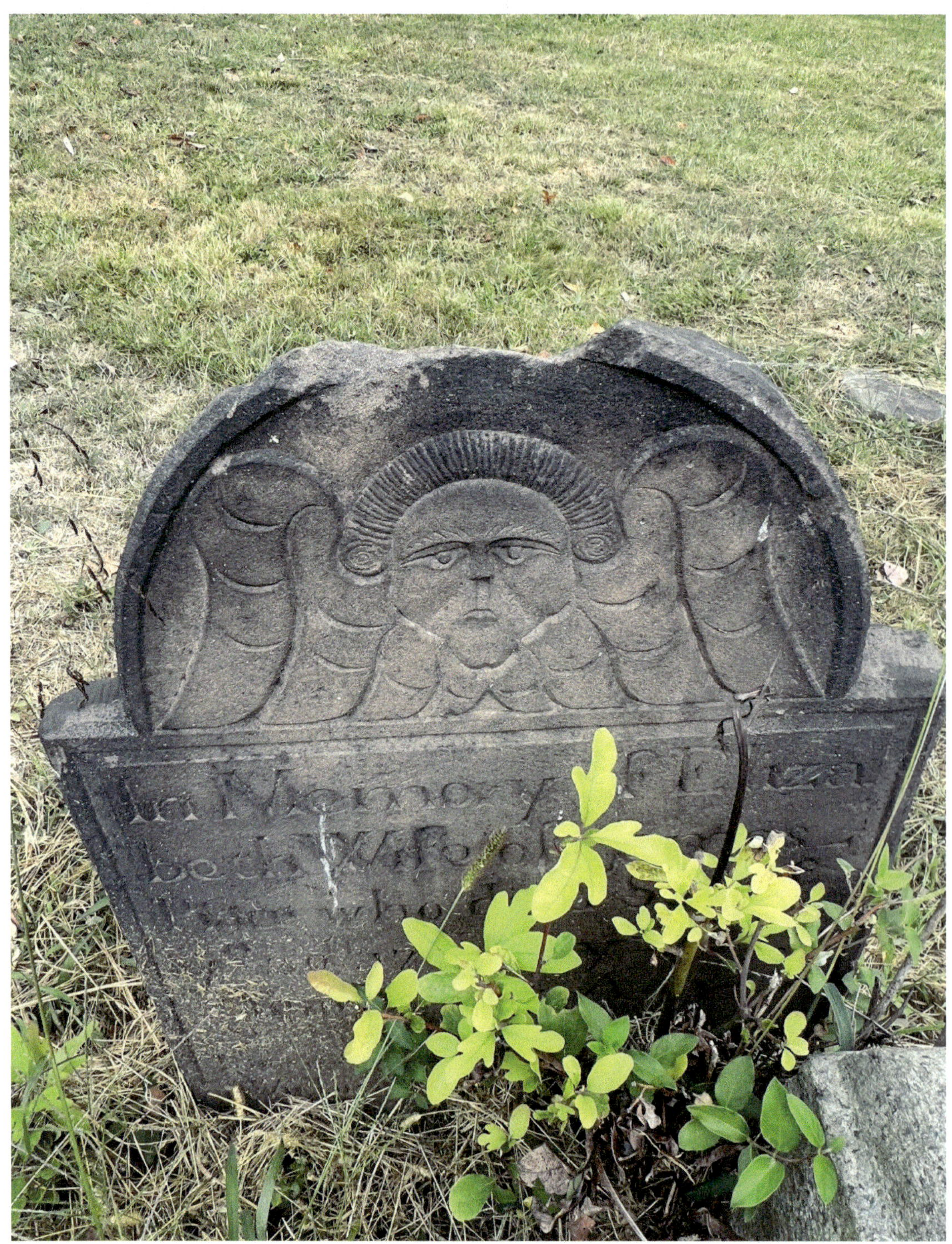

A serious soul effigy with brilliant plants at Piscatawaytown Burial Ground.

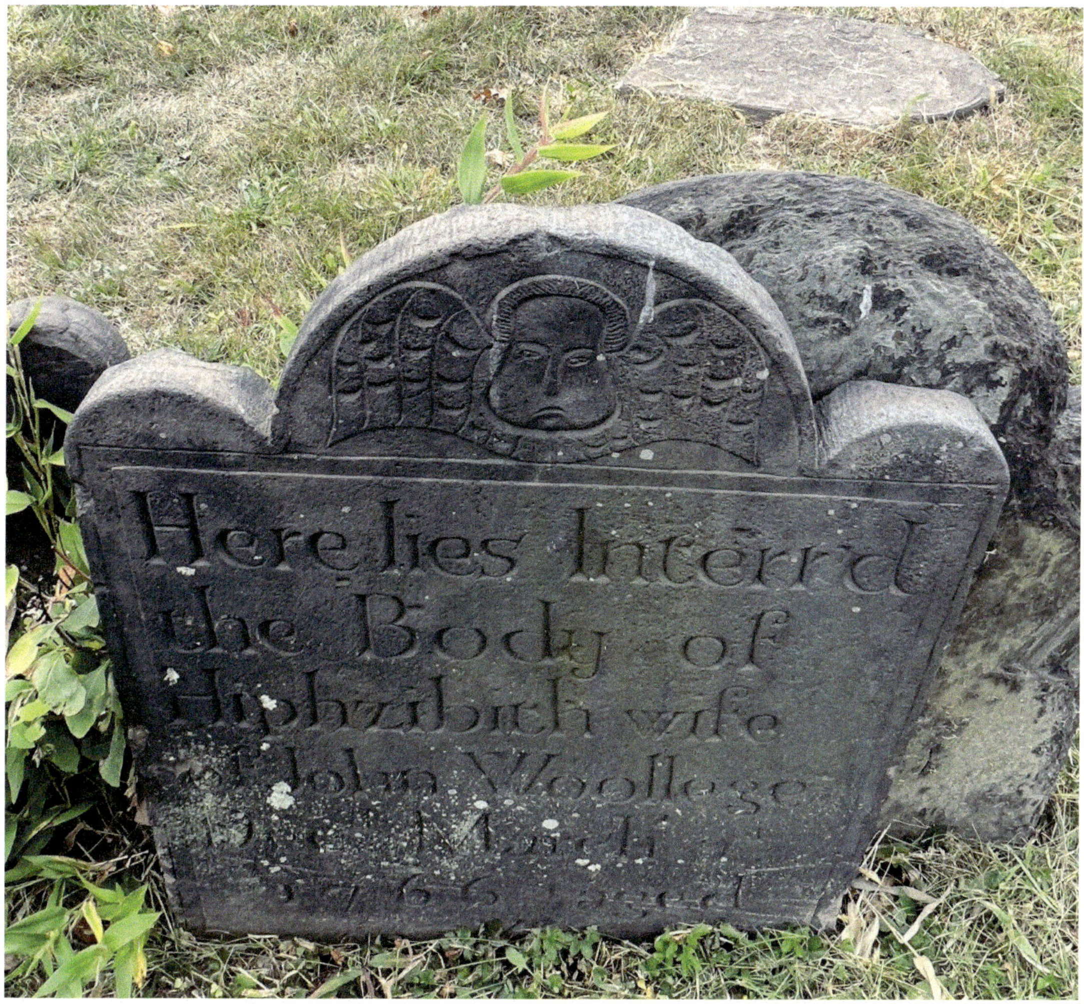

Some of the stones have been toppled at Piscatawaytown Burial Ground but many are still standing and are in good condition.

The cemetery itself is very easy to find. No hiking is required to find it. It's easy to park in the commons behind the cemetery, which is now a park. Some of the graves have collapsed and there are fragments of broken stones on the ground, so you should be cautious walking through it if you decide to visit. The church is very quaint, and it looked like someone was working on repairs when I visited. I found the east side of the cemetery with the older graves to be more interesting. The iconography ranges from colonial to modern.

6
Emilio Carranza Memorial

Wharton State Park, Carranza Rd., Tabernacle, N.J. 08088, 39.777789, -74.633068

The monument for Emilio Carranza Rodríguez is located in Wharton State Park in Tabernacle, N.J. The monument is actually a cenotaph. A cenotaph is a monument built for someone whose remains have been lost or are buried elsewhere. Emilio Carranza's memorial marks the site of his fatal plane crash in 1928, but Carranza is buried in Mexico. Emilio Carranza was considered the Mexican Charles Lindbergh.

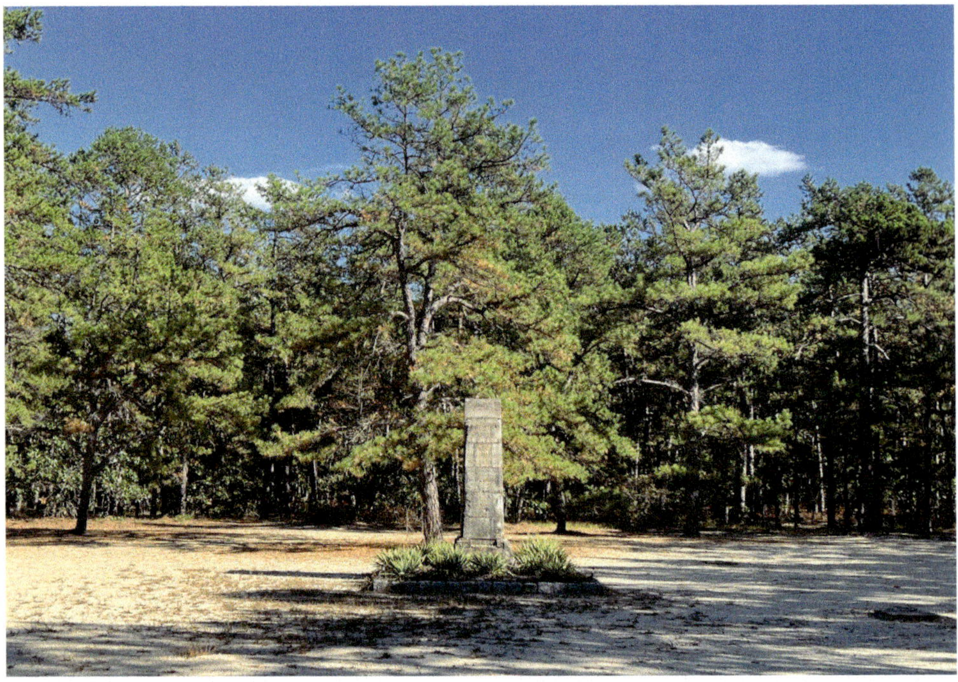

The cenotaph for Emilio Carranza stands in the middle of a sandy clearing at Wharton State Park. Each side has its own inscription and the whole monument is surrounded by yucca plants.

The Carranza Monument was built in 1931 with money fundraised by Mexican and local school children.[1, 2] The monument was built from stone quarried in Mexico.[3] The 4-foot-long bases are surrounded by yucca plants.[4] One side has a carving of an Aztec-style eagle falling to earth and the other side has an arrow flying to heaven. The other sides have two inscriptions, one in English and one in Spanish. The inscriptions read: "Messenger of Peace, The people of Mexico hope that your high ideals will be realized, Homage of the children of Mexico to the aviator captain Emilio Carranza who died tragically on July 13, 1928 in his good will flight."

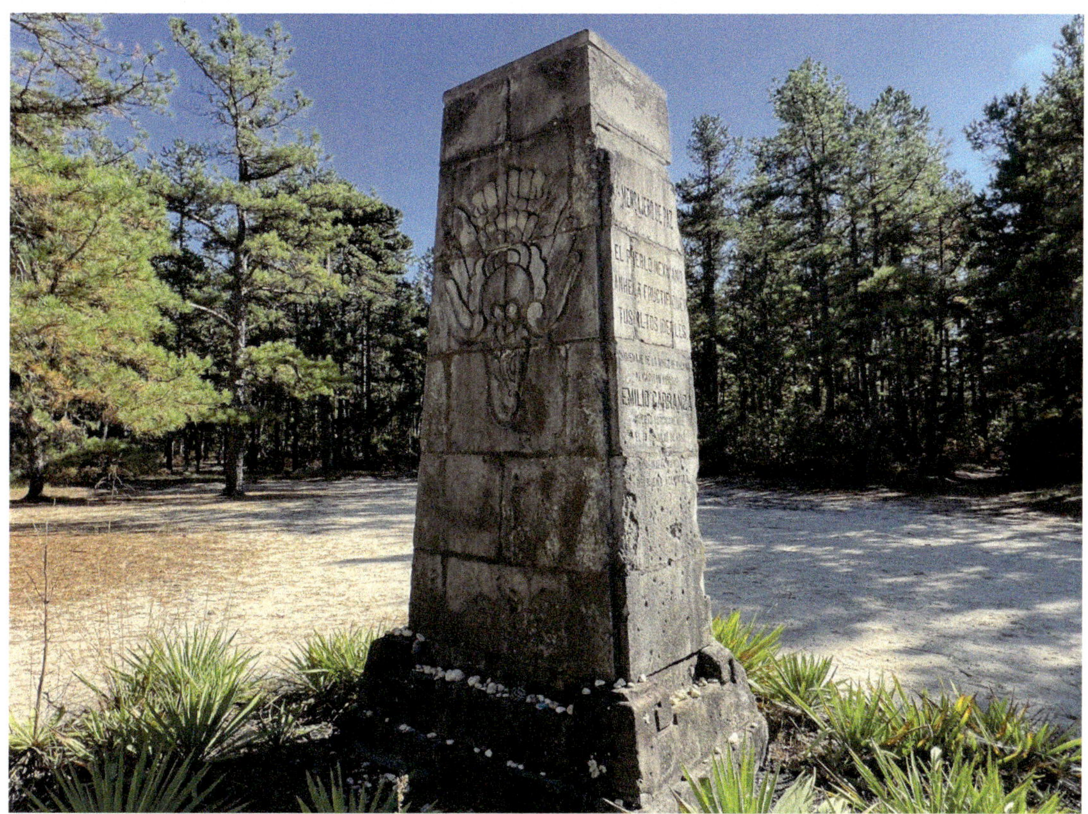

One side of Emilio Carranza's cenotaph depicts an Aztec-style eagle falling to earth. The Spanish side of the monument is visible from this angle.

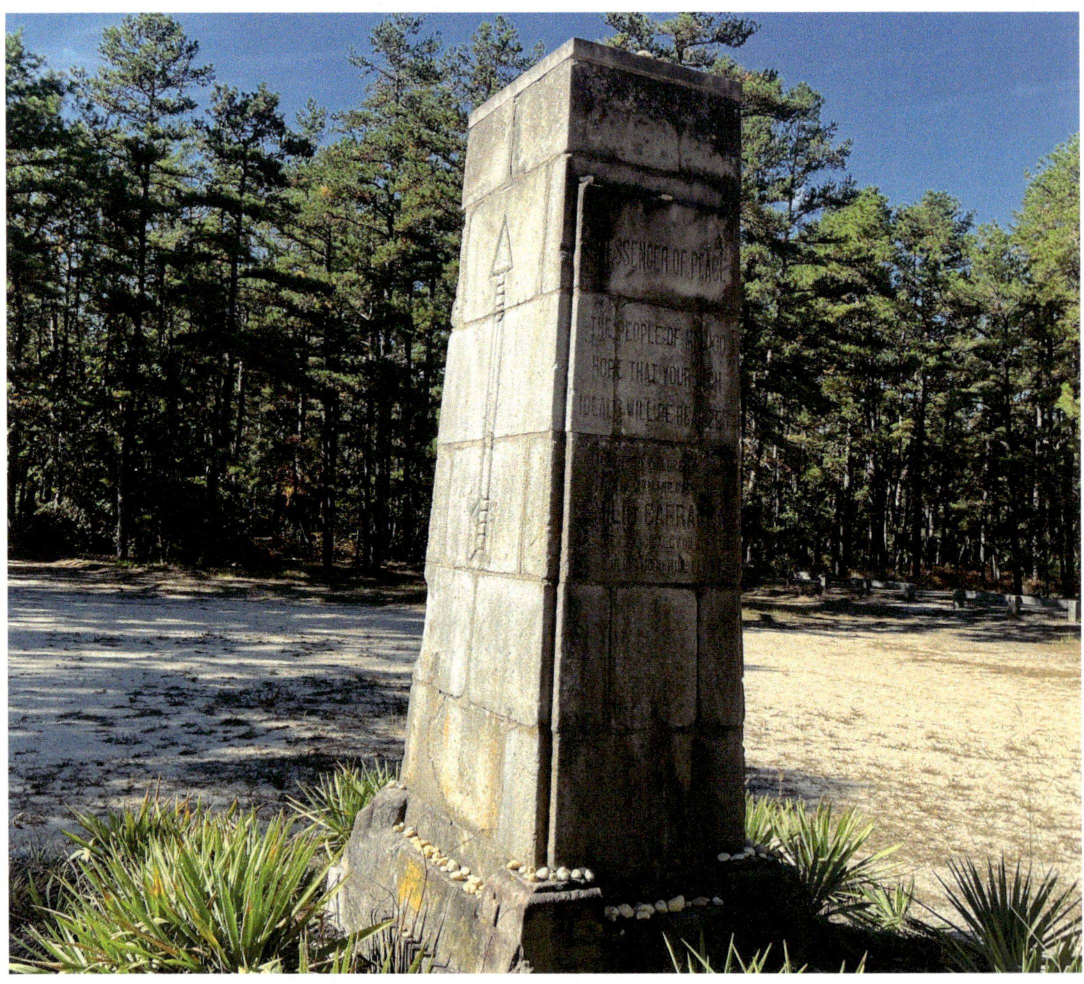

My favorite side of Emilio Carranza's monument is the arrow shooting towards heaven. I think it's a beautiful message of hope and achieving your dreams. Part of the English inscription is visible from this angle.

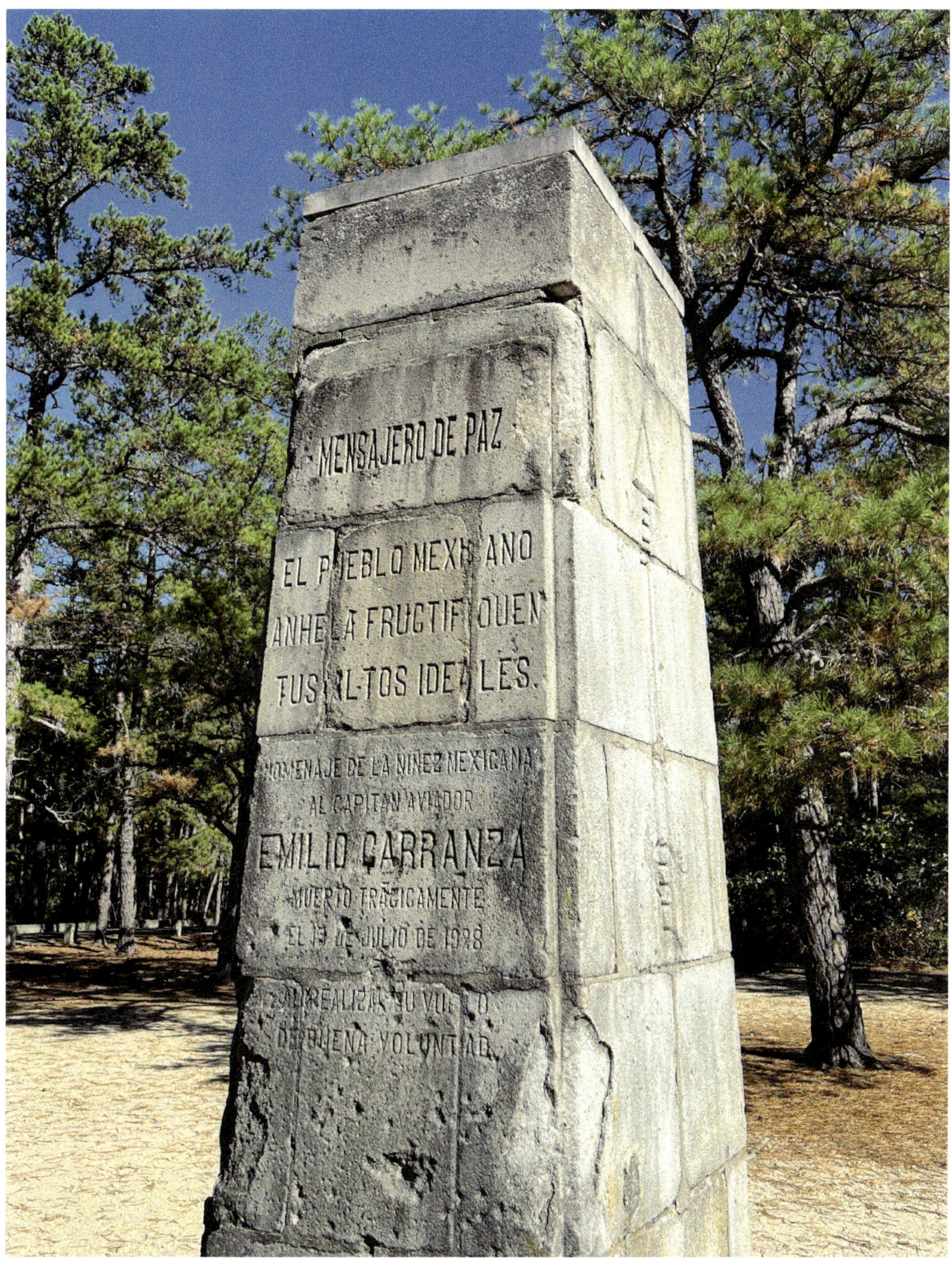

A closer detail of the Spanish inscription on Emilio Carranza's monument with the arrow pointing to heaven visible.

The year 1928 was good for Emilio Carranza until the plane crash. That was the year that Carranza became an international hero and possibly the most famous man in Mexico.[5] Emilio Carranza Rodríguez was born on December 9, 1905, in Ramos Arizpe, Coahuila, Mexico.[6] Carranza's father, Sebastian Carranza Cepeda, was an attaché for the Mexican consulate in New York City.[7] Emilio was the grandnephew of Don Venustiano Carranza, the first president of the Grand Republic of Mexico who was assassinated in 1920.[8] According to his descendants, Carranza loved planes even as a young boy and used to frequently visit the flying academy.[9] Carranza idolized Charles Lindbergh when he was young.[10]

Carranza made the first flight between Mexico City and Juarez, a distance of almost 1,000 miles, in September 1927.[11] Carranza landed the same day that Charles Lindbergh landed in El Paso, Texas.[12] That's when Lindbergh and Carranza first met, and they became reacquainted when Lindbergh made his goodwill flight from Washington, D.C., to Mexico City.[13] Tensions between Mexico and the United States were high in the early twentieth century due to war and business conflicts.[14] This sounds exactly how things are right now.

Carranza was selected to undertake the goodwill flight from Mexico City to New York City. Carranza took off from Mexico City to Washington, D.C., on June 11, 1928, with his bride of six months, Maria Luisa Corbata, seeing him off. The flight to Washington, D.C., was routine until thick fog forced an emergency landing in North Carolina.[15]

Carranza landed in Washington, D.C., on June 12, 1928, where he was congratulated by President Calvin Coolidge.[16] Carranza then flew to Roosevelt Field on Long Island, N.Y.[17] New York City mayor Jimmy Walker gave Carranza the key to the city.[18] A banquet was held in Carranza's honor that included President Coolidge, mayor Walker, Charlie Chaplin, and former heavyweight champion Jack Dempsey.[19] After the banquet Carranza announced that he was planning a nonstop solo flight from New York City to Mexico City.[20] Carranza's return trip to Mexico City would be the longest nonstop solo flight in the Americas.[21]

The summer weather caused difficulties in planning the return flight.[22] Carranza's return flight was repeatedly delayed by summer thunderstorms.[23] On July 12, 1928, Carranza departed from New York for his return trip to Mexico City.[24] Carranza ordered his plane readied while he was eating at the Waldorf Astoria.[25] Carranza took off at 7:18 p.m. from Roosevelt Field during a break in an electrical storm.[26] Experienced pilots warned Carranza to postpone his flight.[27] Lindbergh himself advised Carranza to put off his return flight until the summer storm season was over.[28] Carranza's motivations for departing so suddenly are unclear. His wife was six months pregnant when he left Mexico a month prior. It's possible that he just wanted to be home with his family or he could have been concerned about how the repeated delays were impacting his reputation.

Little is known about the crash aside from what was pieced together from the crash site. Black box recorders wouldn't be put into planes until the 1950s. What's known is that Carranza flew for an hour before he crashed.[29] The plane broke up and crashed in the woods in the Pine Barrens.[30] One wing of the plane and Carranza's flight jacket were charred, which supports the hypothesis that his plane was struck by lightning. The second hypothesis is that Carranza was flying low looking for a place to land when his plane hit trees and flipped. Carranza's body was found with the flashlight that he was holding jammed through the palm of his hand by the force of the crash.[31] It was reported that both wings of the plane were found shorn from the fuselage and there was a debris field spread over a quarter of a mile.[32] There was no trace of the parachute that Carranza was known to carry on board with him in the wreckage.[33]

Carranza's body was found and recovered on July 13, 1928.[34] John Henry Carr was picking huckleberries when he found Carranza's body and wrecked plane.[35] The Mexican government gave Carr $500.00 for his services.[36] Carranza's body was recovered by members of the Mount Holly American Legion Post 11 and carried to a local garage.[37] Colonel C. V. Wickersham, the chief of staff of the 77th Division at Fort Dix, selected an honor guard of six to guard Carranza's body overnight.[38] Carranza's death certificate was signed by coroner Ben F. Farmer and his cause of death was listed as "Accidental fall from airplane."[39]

On July 14, 1928, Carranza's body was escorted by Mexican officials and New Jersey State Troopers to New York City for funeral services. Carranza's body lay in state at the funeral home where the public could view Carranza dressed in his Mexican Air Corps captain's uniform. Then Carranza's flag-draped casket was placed on a caisson and processed from the funeral home to Penn Station. It was reported that 10,000 soldiers led the procession to Penn Station. Mexico's President Calle requested that Carranza's body be sent by train to Laredo, Texas, where family and dignitaries met Carranza and escorted his body to Mexico City where he was buried in the Rotunda of Illustrious Persons.[40, 41]

Yearly services in Carranza's honor were held at the crash site starting in 1929.[42] American Legion Post 11 organized the first anniversary memorial in 1929 at the crash site and pledged to honor Carranza's memory and his mission of goodwill and peace.[43] Services are still held on the Saturday closest to the anniversary of the crash at 1:00 p.m. with members of American Legion Mount Holly Post 11, and an entourage of attendees from the Mexican consulates in New York City and Philadelphia.[44]

The monument is easy to find. It's possible to follow either the GPS coordinates or to search Carranza Memorial in Google Maps. It's located off of Carranza Road, past the juvenile camp. Be aware that cell service isn't great this deep in the Pine Barrens. Parking is easily located off of Carranza Road and a short path takes you right to the monument. The whole park is gorgeous and is worth exploring as part of your visit. A friendly cyclist pulled over while I was taking photographs and warned that this is one of the only locations in New Jersey that still has timber rattlesnakes.

This monument made me the most emotional out of all the cemeteries and graves that I've photographed. It's strangely beautiful. It doesn't look like the obelisks at Mount Pleasant or the hundreds of columns with draped urns that I've seen. The stone is rough-hewn, and it's not polished. My favorite side is the arrow pointing to heaven. It reminds me of some of my favorite Victorian-era cemetery iconography, a hand with a finger pointing towards heaven. Carranza lived to fly but it's also like that arrow is a reminder to look for something bigger in life. Reading the words on Carranza's monument made me sad. "Messenger of Peace ... The people of Mexico Hope that your high ideals will be realized." It's almost 100 years since Carranza's flight and our countries are still bickering.

7
Honorable Mentions

I visited and photographed more cemeteries than I could fit into this book. I could probably fill three books with the cemeteries that I visited. Here are some cemeteries that are no less beautiful or worthy than the previous cemeteries.

Good Luck Cemetery

Lacey Township, N.J.

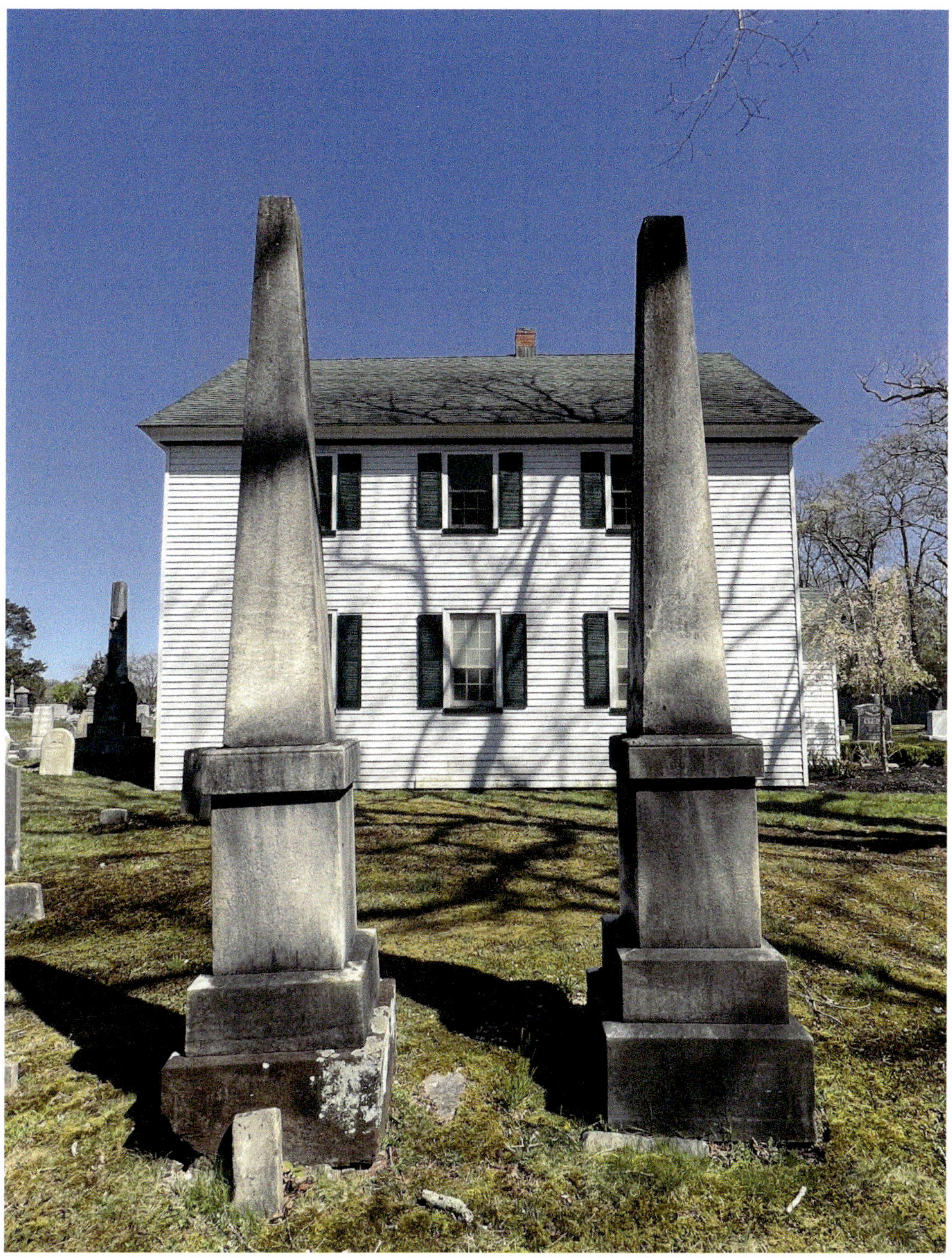

Potter Church at Good Luck Cemetery was the birthplace of Universalism in the United States.

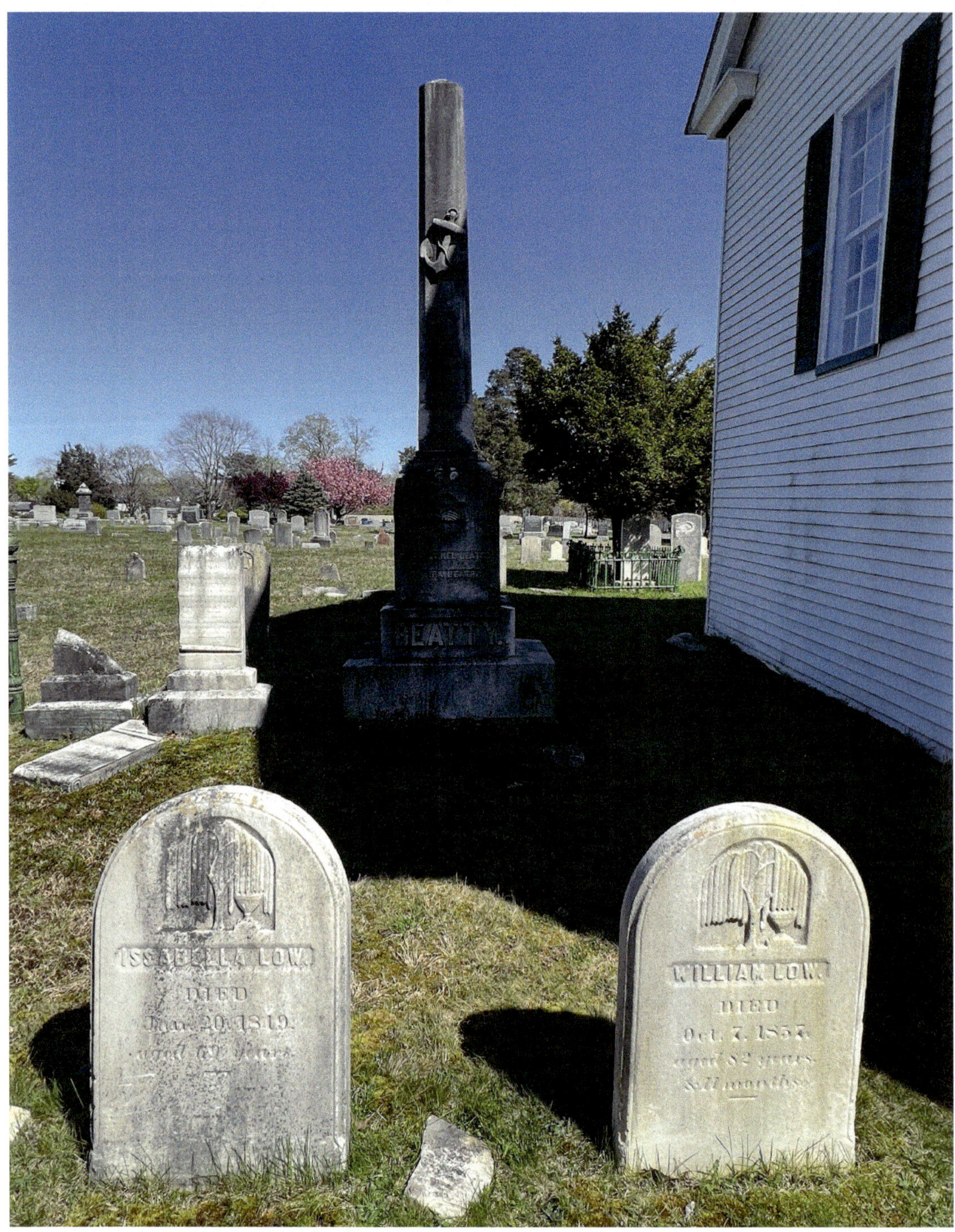

The stones at Good Luck Cemetery show a range of iconography from colonial to Victorian. There is also an extensive modern section. These headstones have weeping willows that would become very popular in the Victorian era.

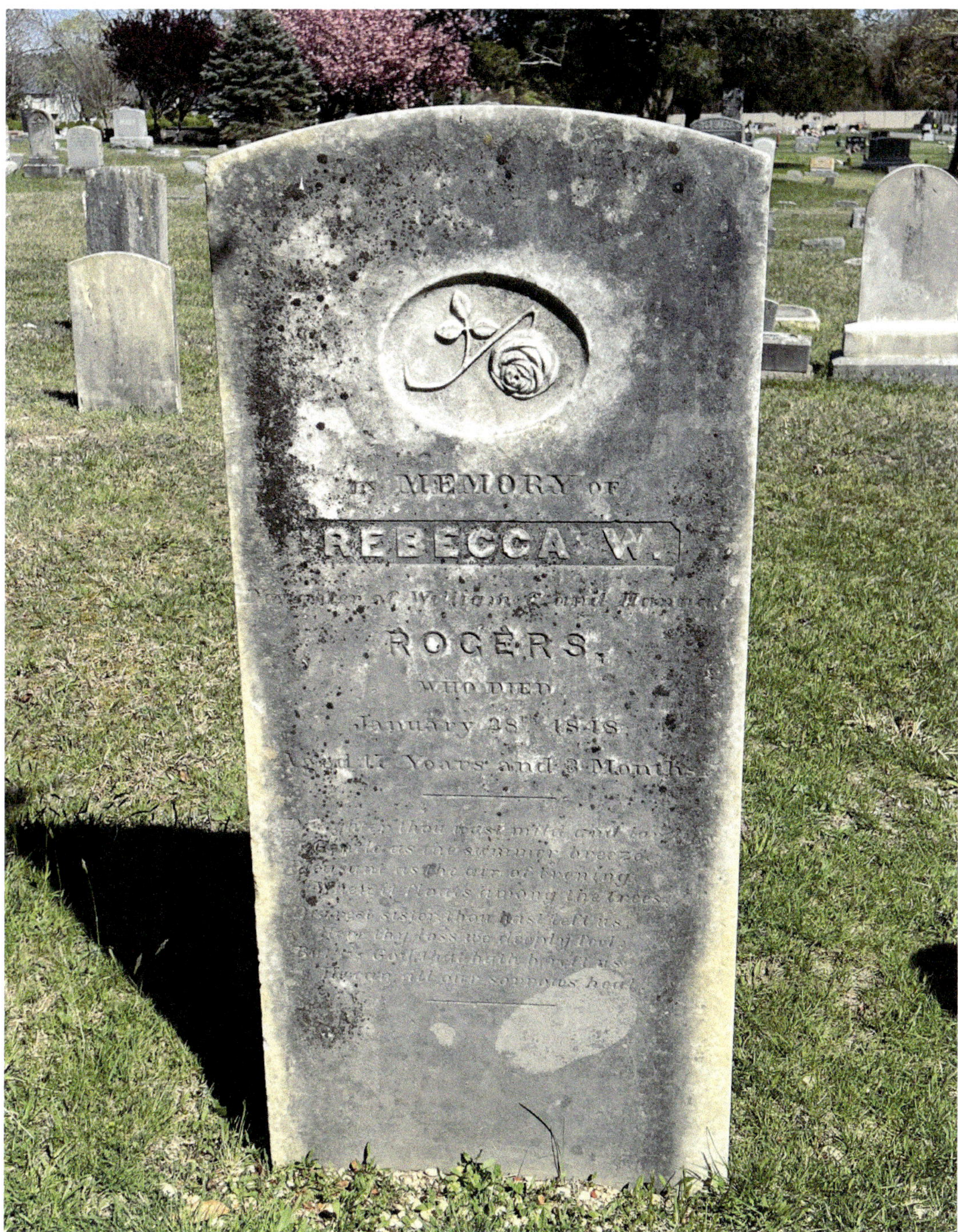

A headstone featuring a rose with a snapped stem at Good Luck Cemetery. A flower with a snapped stem was a popular way of conveying the death of a young person. Rebecca was seventeen years old when she died.

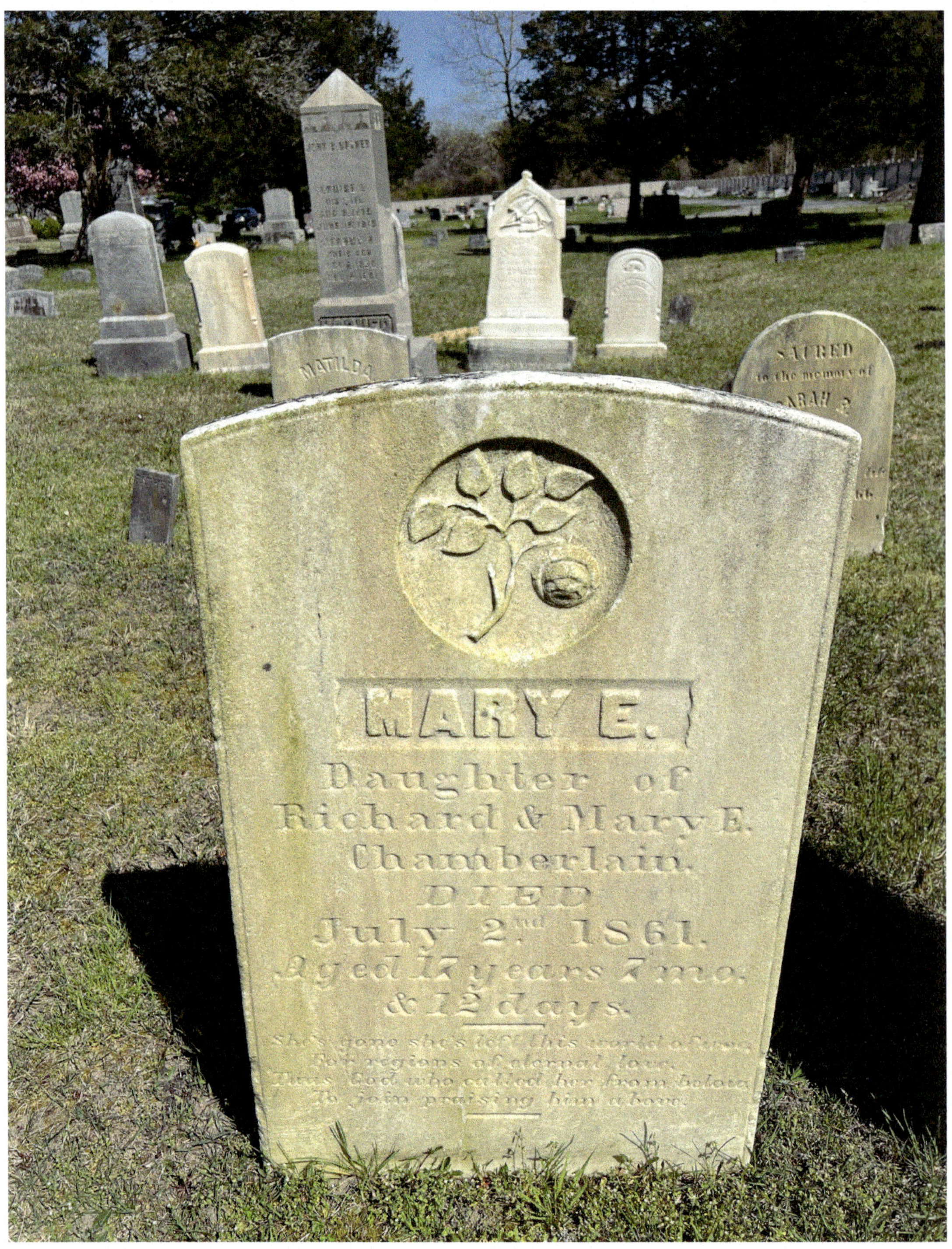

A flower that was not fully blossomed was also a popular Victorian way of conveying the loss of a young person. Mary was also seventeen when she died.

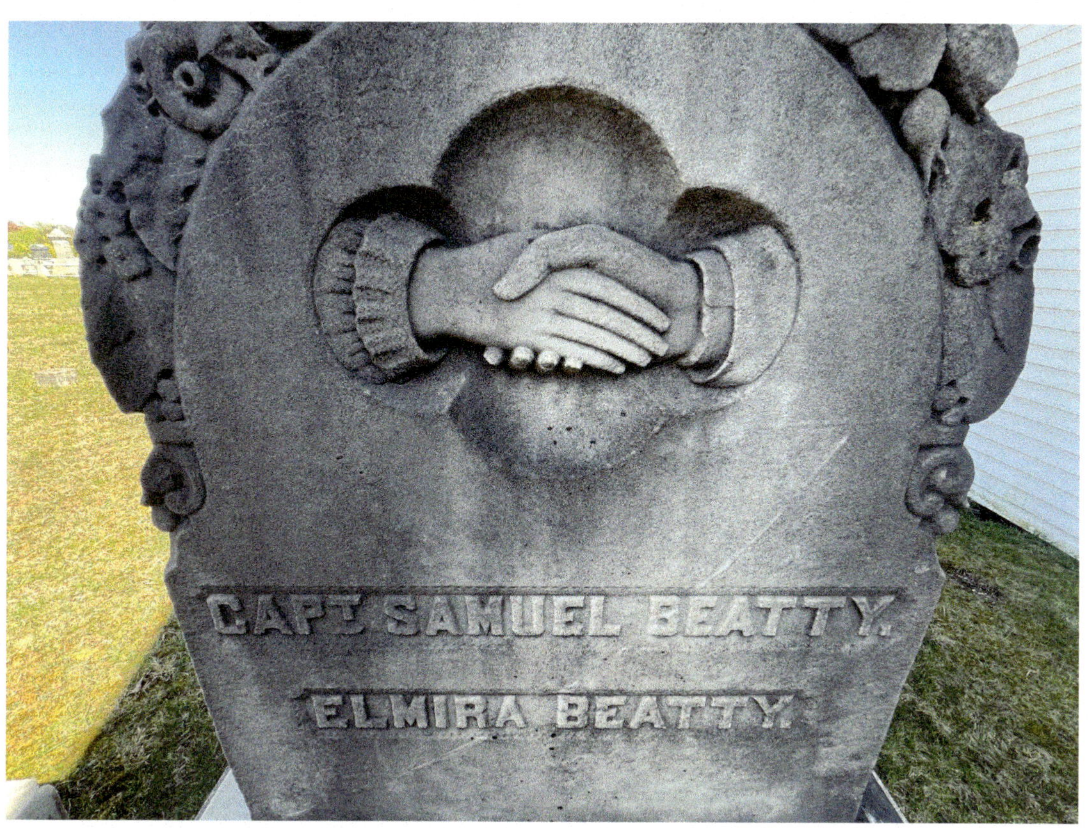

This monument depicting a pair of clasped hands for Captain Samuel Beatty and Elmira Beatty has one of the most striking designs I've ever seen. Notice the differing style of cuffs, allowing the viewer to tell which hand is Elmira's and which hand is Samuel's.

Congregation Ahavath Joseph

Hawthorne, N.J.

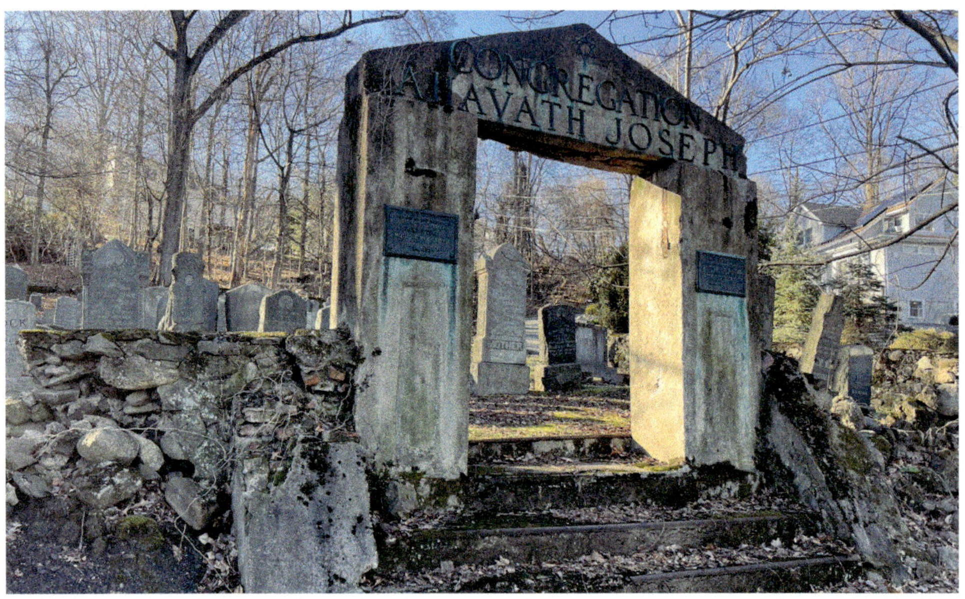

Above: The gate to Congregation Ahavath Joseph Cemetery is impressive despite the deterioration of the cemetery wall.

Below: Congregation Ahavath Joseph Cemetery is very small and across the street from a suburban neighborhood. It's built on a hill that becomes quite steep.

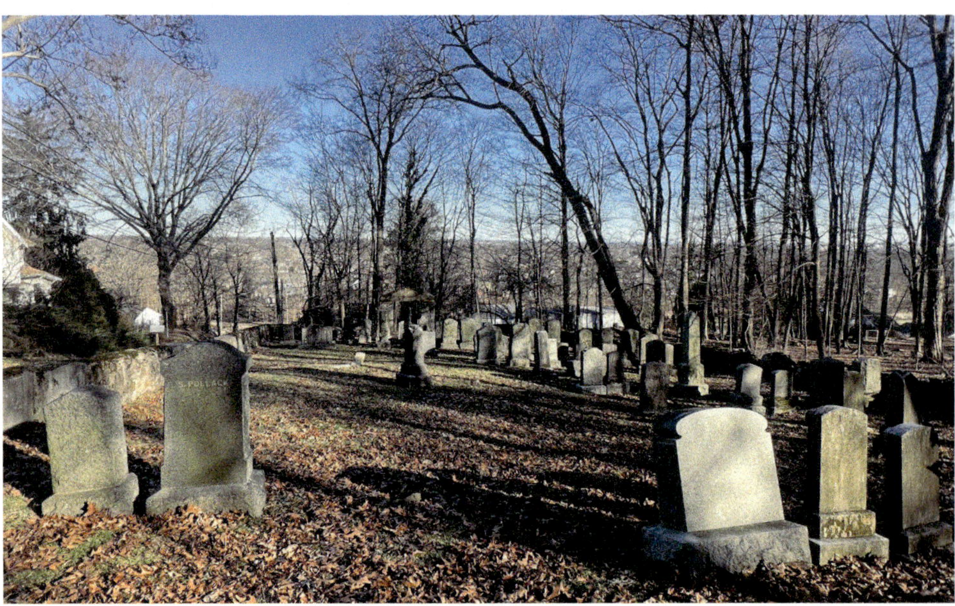

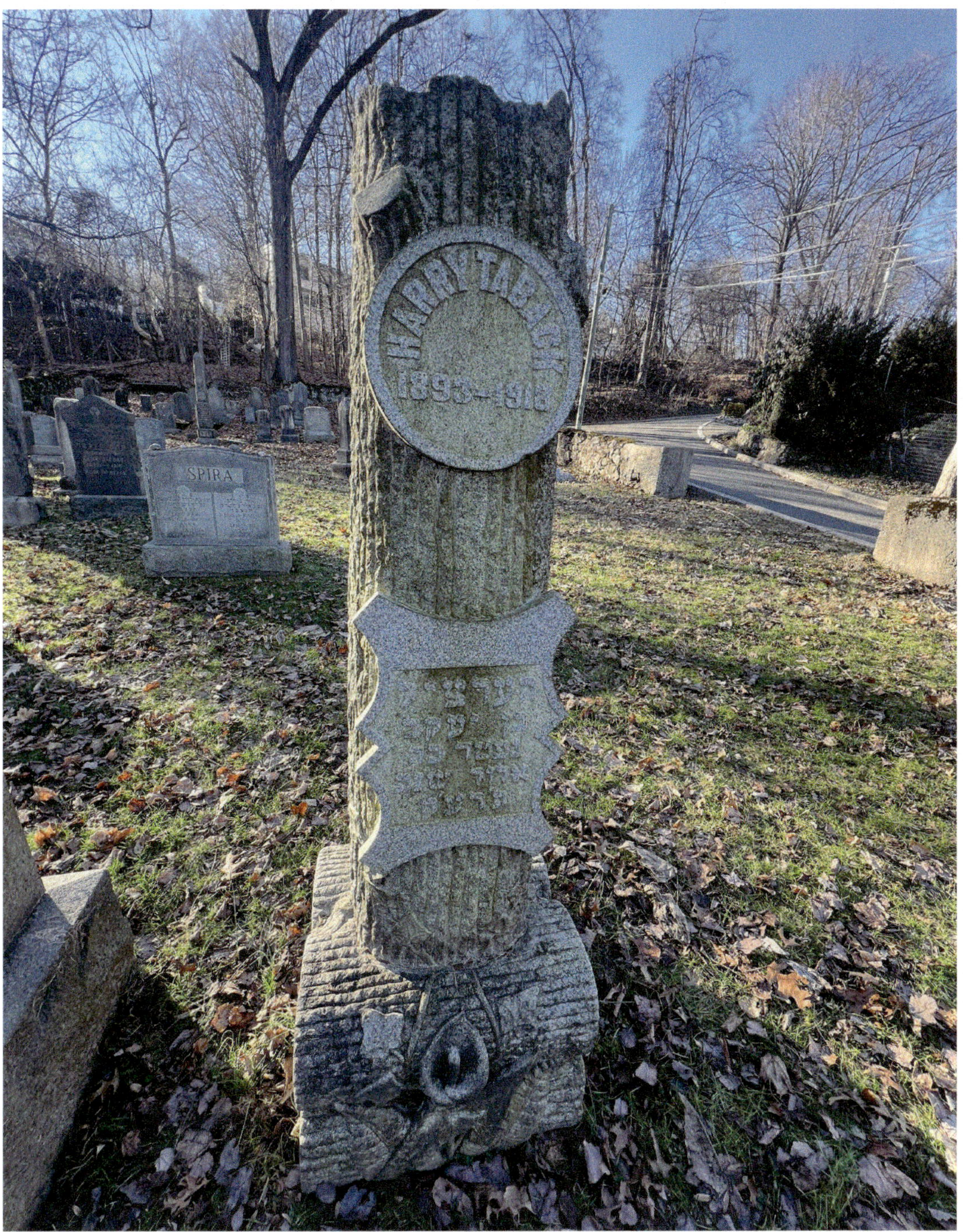

A headstone at Congregation Ahavath Joseph is shaped like a tree that's been chopped down. This symbolizes an early death, like the earlier headstone with a snapped flower. Harry died in 1918; it's possible he was a victim of the Spanish flu.

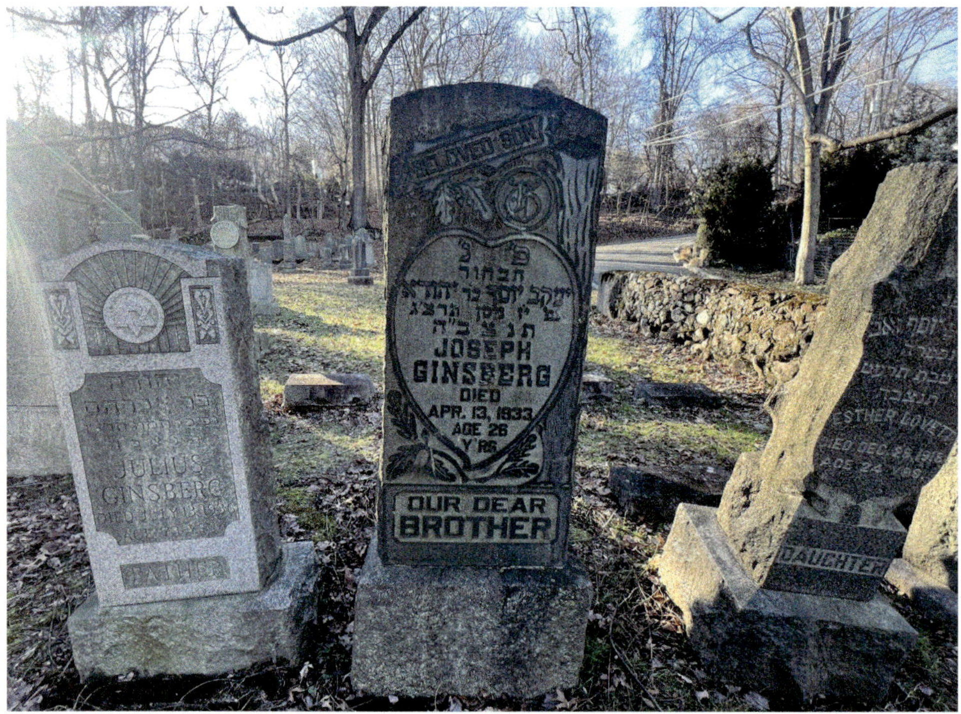

Above: Instead of being shaped like a tree that's been chopped down, Joseph Ginsberg's family had the tree engraved on his stone. He was also young.

Below: The Cohen stone is engraved with the symbol of the Kohanim blessing.

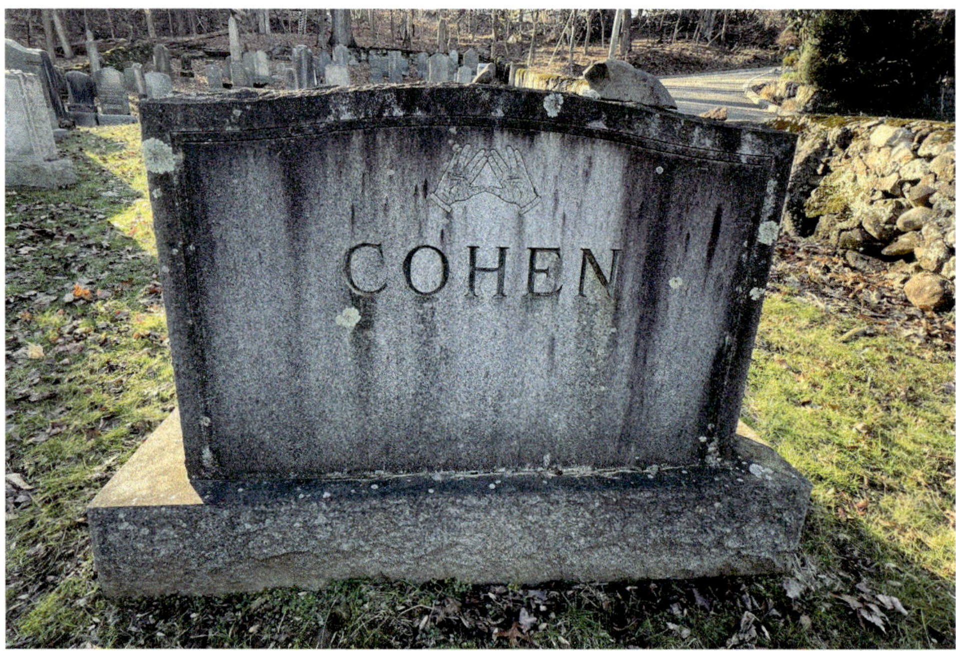

VERMEULEN CEMETERY

Hawthorne, N.J.

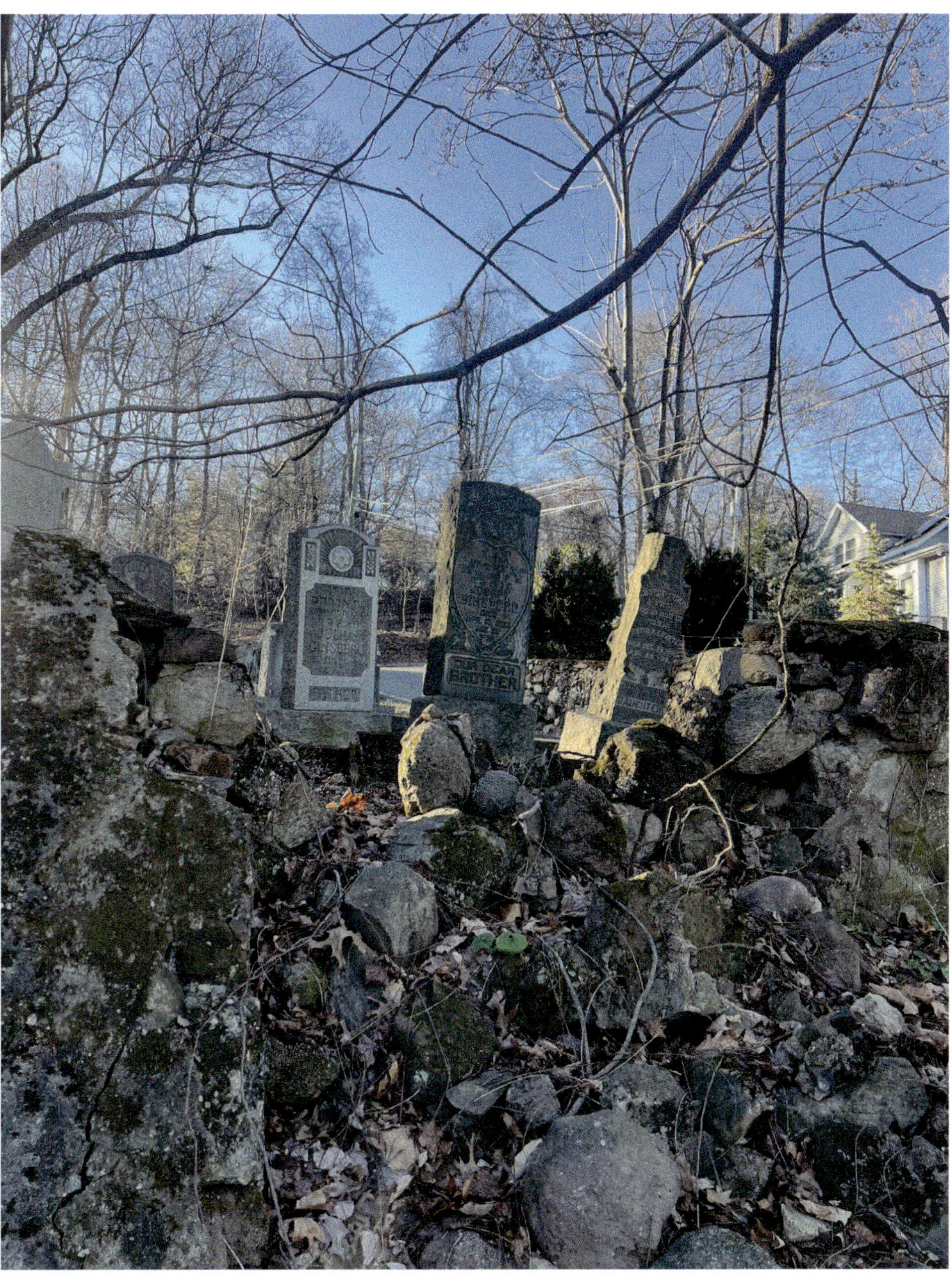

The view of Congregation Ahavath Joseph Cemetery, from Vermeulen Cemetery. Vermeulen Cemetery was the original cemetery on this plot of land Congregation Ahavath Joseph Cemetery was built at a later date.

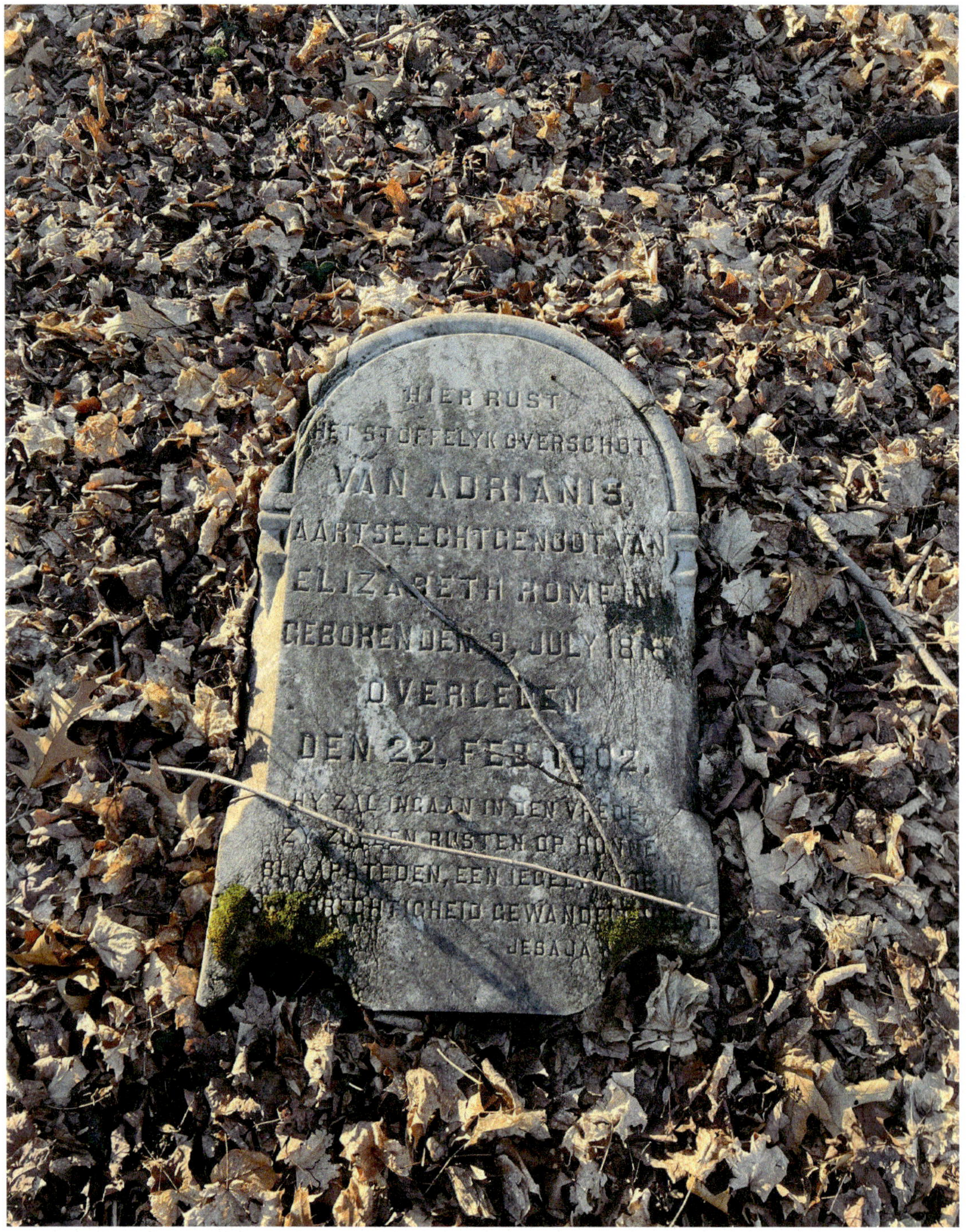

Vermeulen Cemetery served members of the Dutch reformed churches of the community. Many of the headstones are in Dutch.

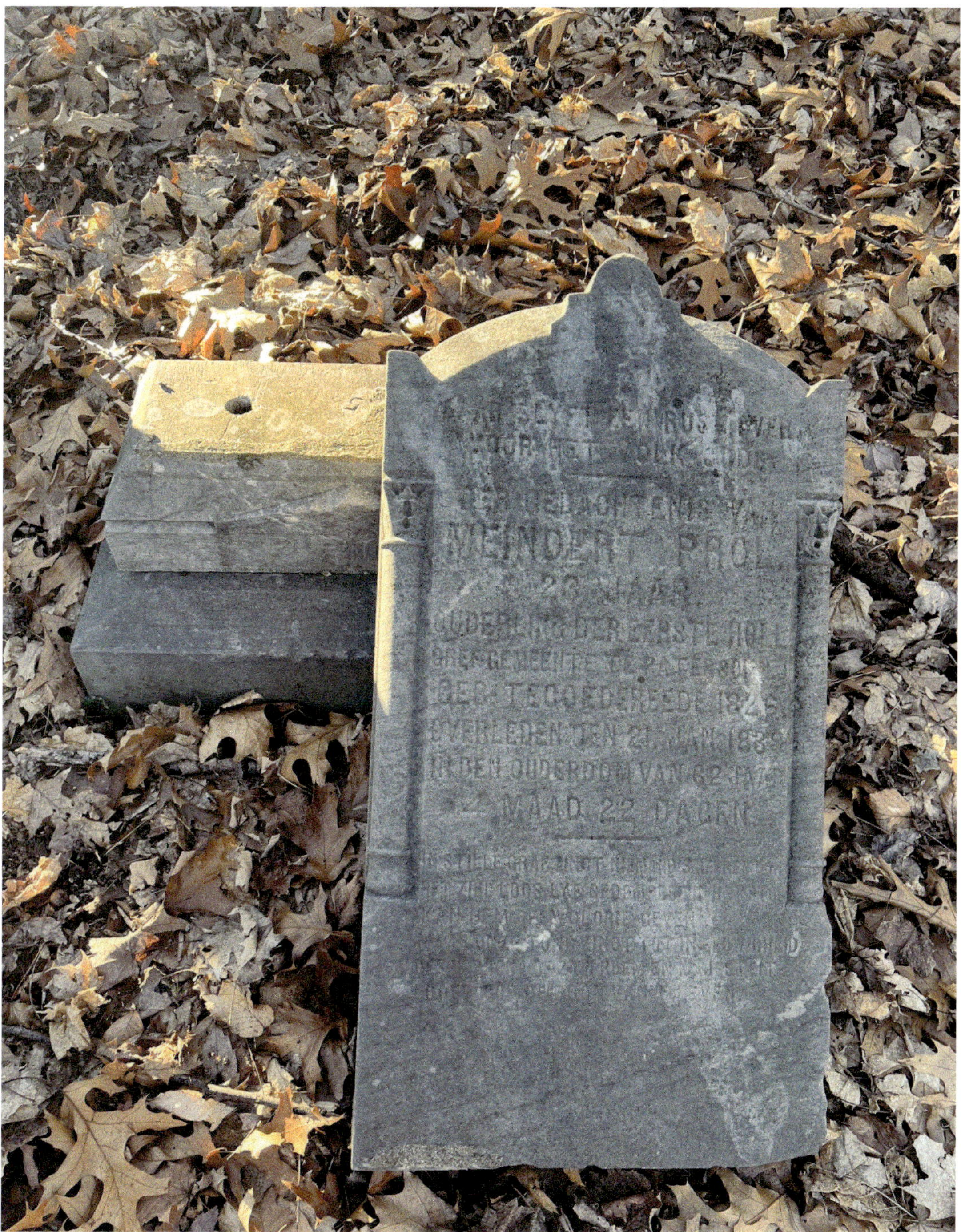

Most of the graves at Vermeulen Cemetery were exhumed and moved with their stones to Fair Lawn Memorial Cemetery in the 1920s.

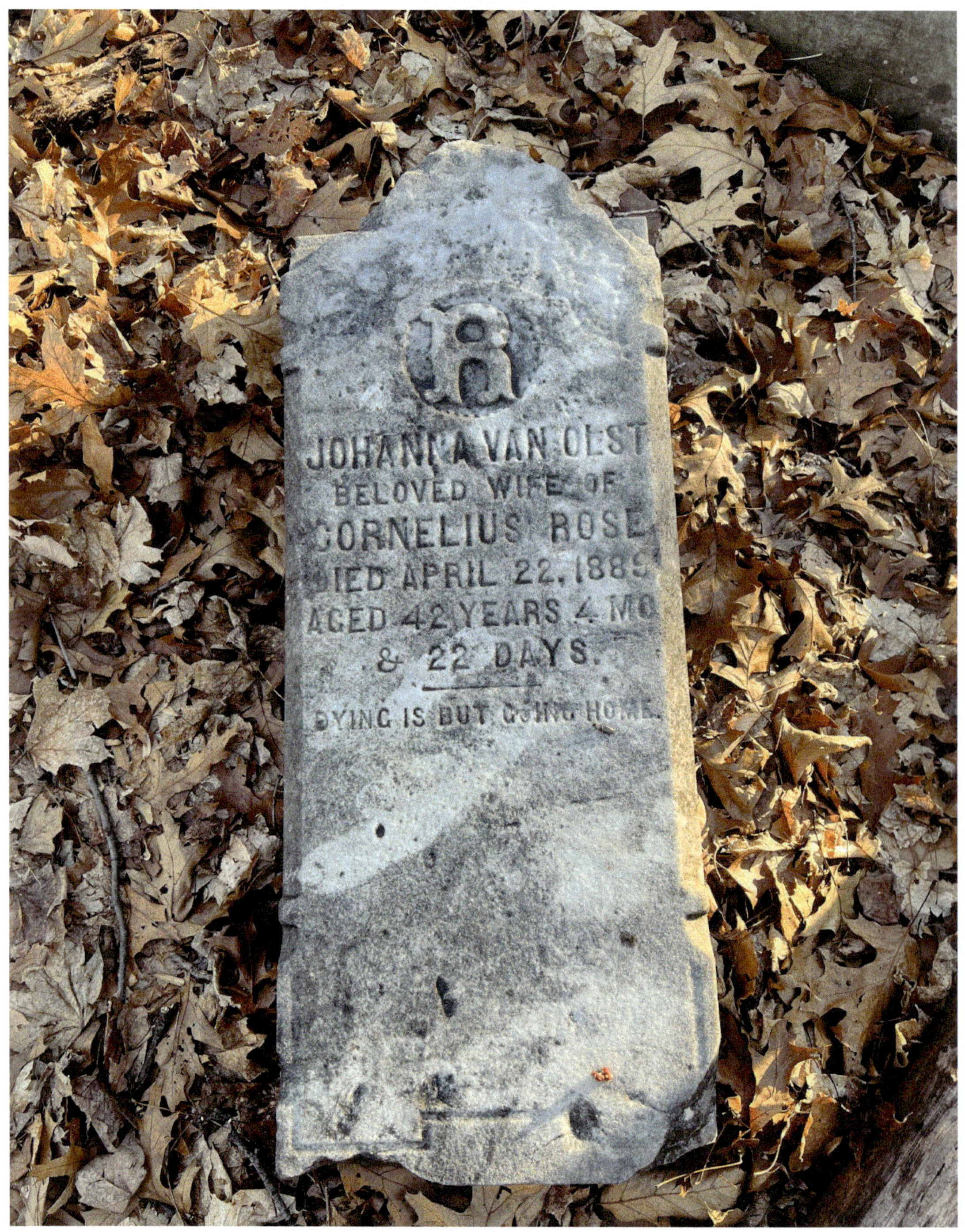

A poignant epitaph at Vermeulen Cemetery notes that dying is but going home.

Dr. Truman Betts's Edgar Allan Poe-Inspired Grave

Riverview Cemetery, Trenton, N.J.

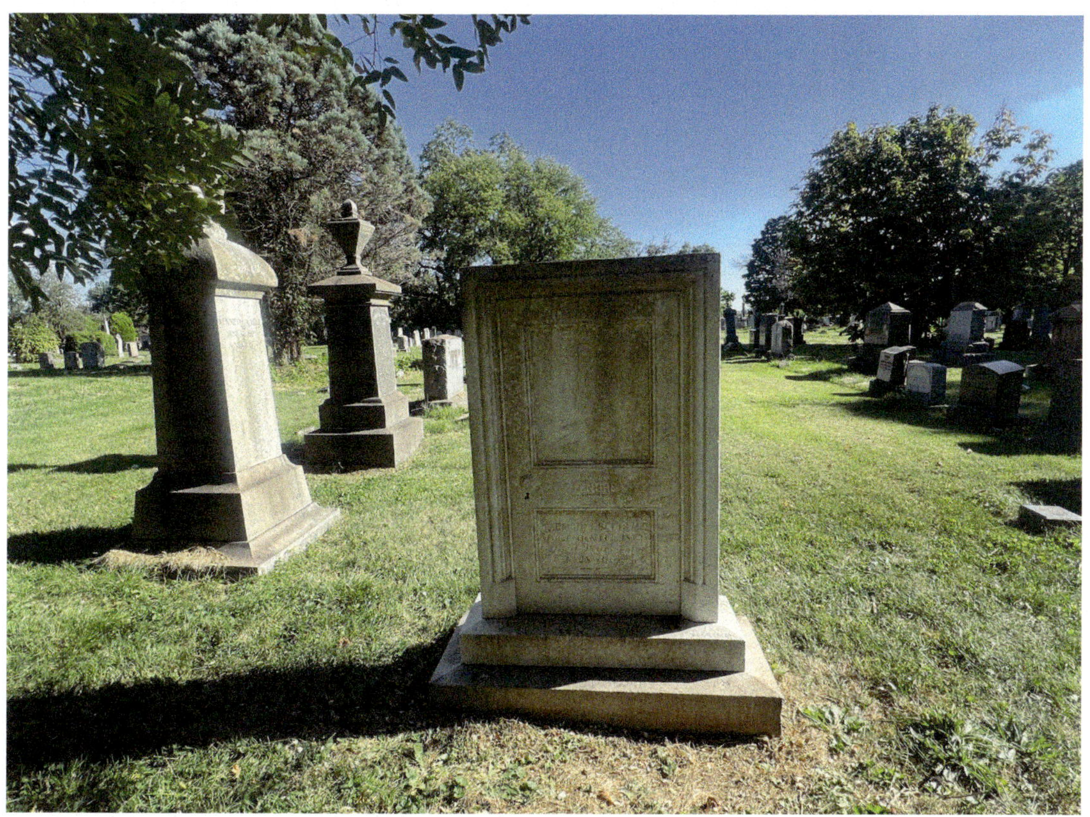

The headstone for Dr. Truman Betts at Riverview Cemetery is shaped like a door. It had a doorknob, and a bust of Pallas Athena with a raven on top of it, but those have been lost to vandalism and the elements.

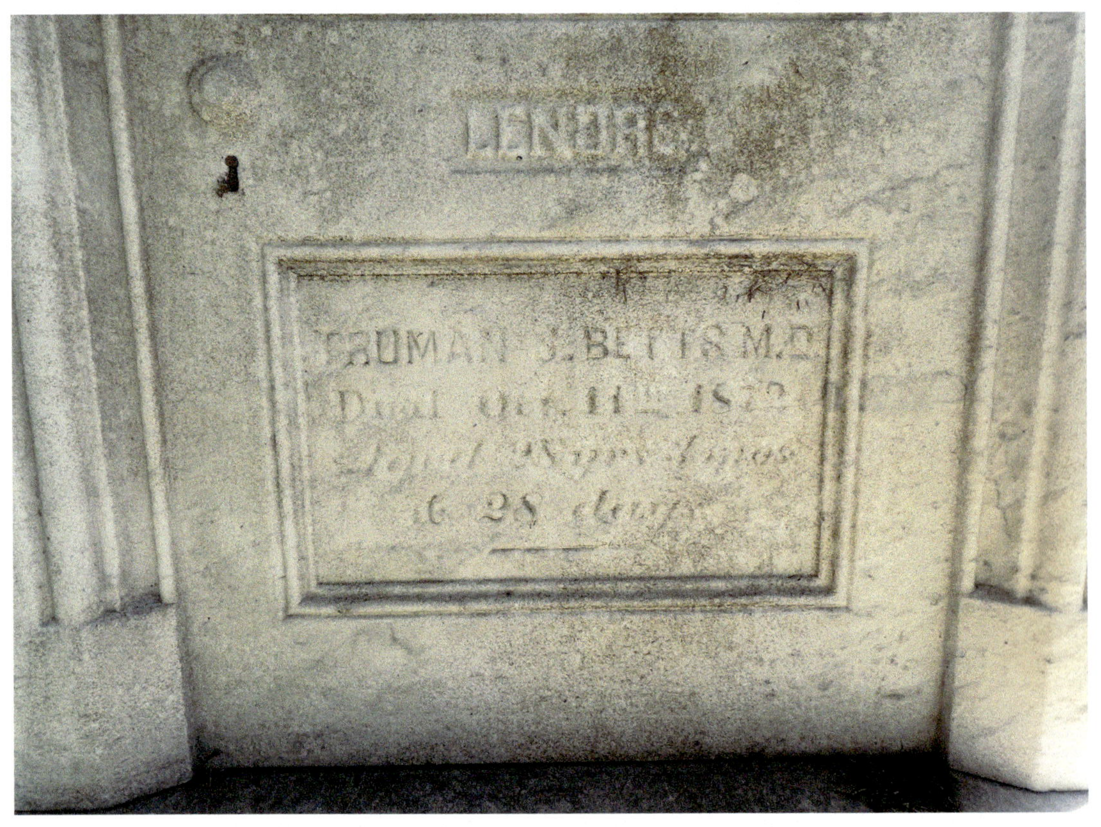

Detail of the inscription of Dr. Betts's stone noting the name "Lenore."

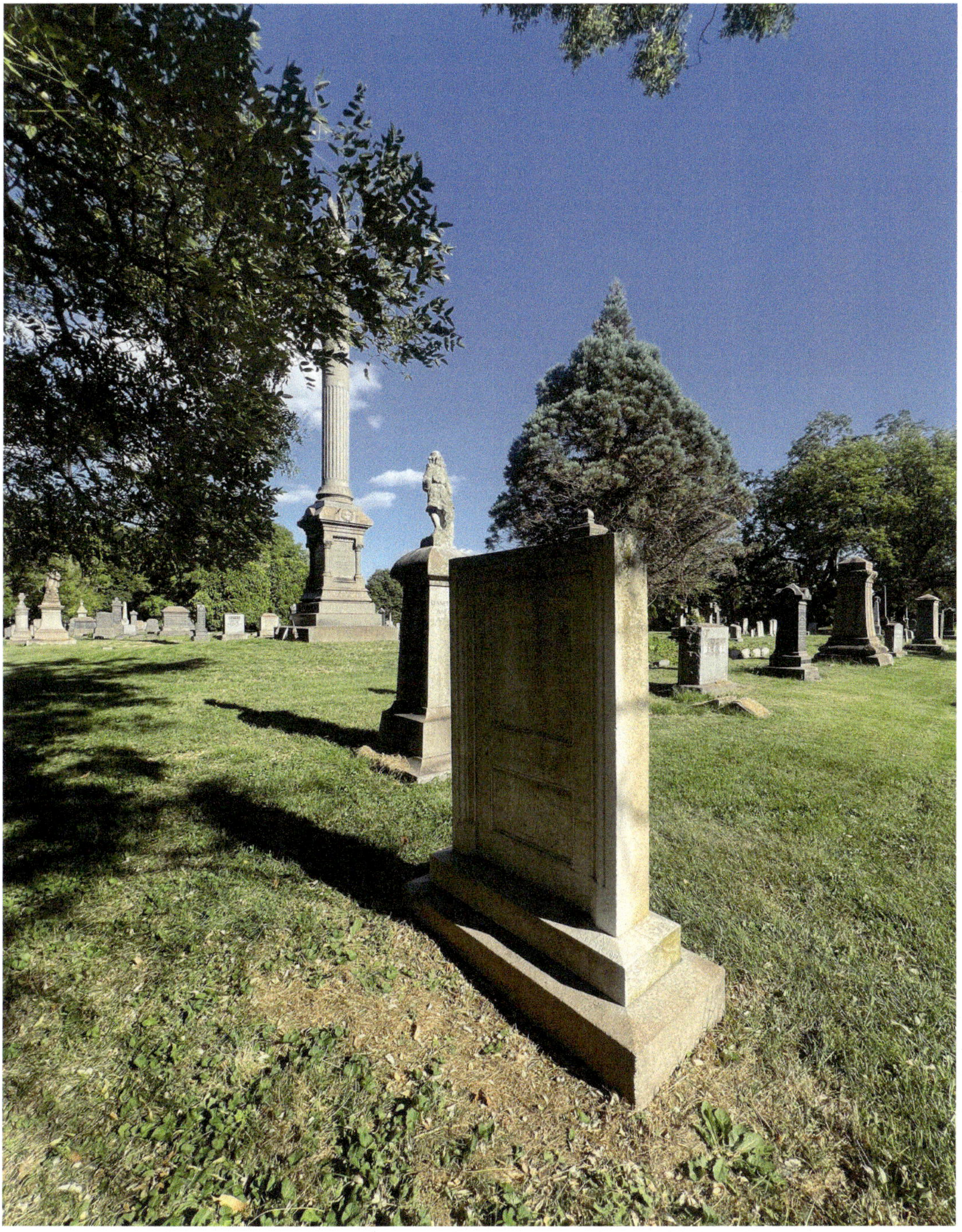

The easiest way to find Dr. Betts's stone is to look for the column that's former governor George B. McClellan's monument. It's the tallest monument in the cemetery.

Hall Cemetery

Neshanic Station, N.J.

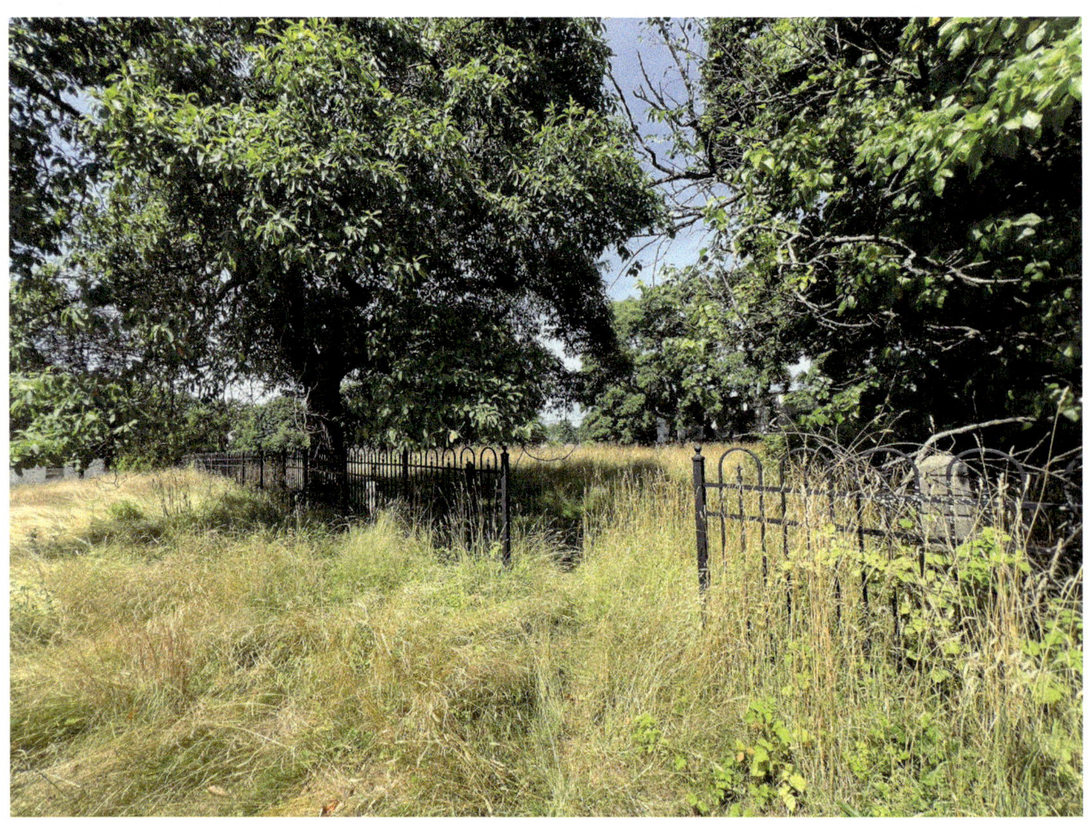

Hall Cemetery is a small, abandoned cemetery hidden in the middle of an abandoned warehouse complex in Neshanic Station, N.J.

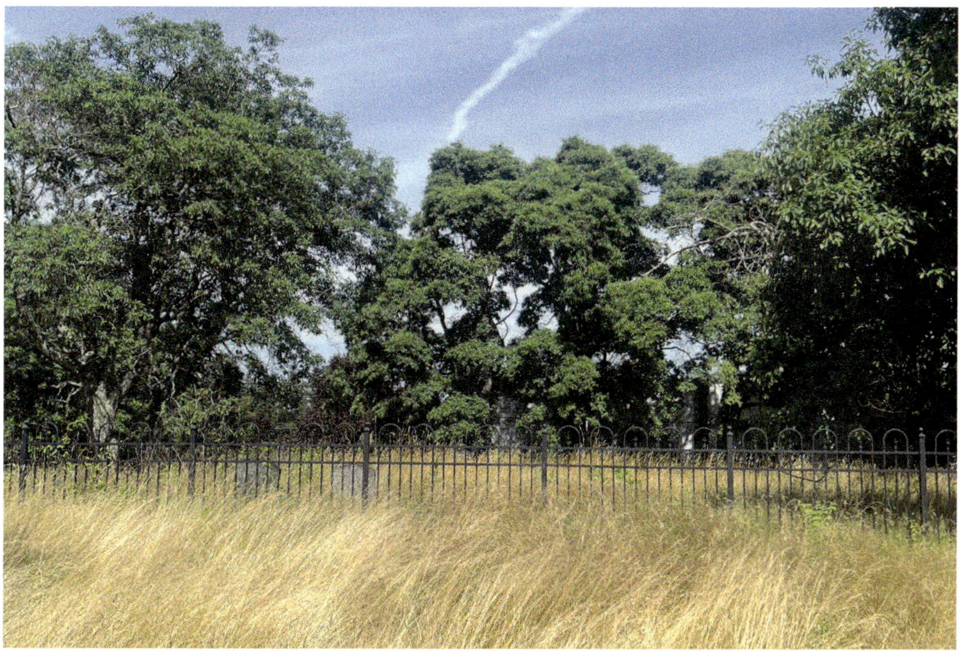

Above: The high grass at Hall Cemetery is quite beautiful, especially in summer, but it's also scary. This cemetery is the most treacherous one I've been to due to the holes from grave collapses, fallen stones, and risk of ticks and chiggers.

Below: The abandoned warehouse and factory buildings are ever present in the background at Hall Cemetery.

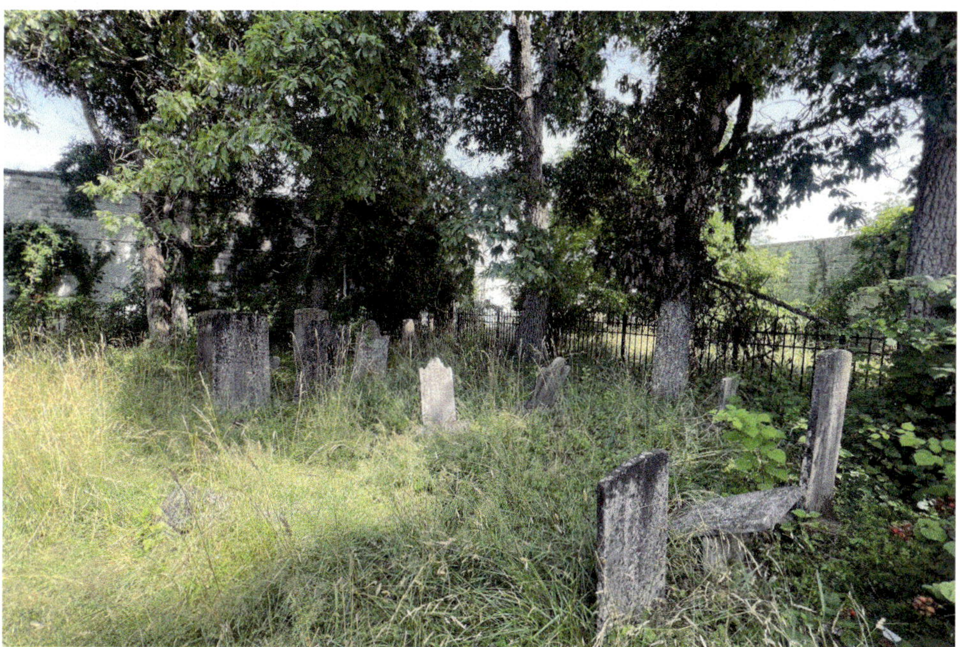

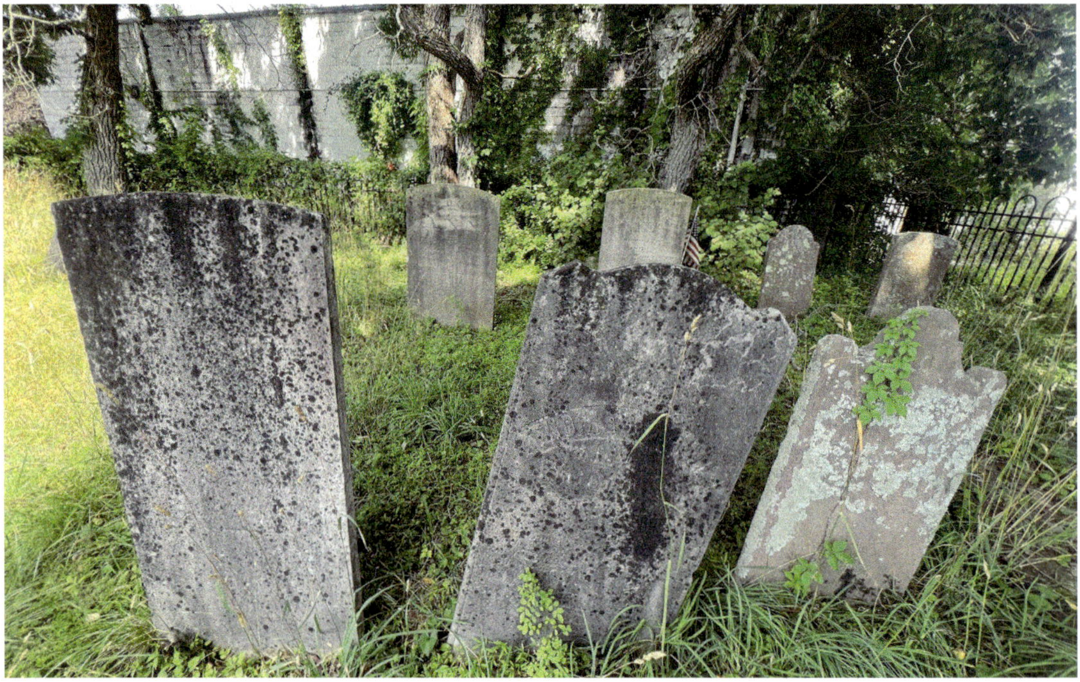

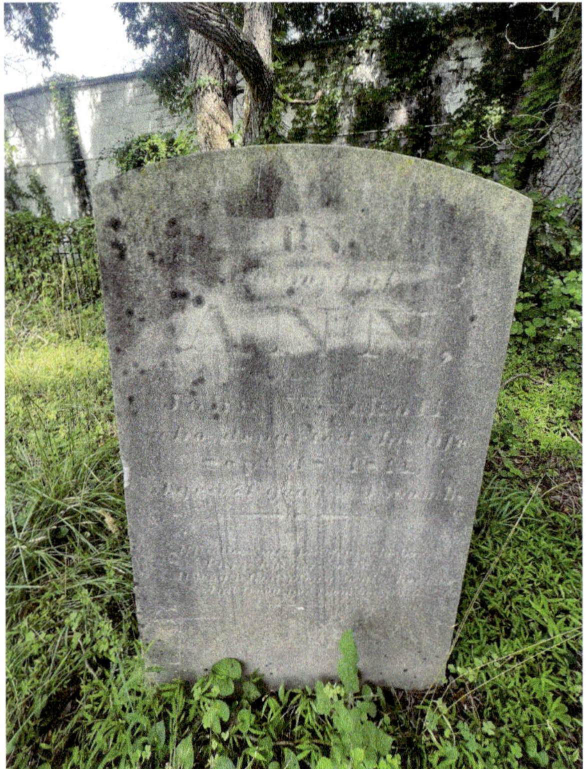

Above: I found very little written about the history of the building complex or Hall Cemetery. It's an odd choice to build an industrial complex so close to a cemetery.

Left: Very few stones at Hall Cemetery are still legible. I'm not sure if this discoloration is a half-hearted attempt to clean the stone. I'd urge anyone against doing this, it's possible to cause more damage attempting to clean a stone if you don't have the proper experience.

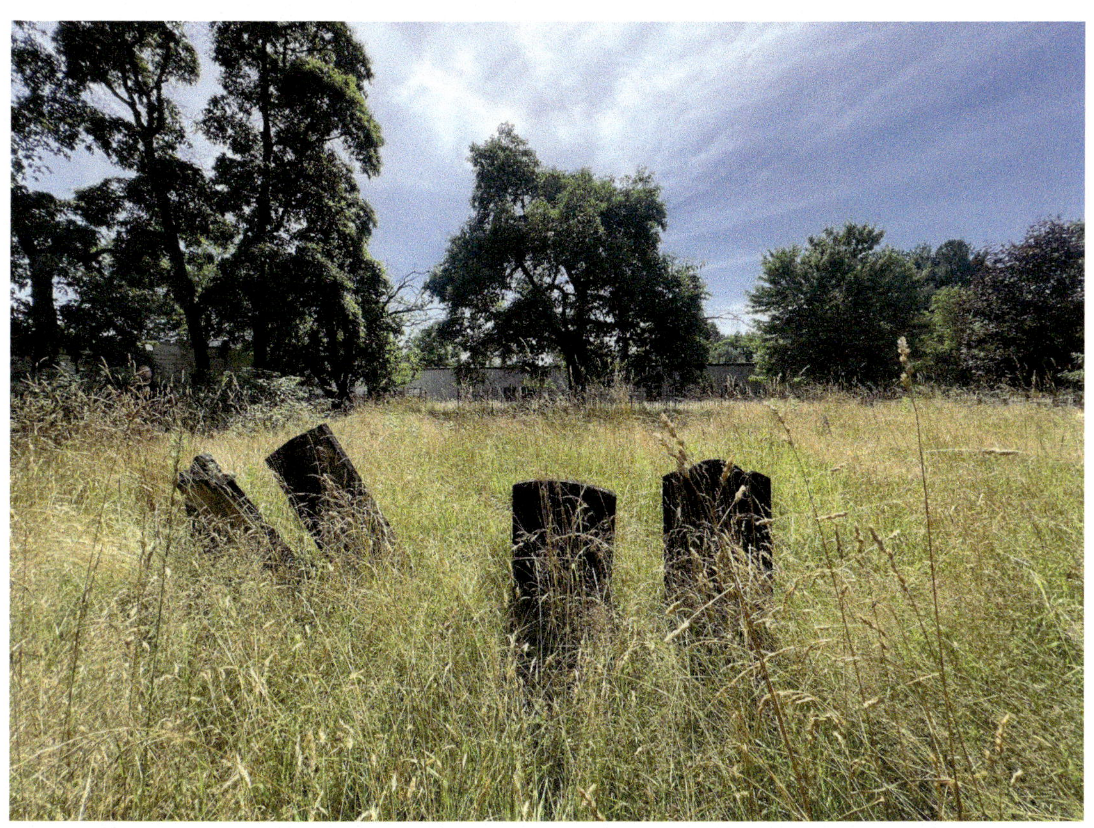

I can't emphasize how high the grass is at Hall Cemetery. My visit was brief because I forgot to bring bug spray.

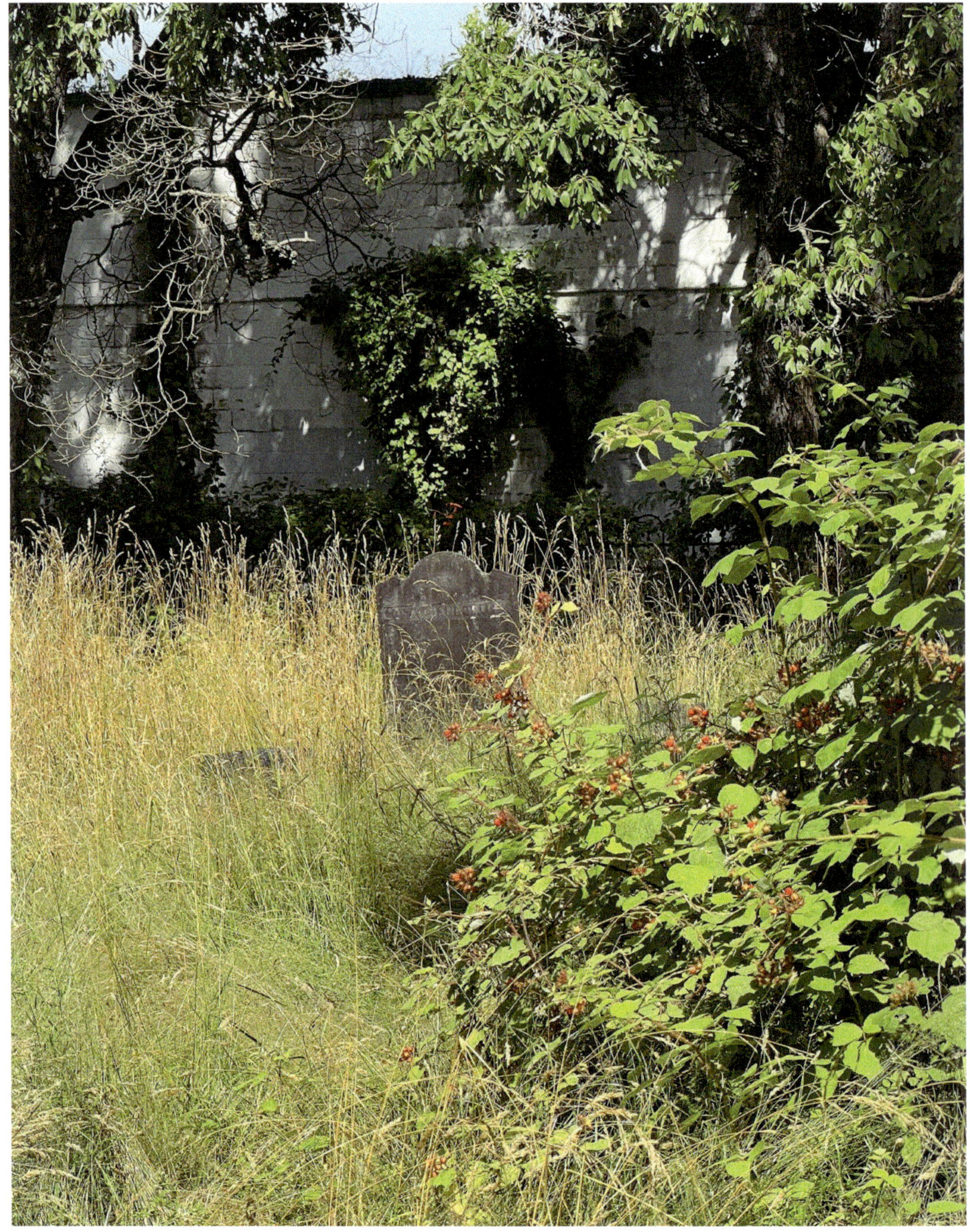

There's a strange beauty at Hall Cemetery. It's so quiet that I could hear radios from the neighborhood nearby, but there wasn't a living soul around when I visited.

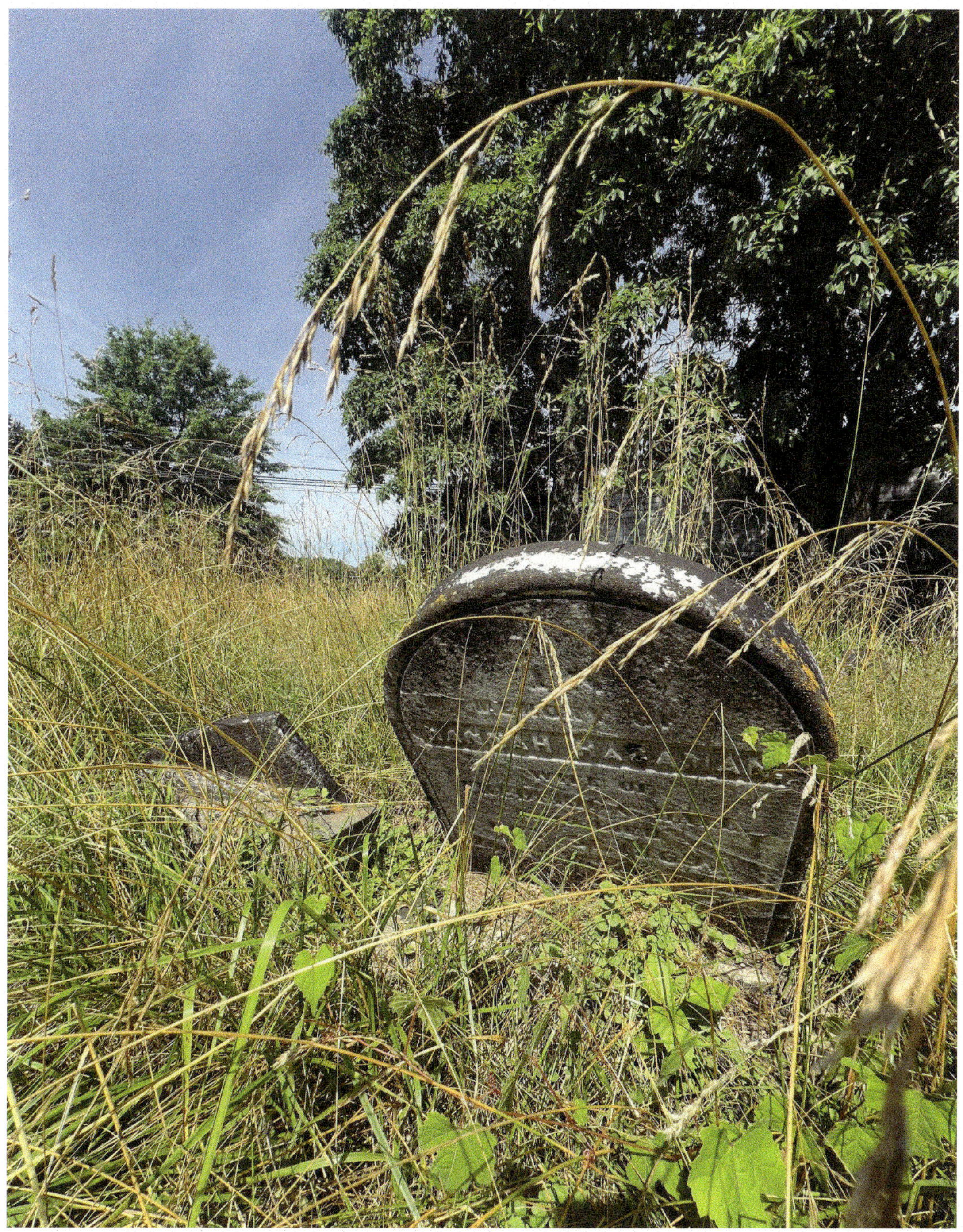

Many of the stones at Hall Cemetery are in the process of toppling over.

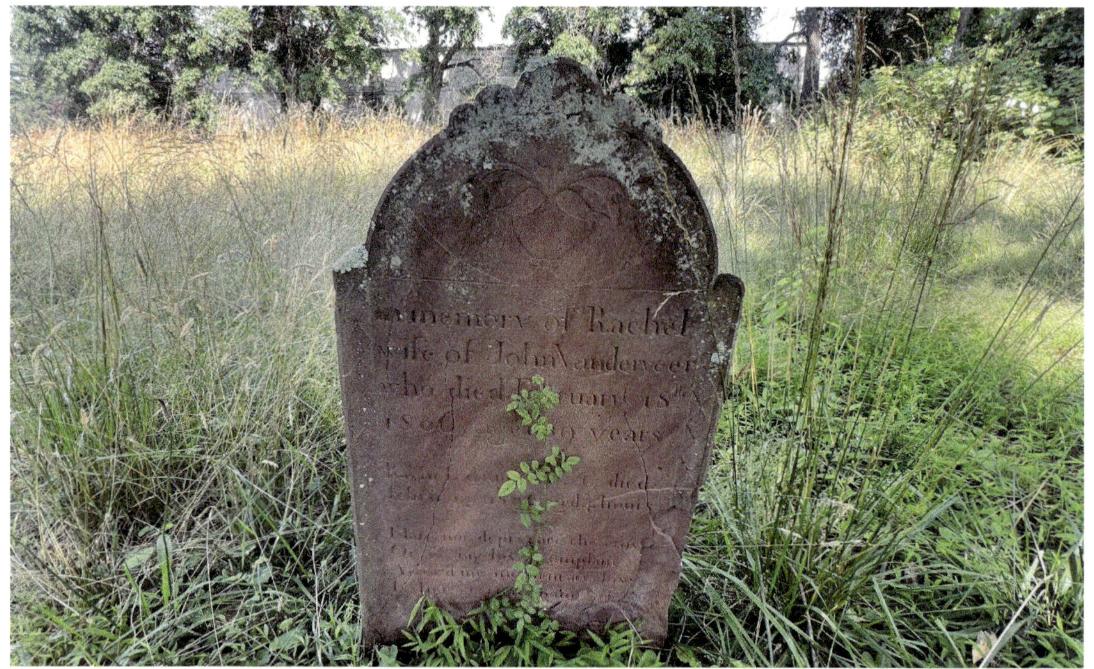

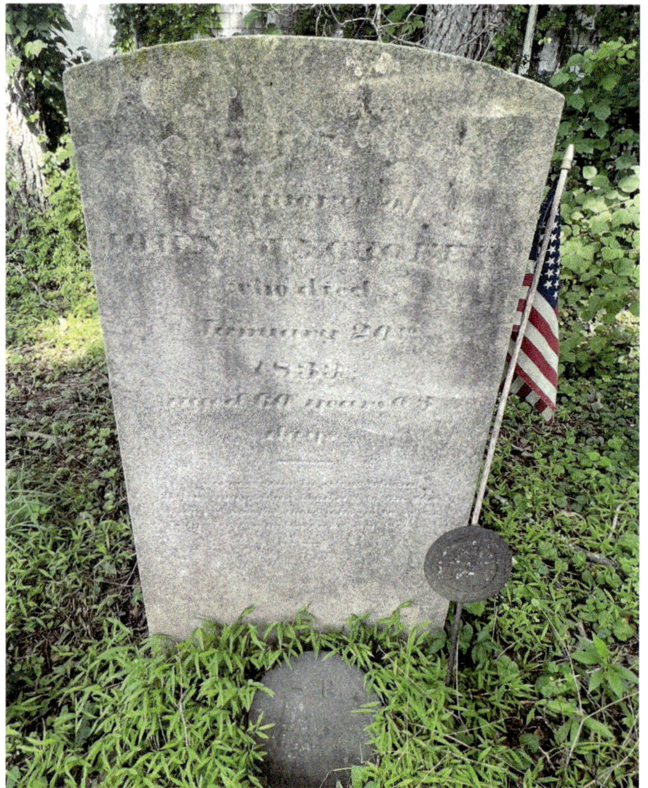

Above: Rachel's stone at Hall Cemetery is one of the most legible ones. It's old enough to have been made of Jersey brownstone but the iconography reflects the movement away from mortality images. I did notice quite a few Dutch names.

Left: Some of the stones at Hall Cemetery had weathered flags so someone had been caring for the cemetery at some point.

WHIPPANY BURYING YARD

Whippany, N.J.

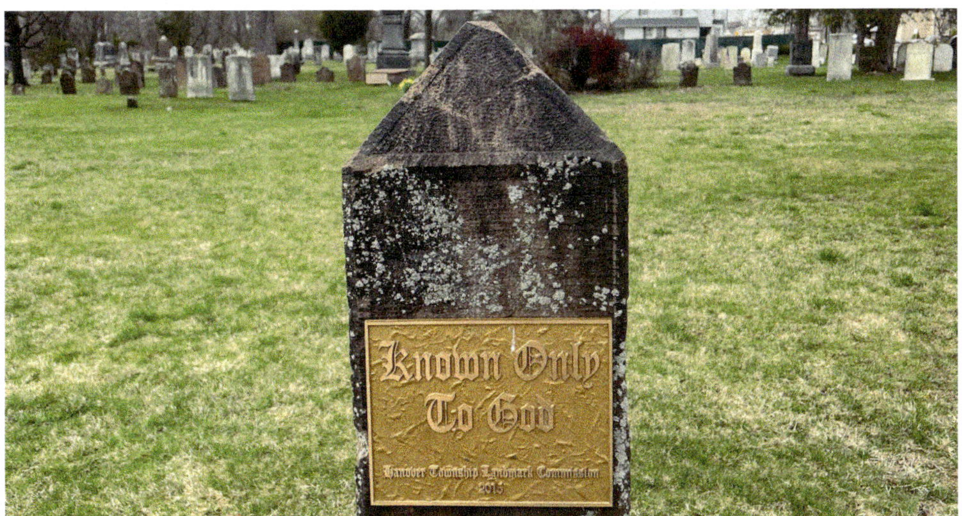

Above: Whippany Burying Yard is the oldest documented cemetery in Morris County. Many of the graves aren't marked and the exact number of people buried here is unknown.

Below: John Richards donated the land that would become Whippany Burying Yard to the town in 1718, died three months later, and became what is believed to be the first person buried there.

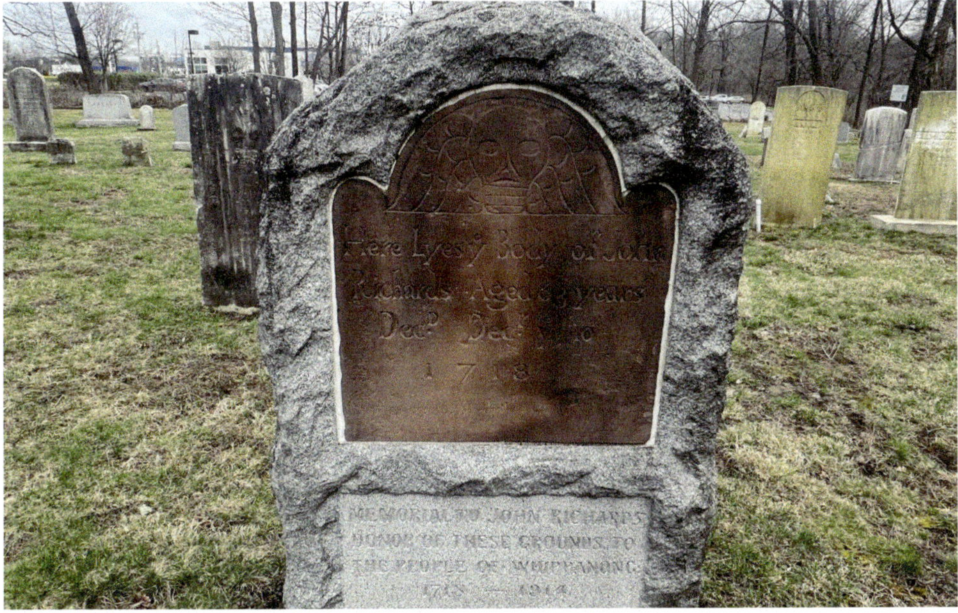

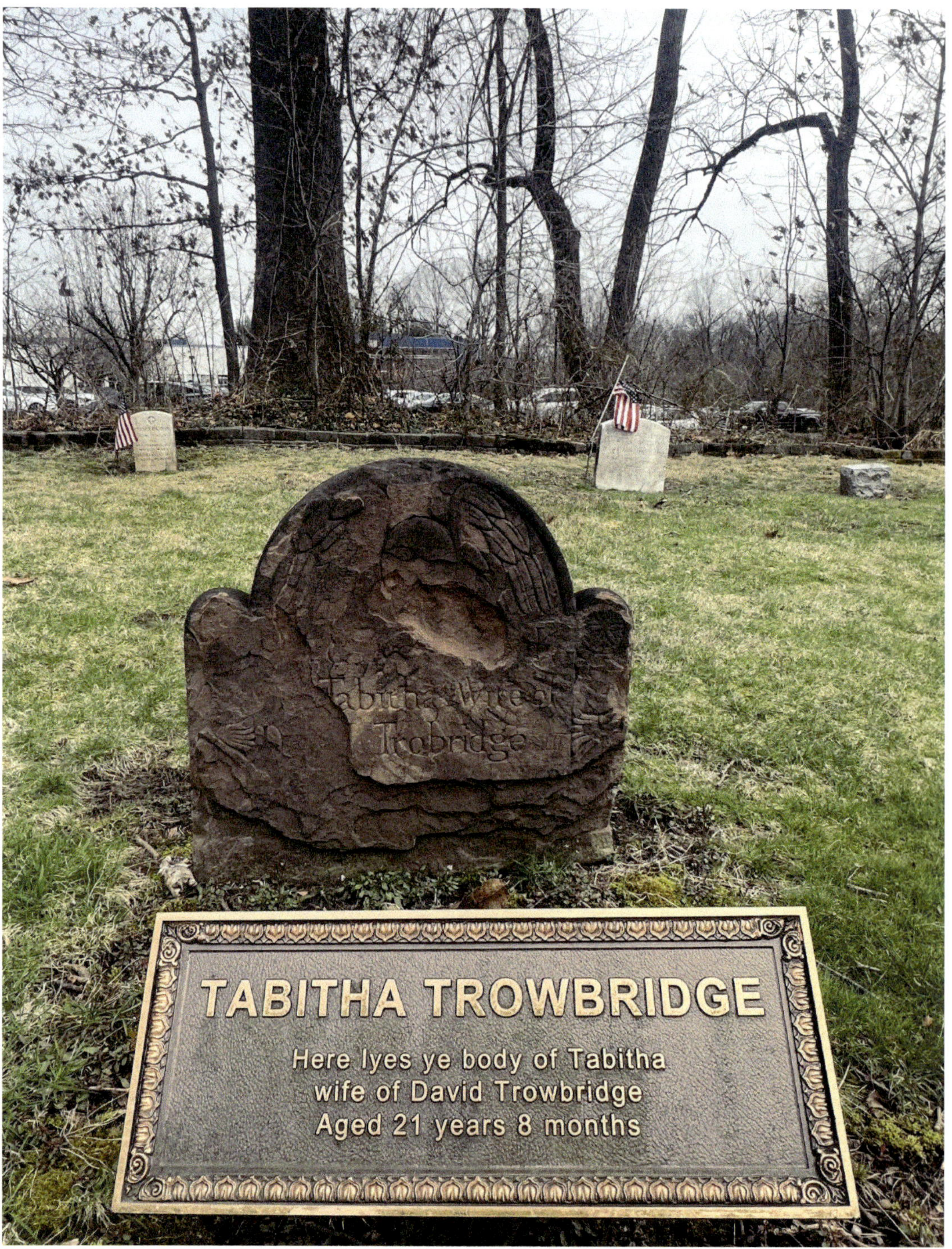

The iconography at Whippany Burying Yard ranges from colonial through modern. There's a wide variety of styles and an active effort to preserve the headstones.

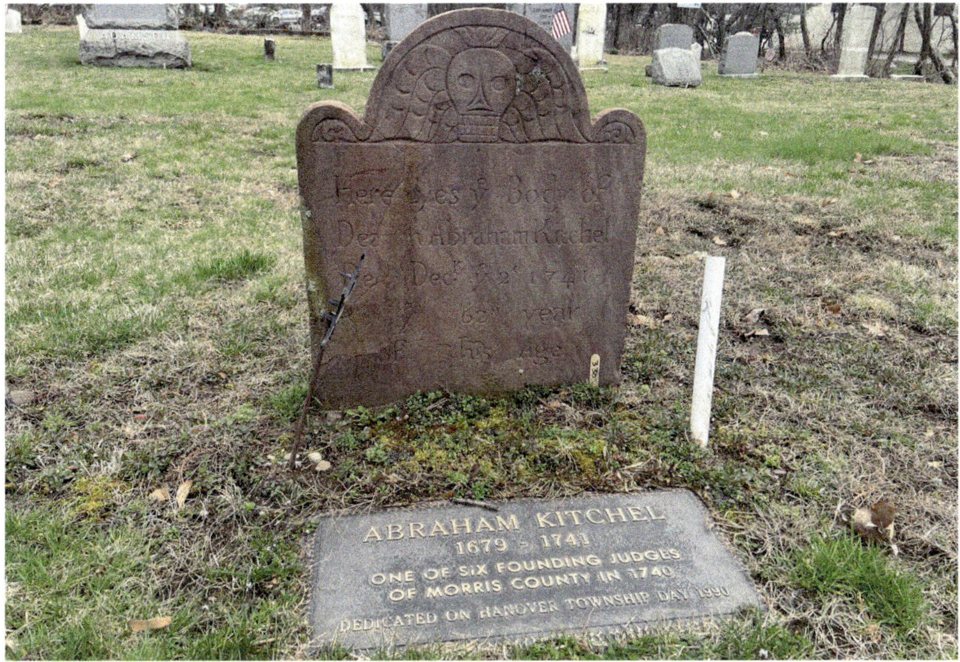

Above: The iconography at Whippany Burying Yard includes mortality images, like the winged skull that adorns Abraham Kitchel's grave.

Below: A headstone with a soul effigy is flanked by two stones with winged skulls at Whippany Burying Yard.

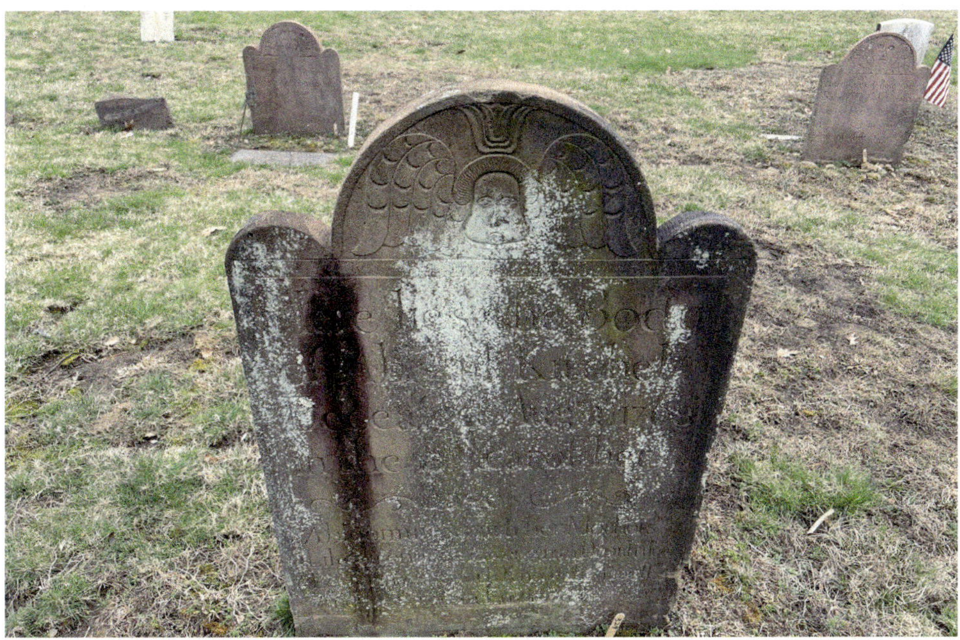

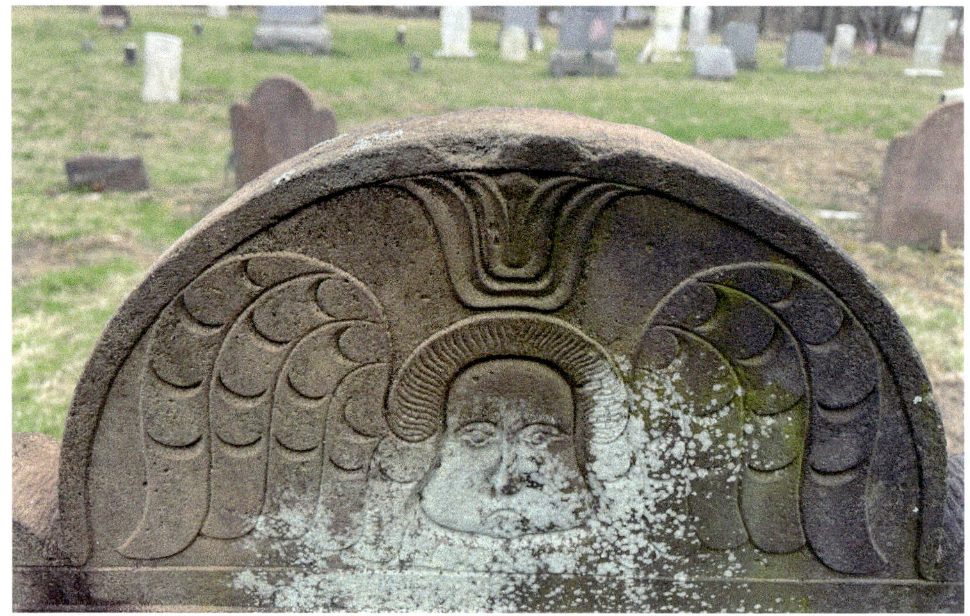

Above: A detail of a melancholy soul effigy at Whippany Burying Yard.

Below: John Biglow's stone is very well preserved and features a very detailed soul effigy.

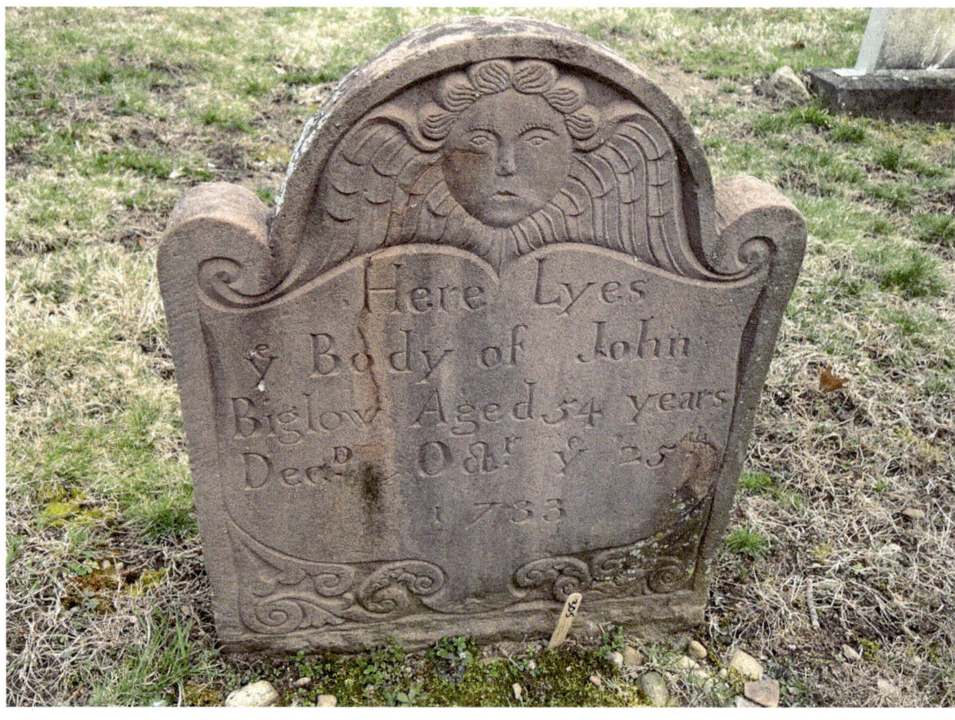

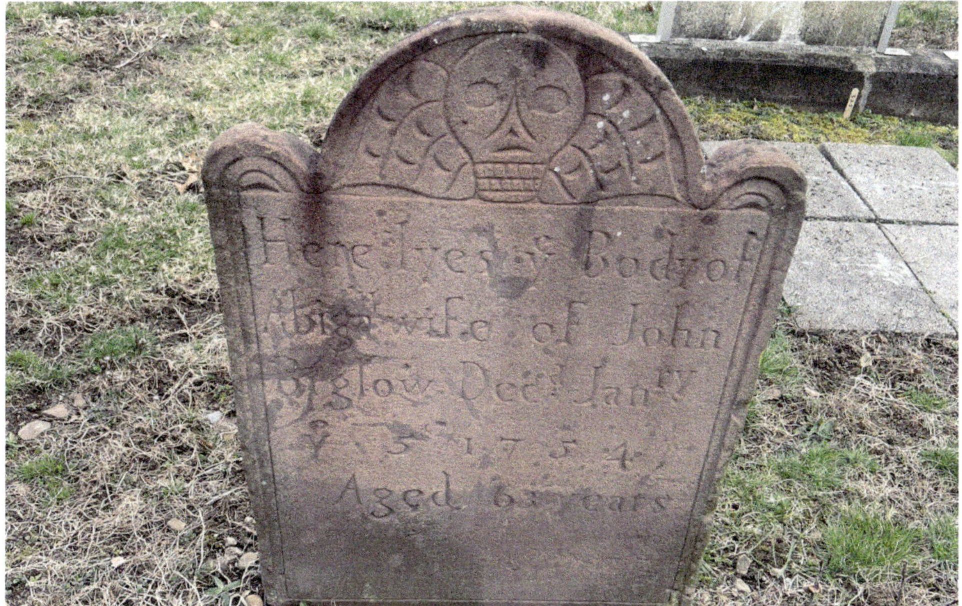

Above: John Biglow's wife, Abigail, features a stern winged skull.

Below: Headstones for children and babies in colonial times featured similar iconography to adult stones. John Heavens died at almost two years old. His epitaph notes that "Here lies the greef [*sic*] of a fond mother and the blasted expectations of an indulgent father."

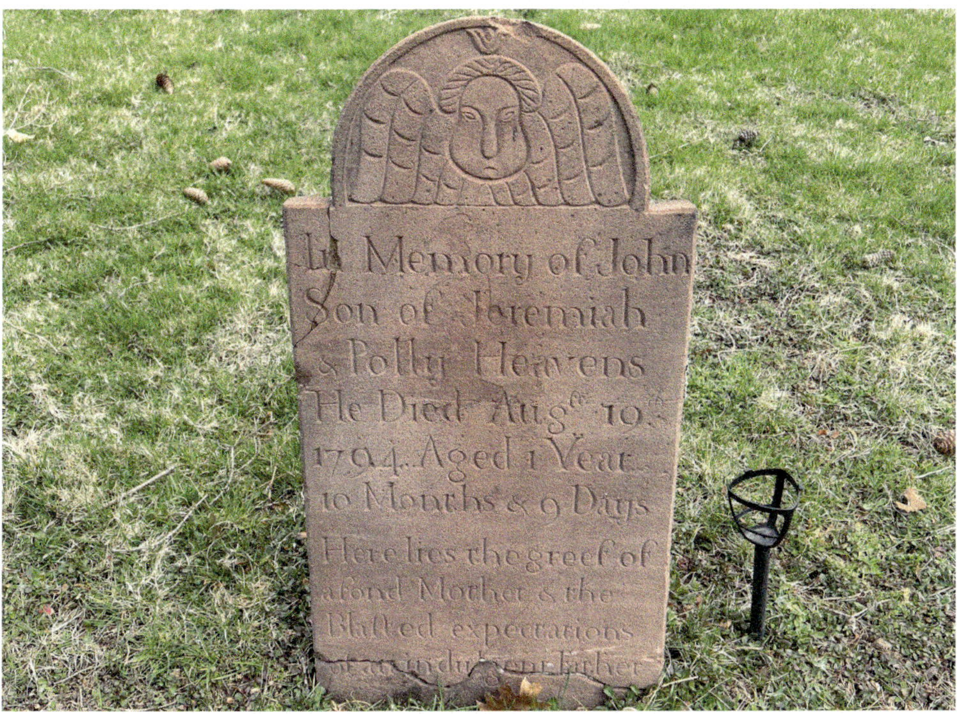

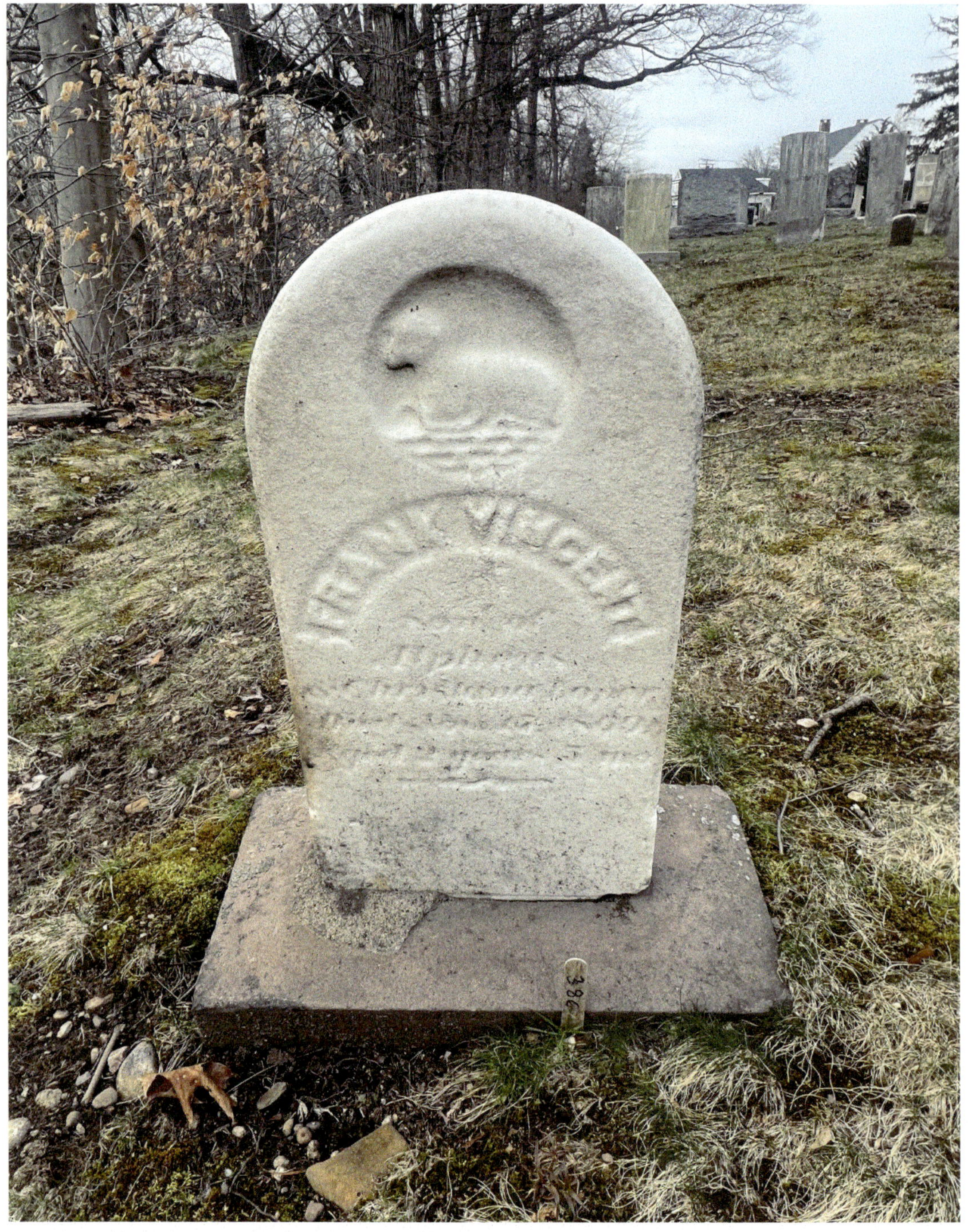

Unique iconography and epitaphs for children and babies started to become popular in the Victorian era. Lambs were particularly popular.

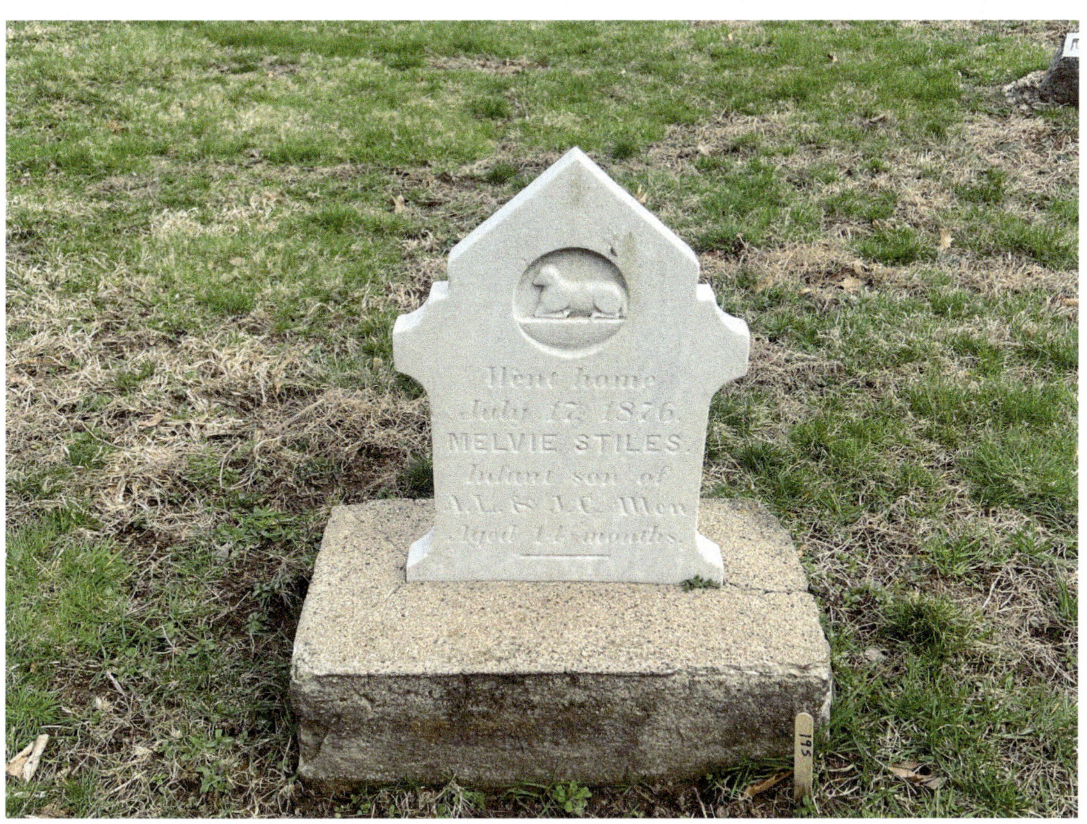

Melvie Stiles died eighty-two years after John Heavens, but there's a marked change in the iconography used for his stone.

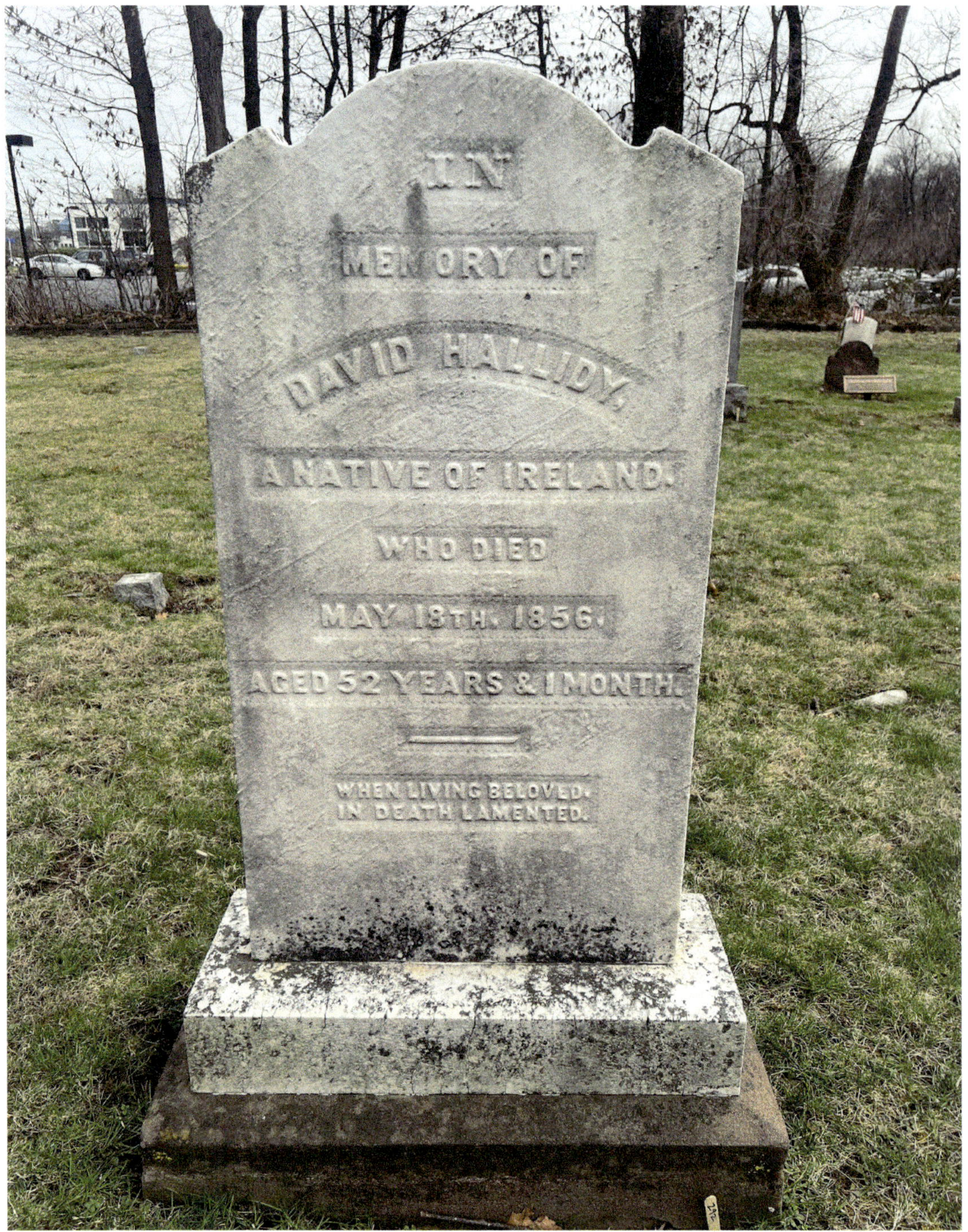

David Halliday's stone at Whippany Burying Yard caught my attention with its epitaph: "When living beloved, in death lamented."

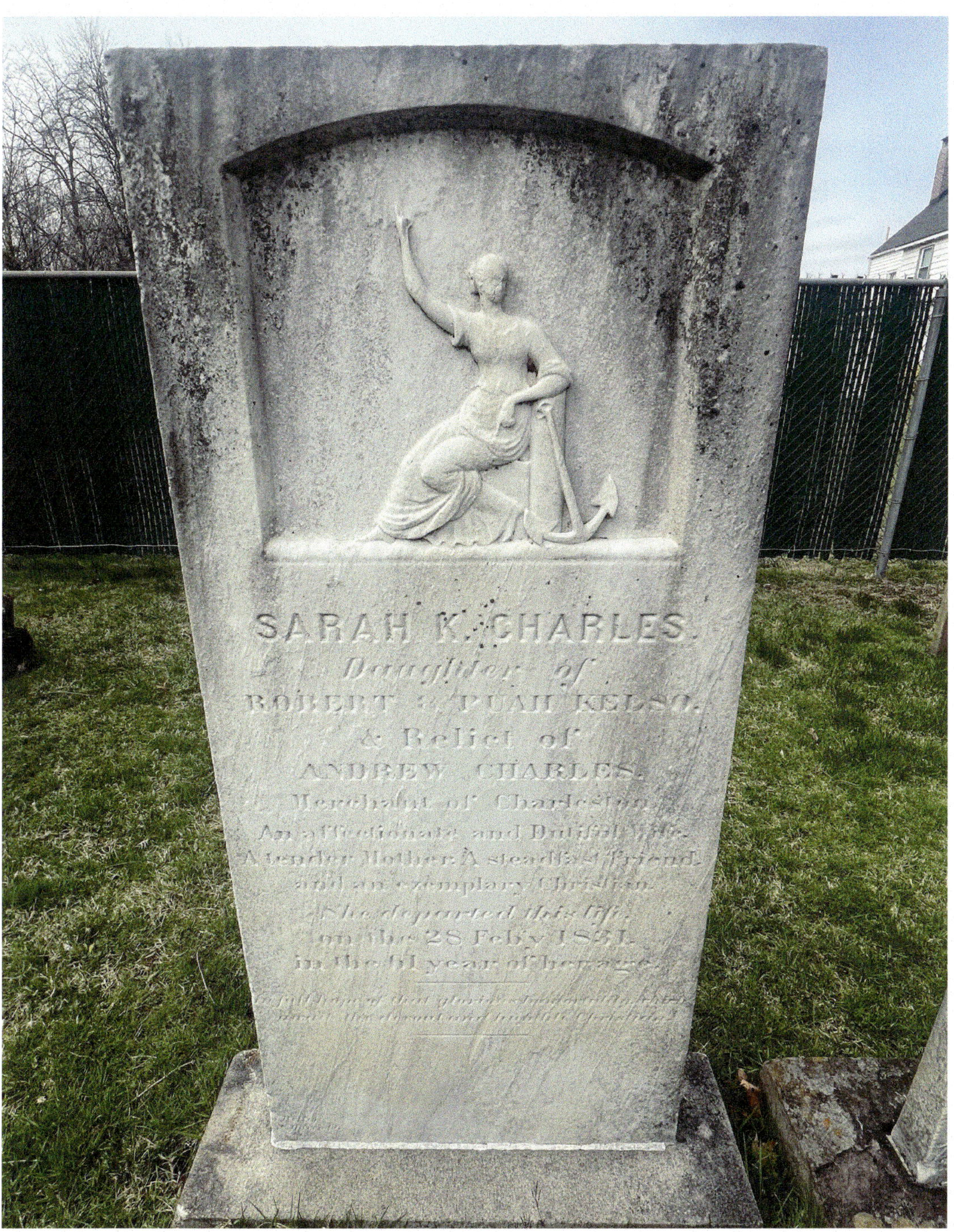

The unique iconography of Sarah K. Charles's stone also attracted my attention.

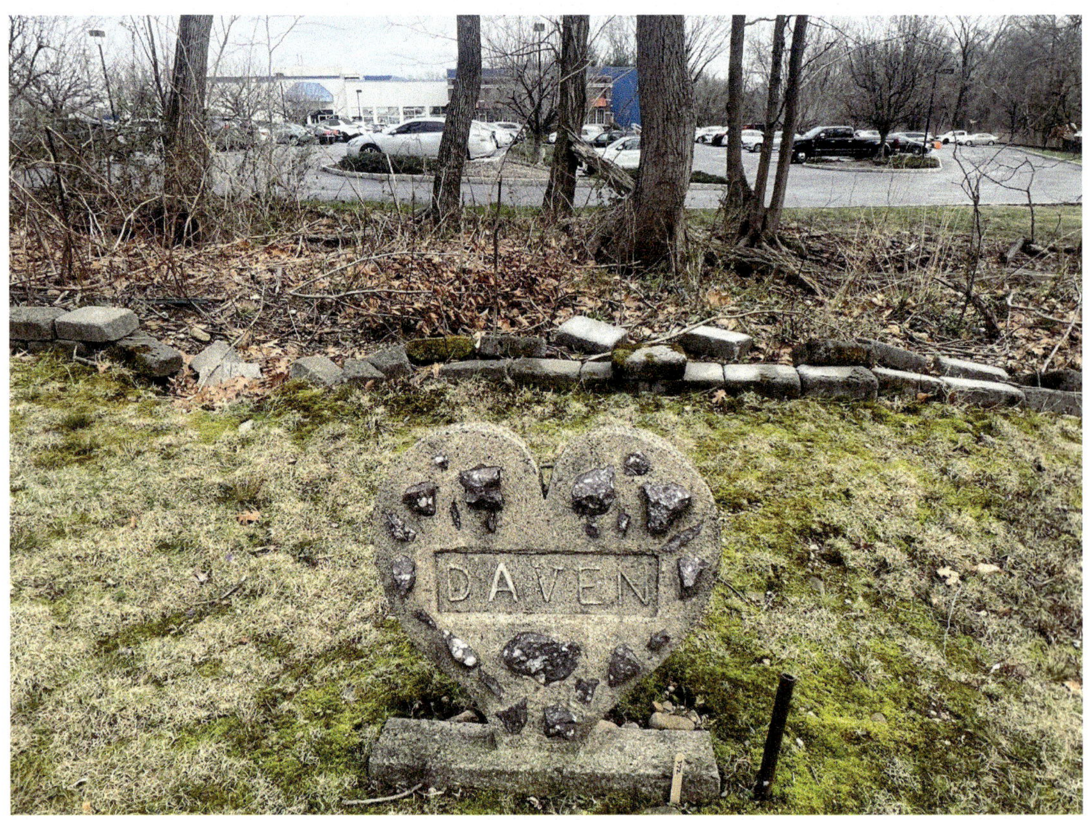

The Daven stone at Whippany Burying Yard is strange and unique. It's by itself in a corner of the cemetery with no stones near it. It's completely different in style from any other monument in the cemetery. I couldn't find any information about who was buried there.

AFRICAN METHODIST EPISCOPAL CHURCH CEMETERY

Tabernacle, N.J.

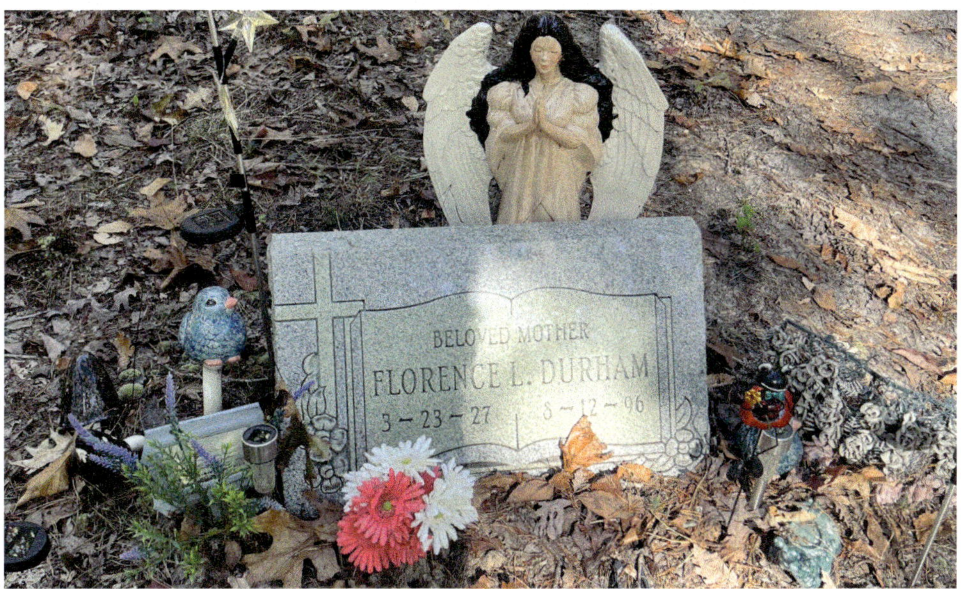

Above: I found the African Methodist Episcopal Church Cemetery on Carranza Road by accident when I was looking for Emilio Carranza's cenotaph. This cemetery is next to someone's house.

Below: The African Methodist Episcopal Church that once stood on the land and was affiliated with this cemetery is gone, but the graves are still maintained.

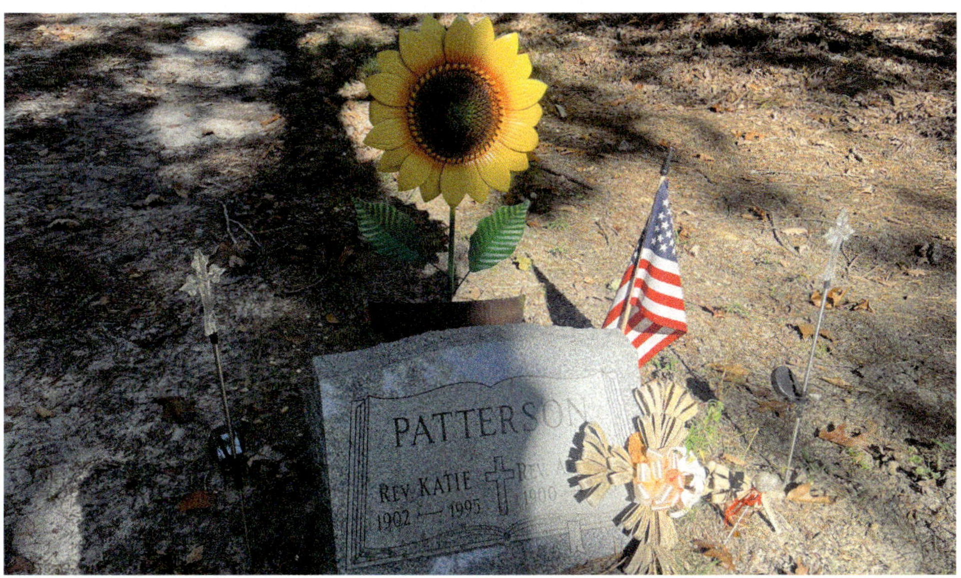

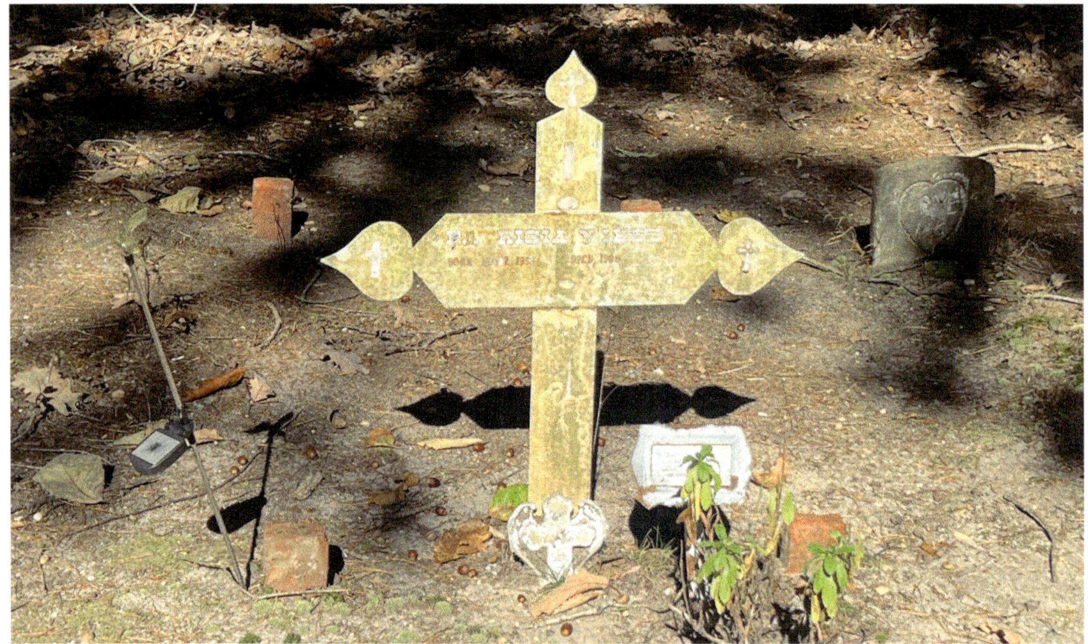

Patricia V. Imes's marker might be my favorite. I love the care that went into making it.

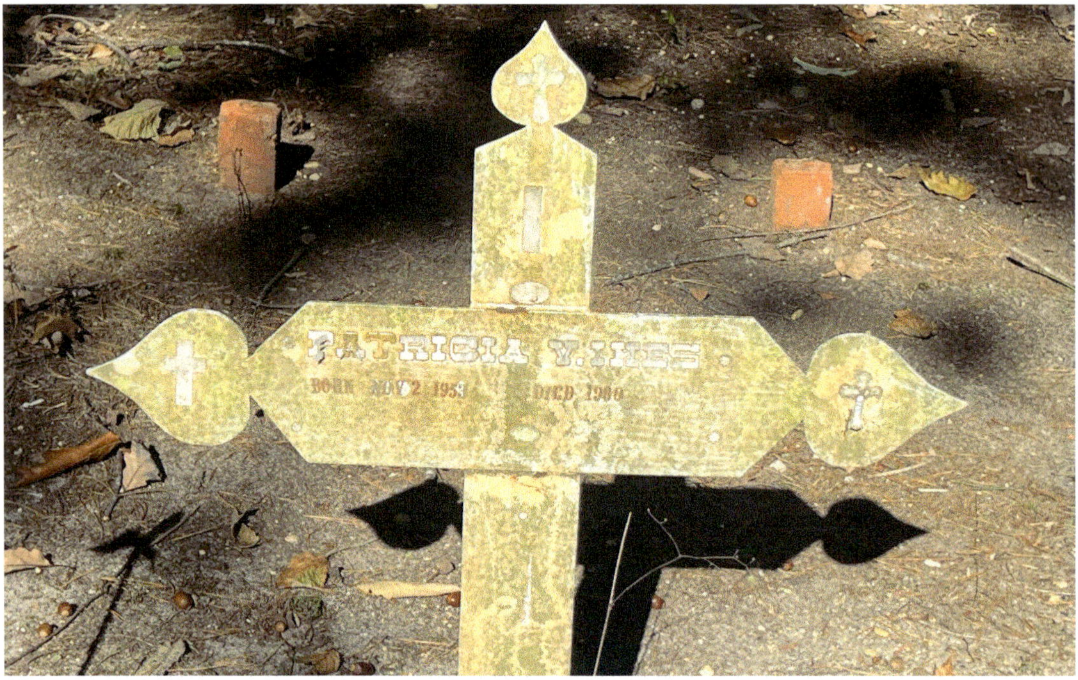

A detail of Patricia V. Imes's marker.

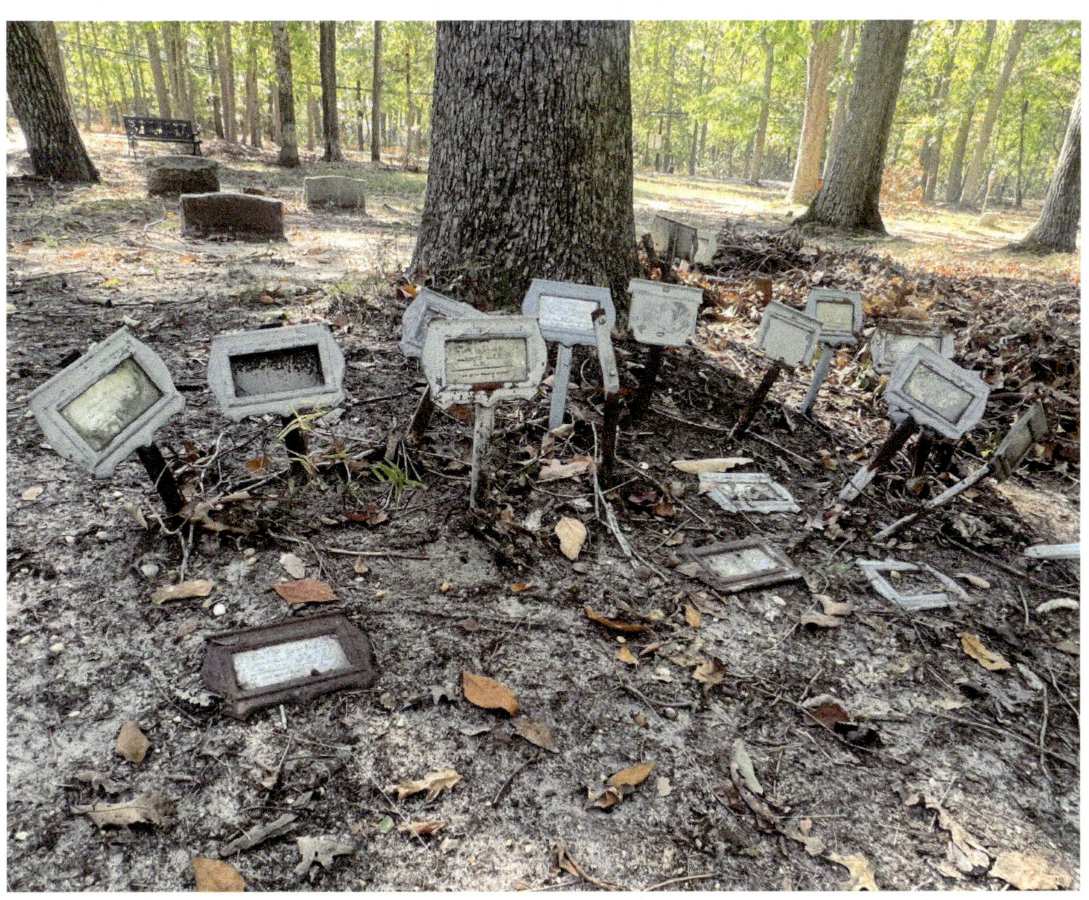

I found an alarming number of temporary markers under a tree. I use temporary markers at cemeteries when there's no monument to mark the grave. I have no clue why there's such a proliferation of temporary markers. Many are decades old and illegible.

HIBERNIA/ST. PATRICK'S CEMETERY

Rockaway Township, N.J.

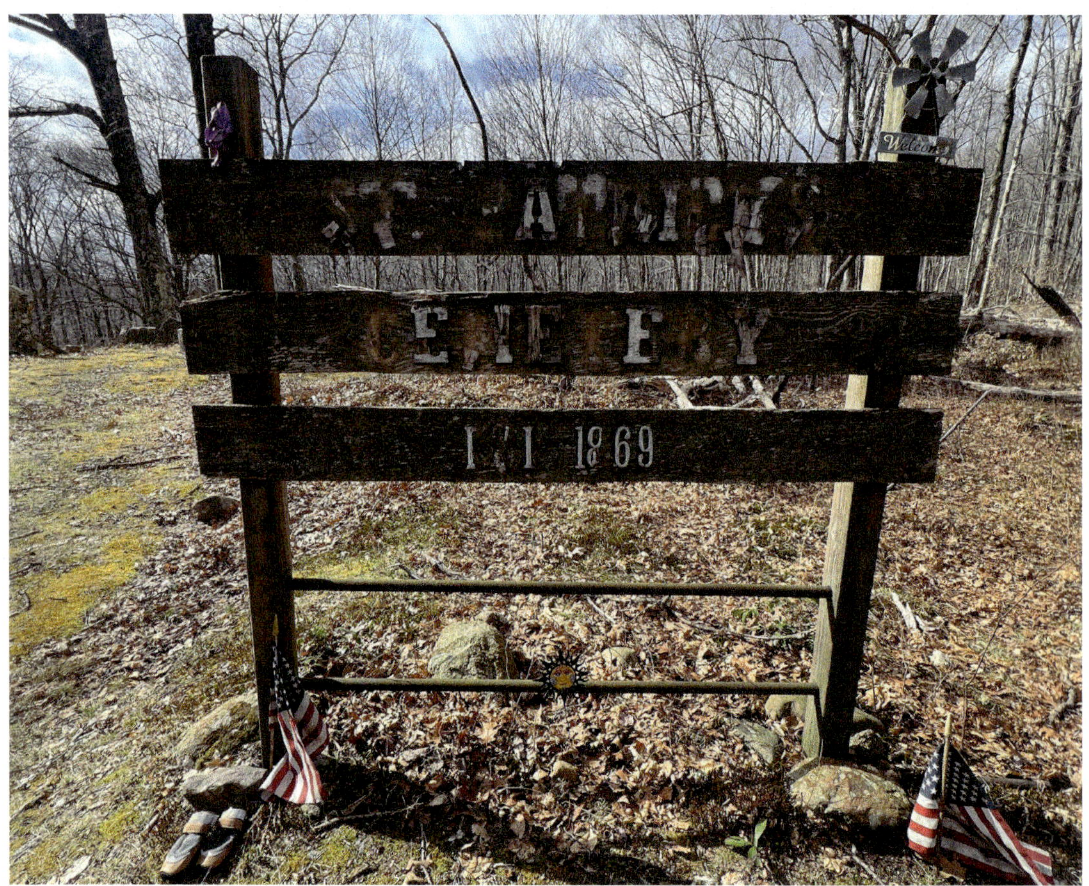

Hibernia Cemetery is in the Wildcat Ridge Wildlife Management Area. It requires a hike to get there and part of the trail is quite steep.

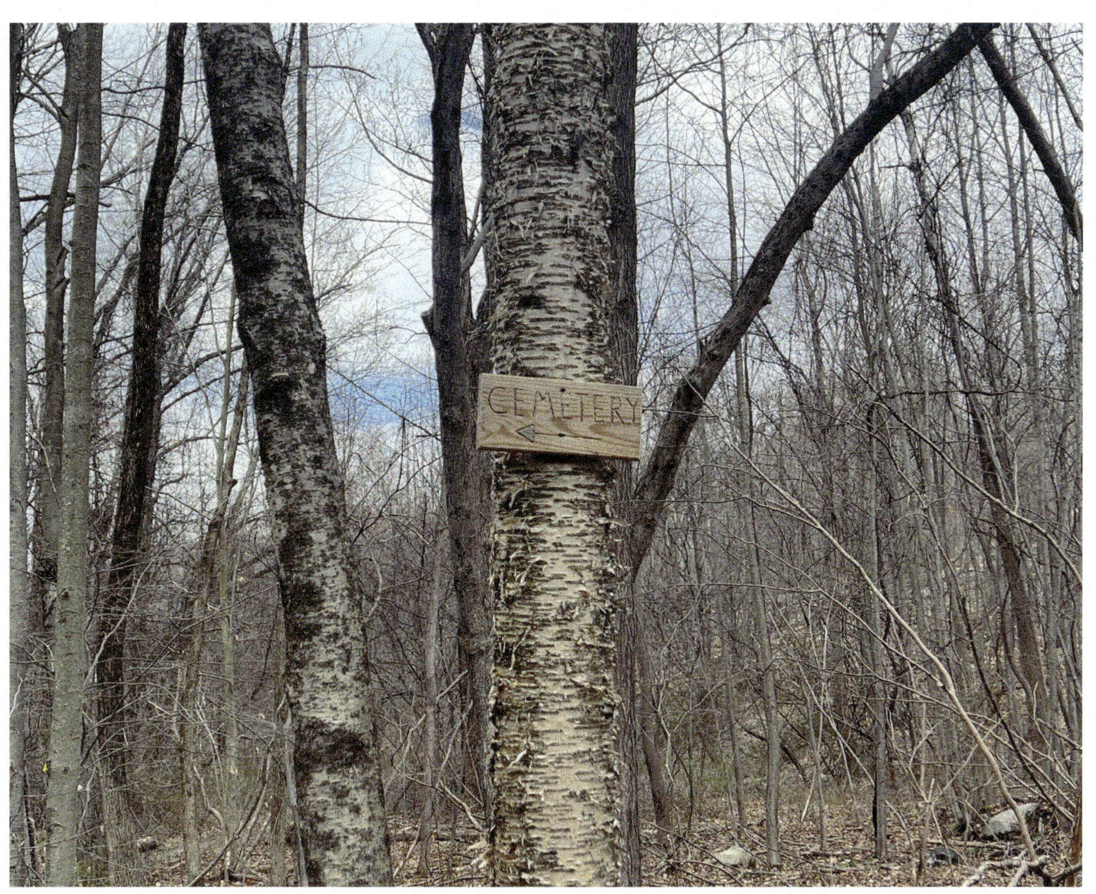

Signs on the trail let you know when you're close to the cemetery.

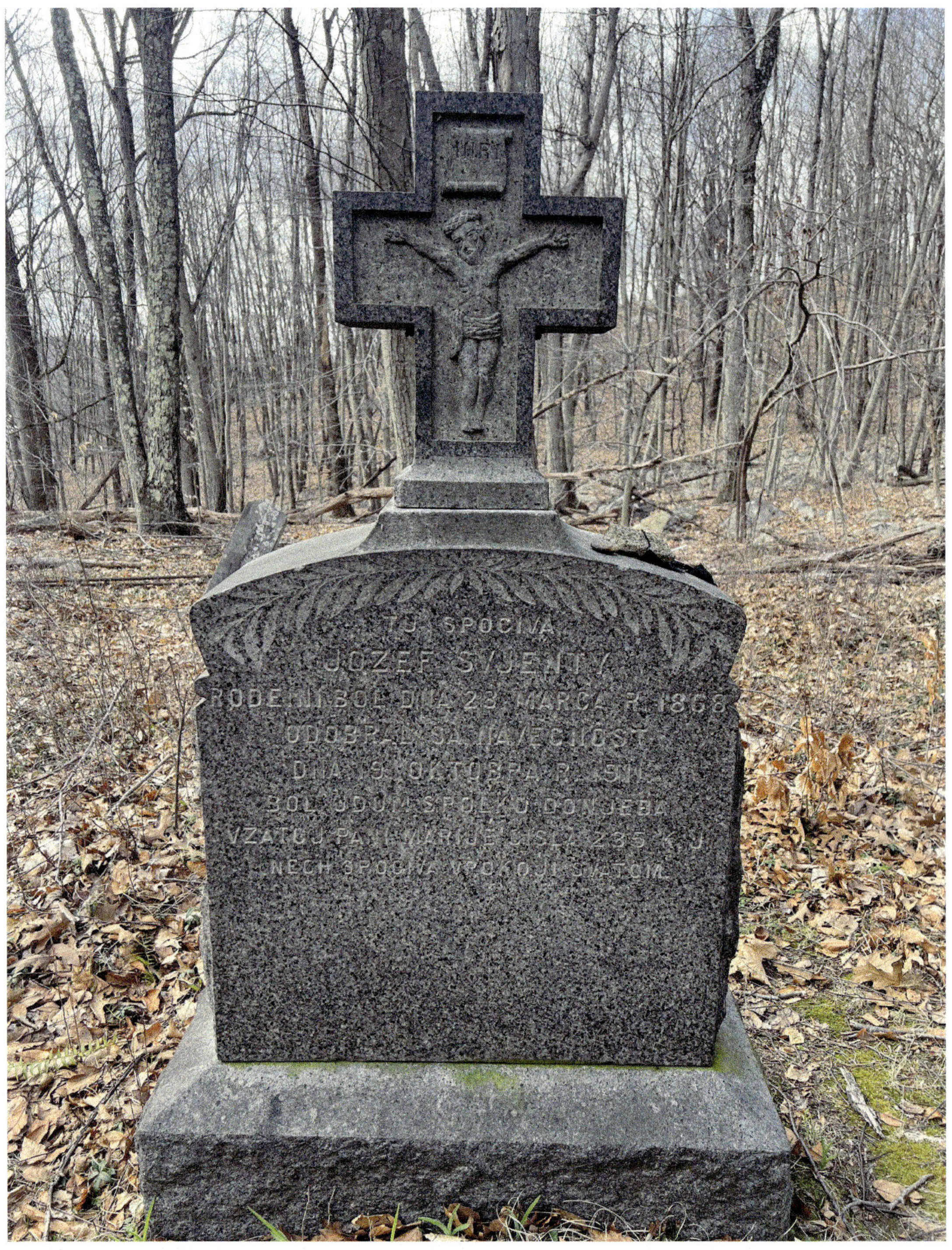

The cemetery once served a mixture of English, Irish, Scottish, and Slovakian miners.

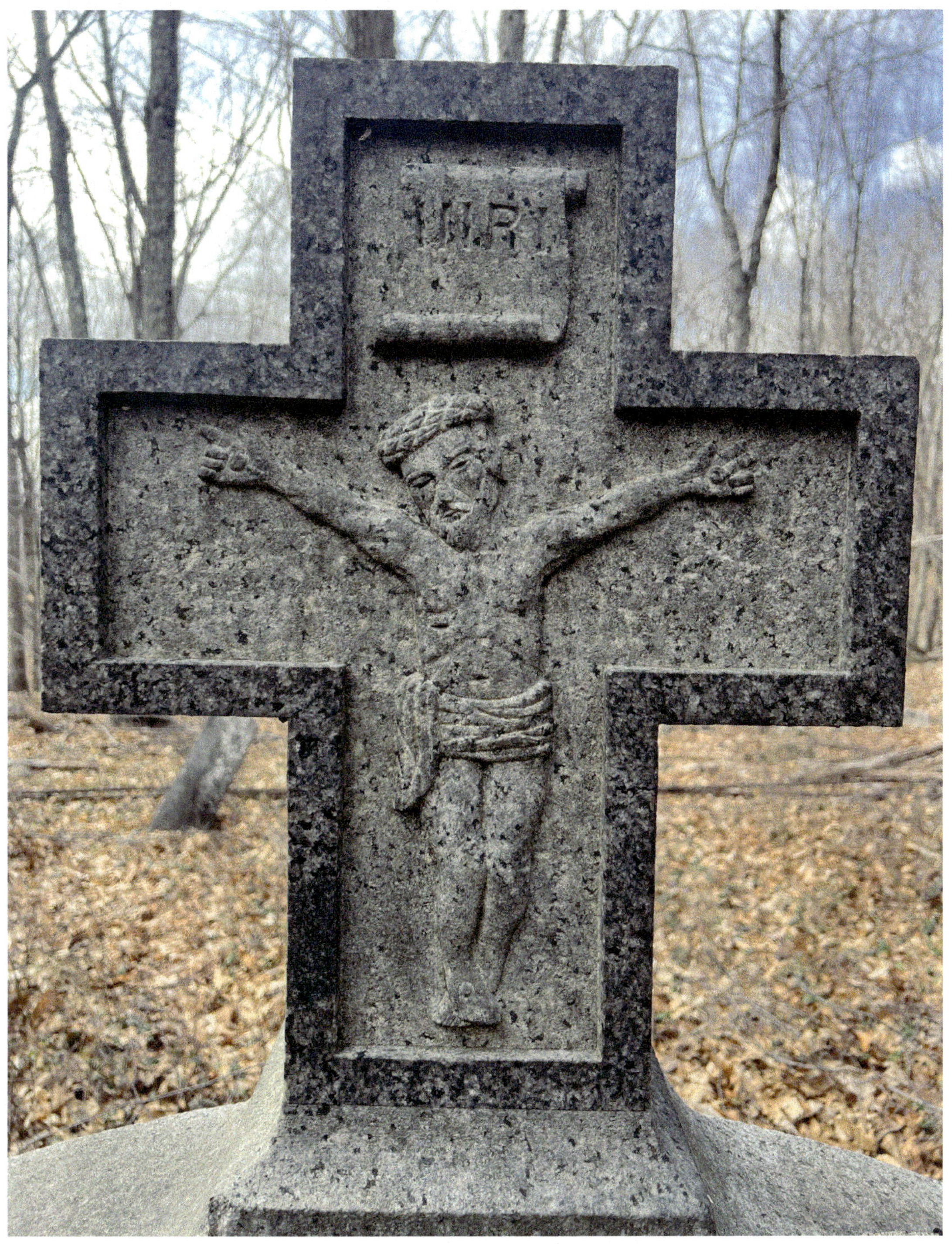

Detail of Jesus on a headstone at St. Patrick/Hibernia Cemetery.

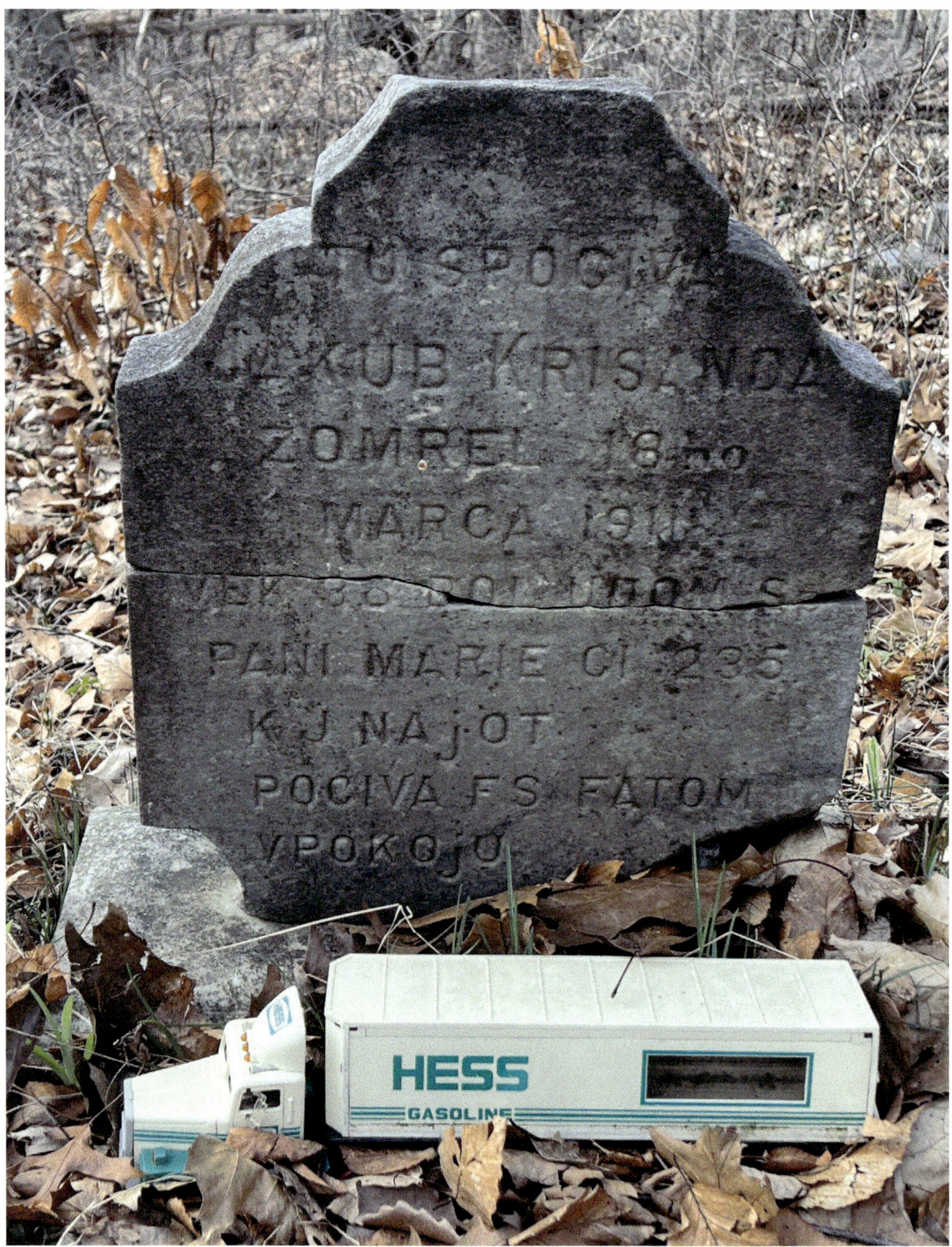

I noticed many gifts left at the graves at St. Patrick/Hibernia Cemetery. I'm unsure if they're pranks or if they have meaning to the families.

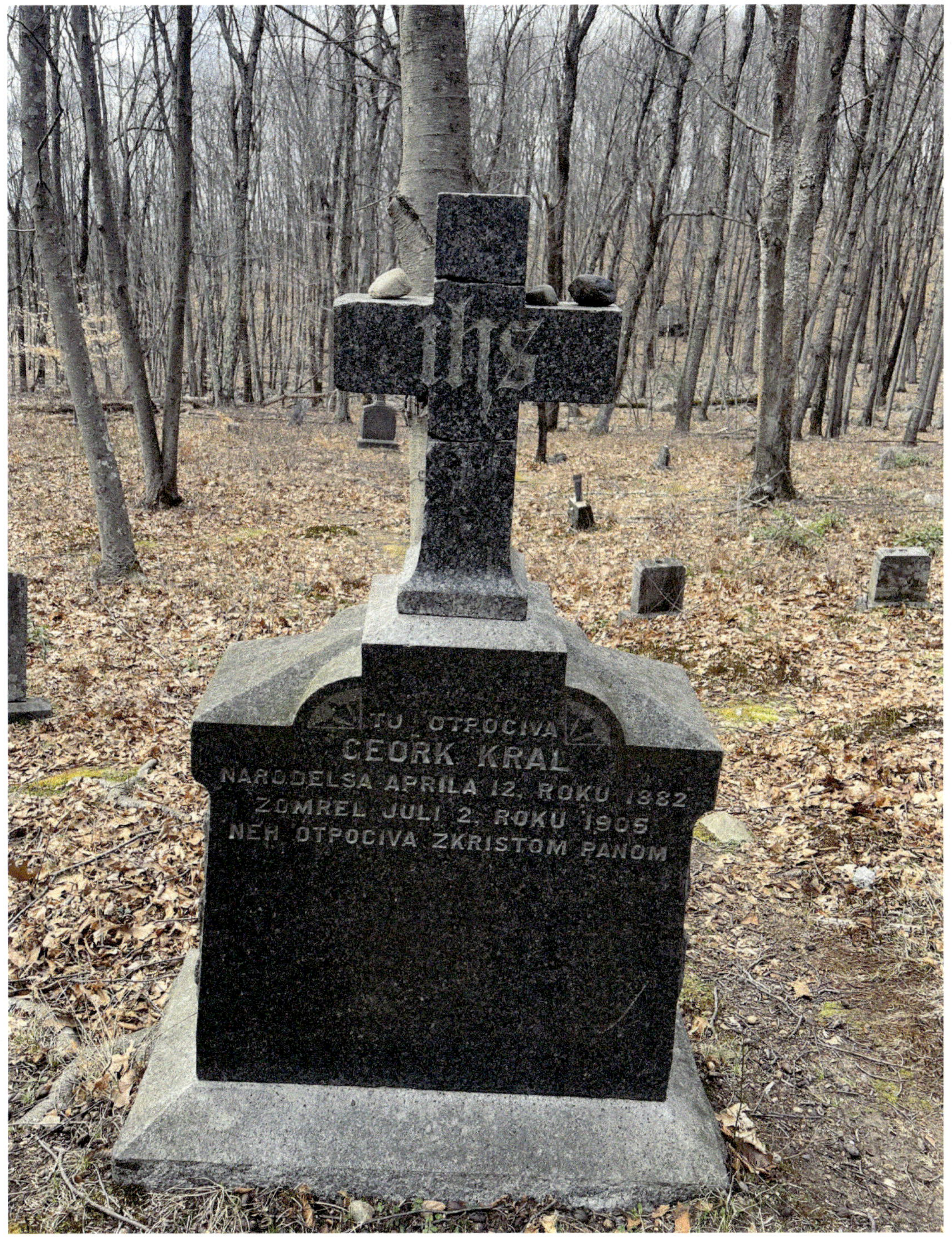

Mining is dangerous and many of the graves are for people in their early twenties.

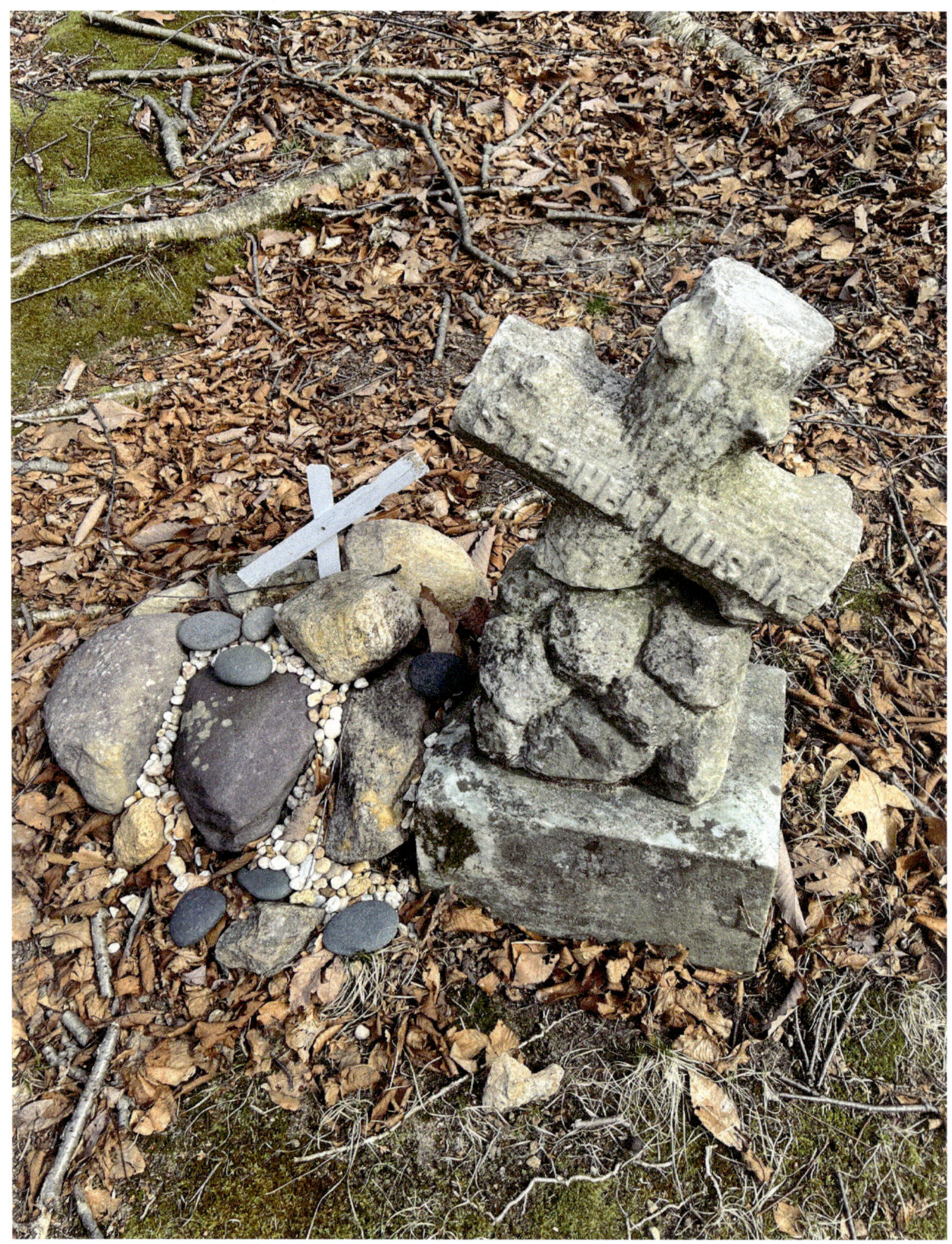

Many of the stones have suffered from time, the elements, and desecrations.

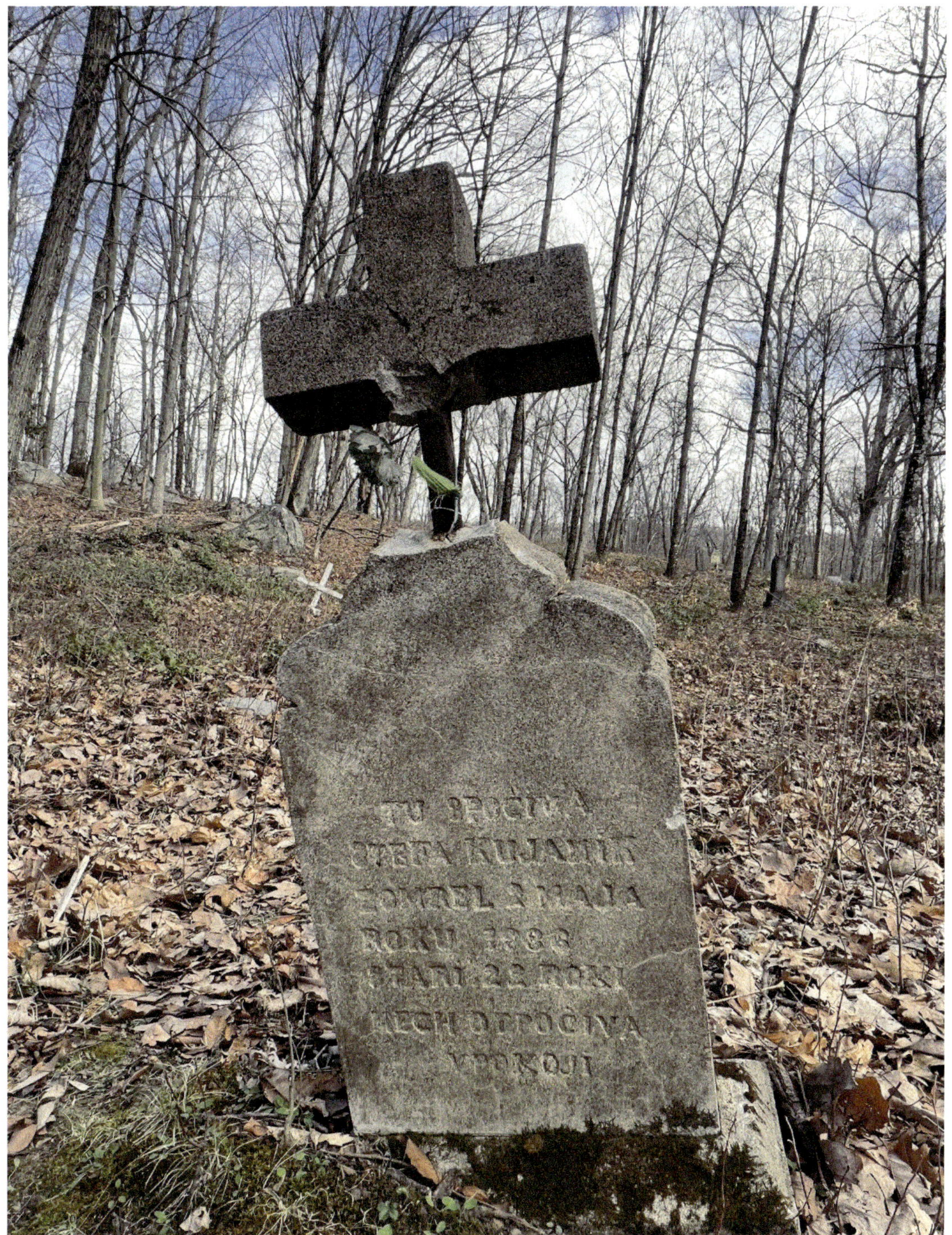

The Friendly Sons of Saint Patrick, an Irish American organization, have adopted the cemetery as a project and have cemetery cleanups and hope to build a new fence.

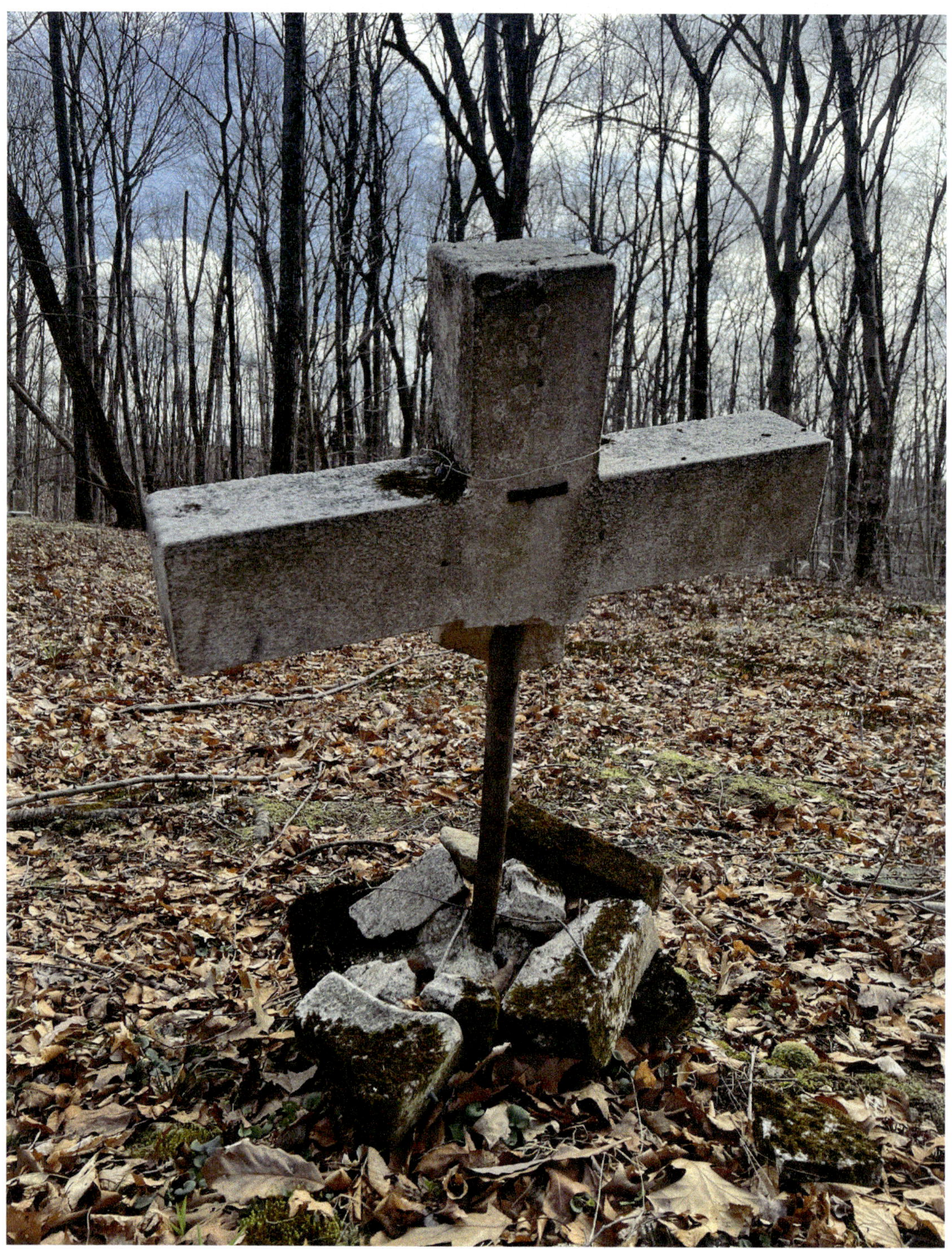

It's unclear which damage is from time or vandalism.

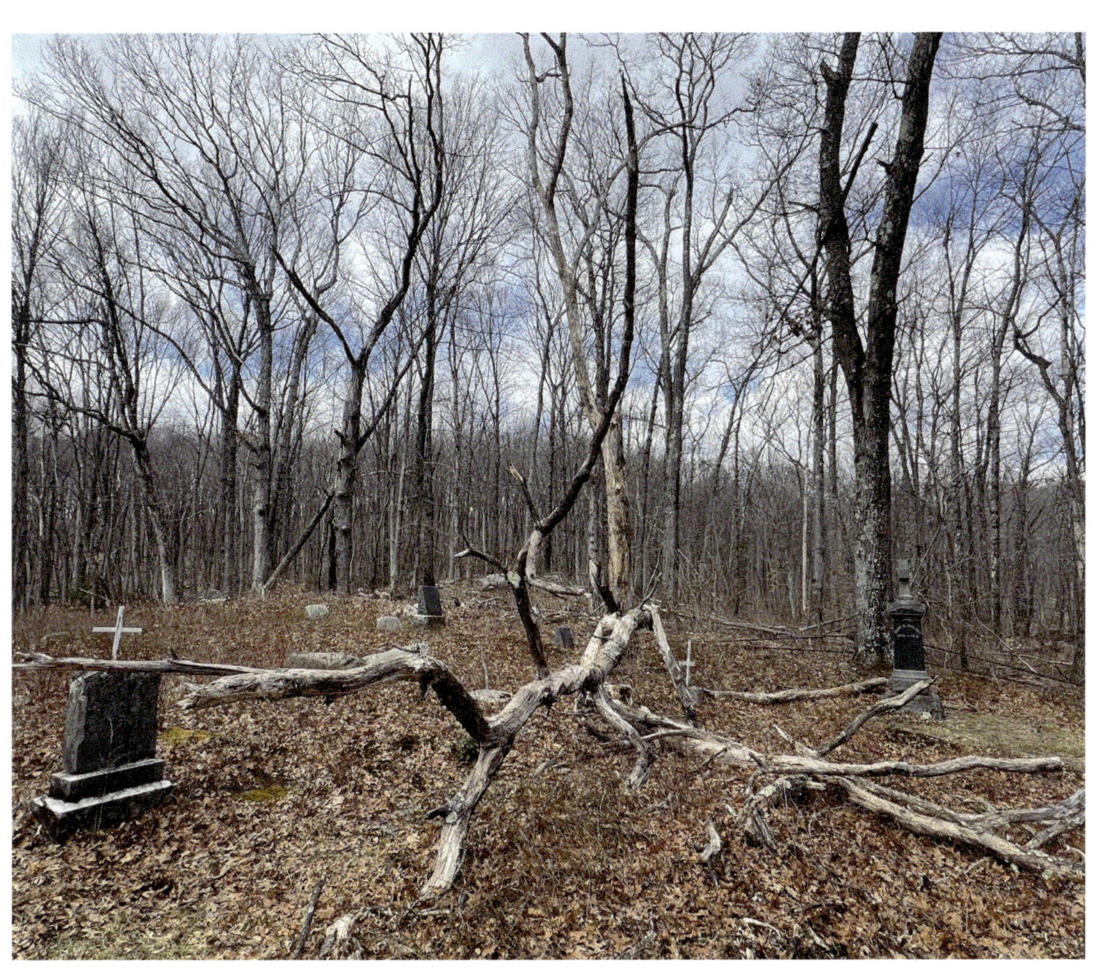

Hibernia/St. Patrick Cemetery has also suffered from damaged caused by Superstorm Sandy.

Walpack Cemetery

Walpack, N.J.

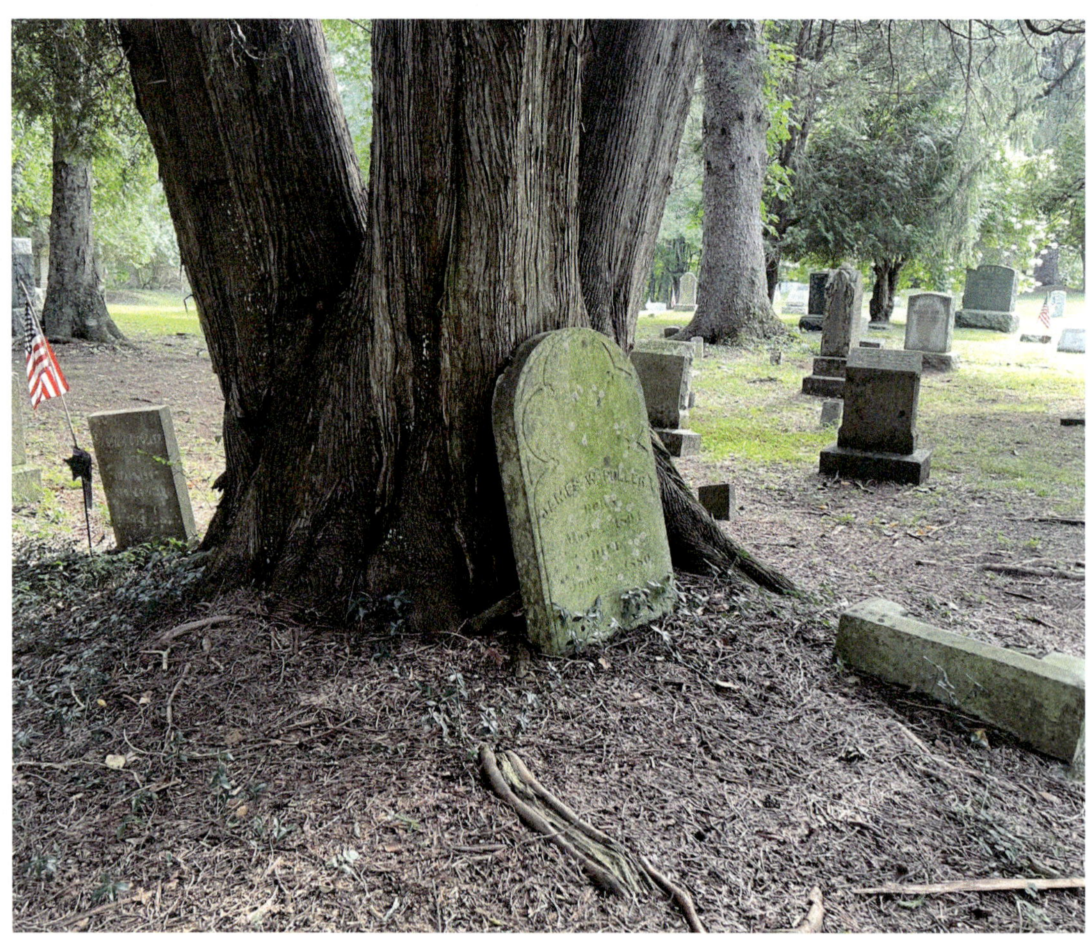

The residents of Walpack were forced to move when the land in their town was seized by eminent domain as part of a plan to dam the Delaware River. The dam was never built, and the residents were unable to return, but the cemetery remains. Walpack Cemetery has graves dating from the Victorian era through modern times.

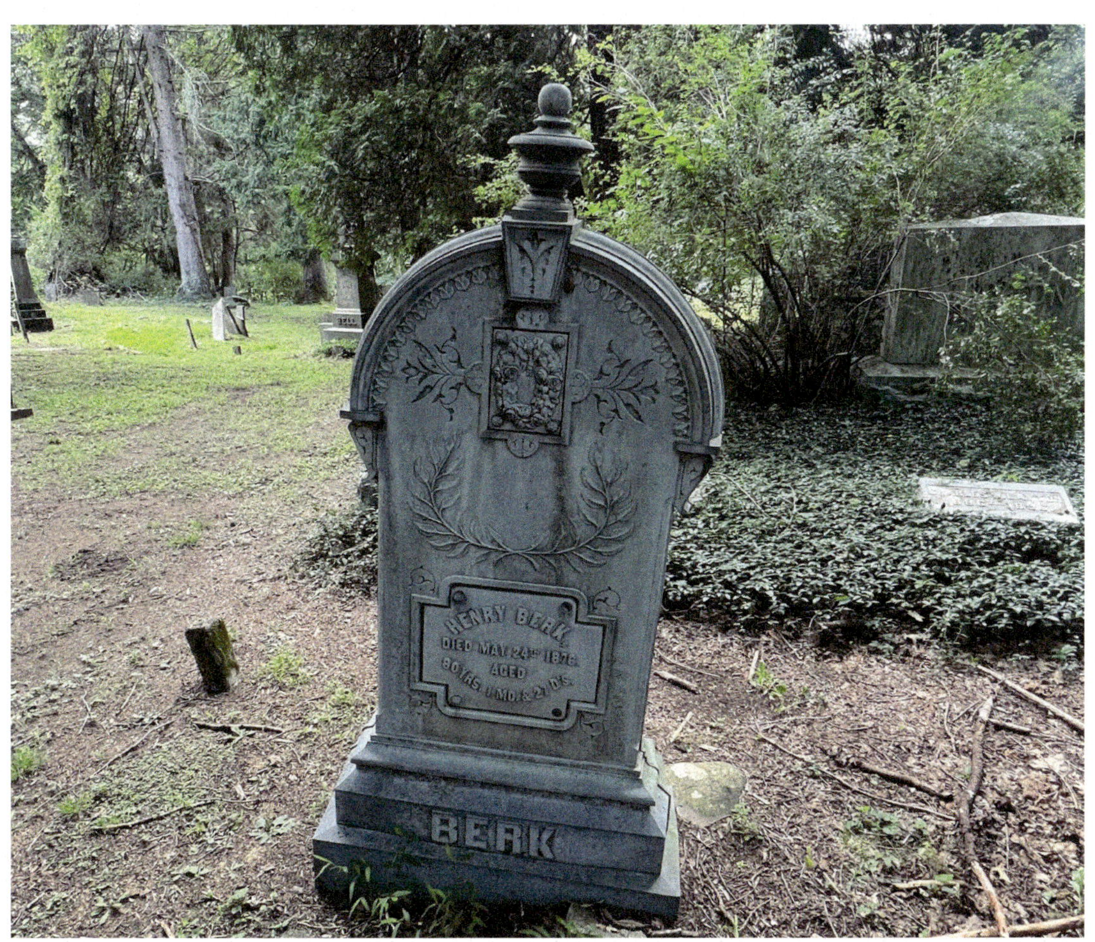

Whenever I visit Walpack Cemetery, I make it a point to visit the Berk family stone.

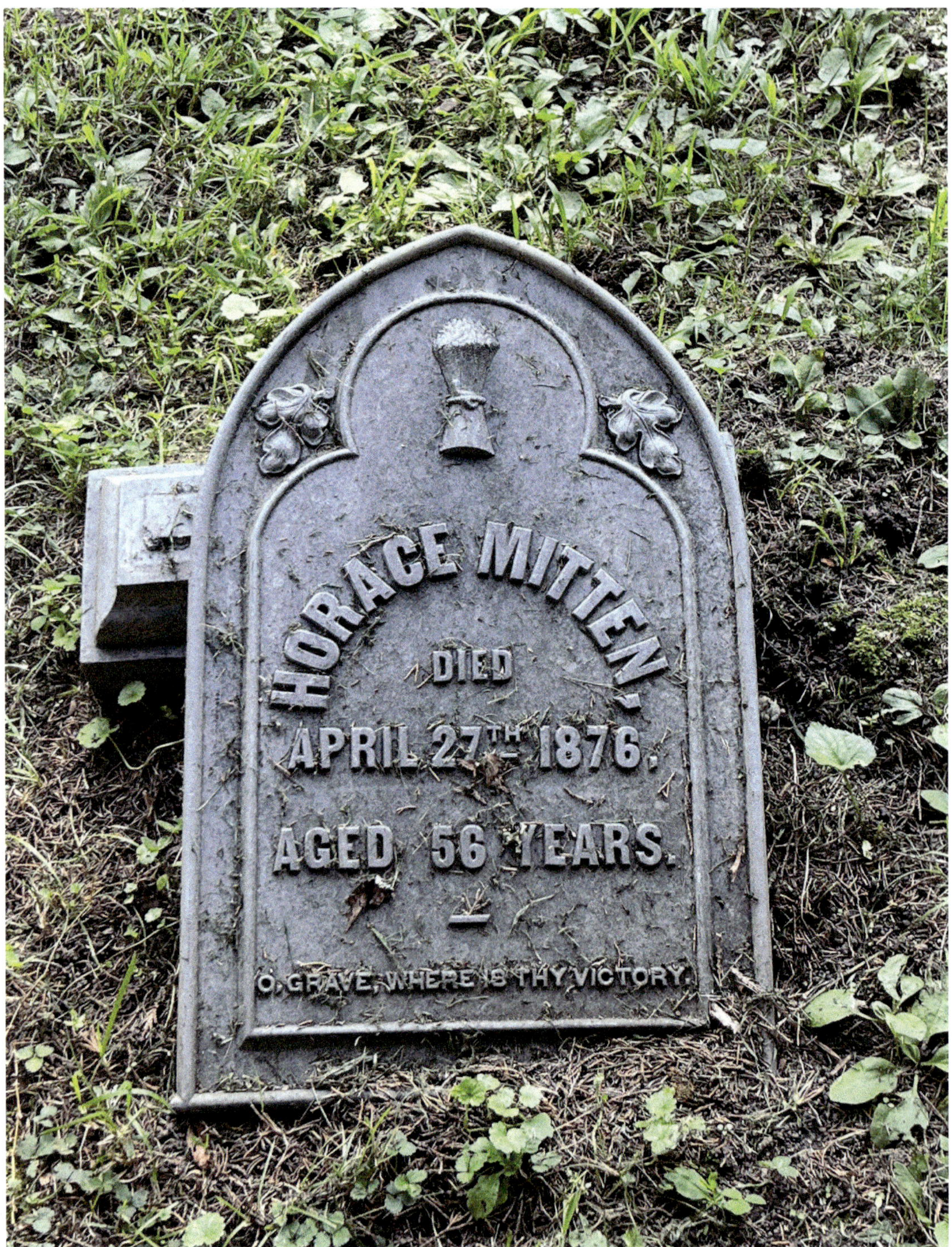

Horace Mitten's stone references 1 Corinthians 15:55. I'm not a religious person but it's one of my favorite Bible verses.

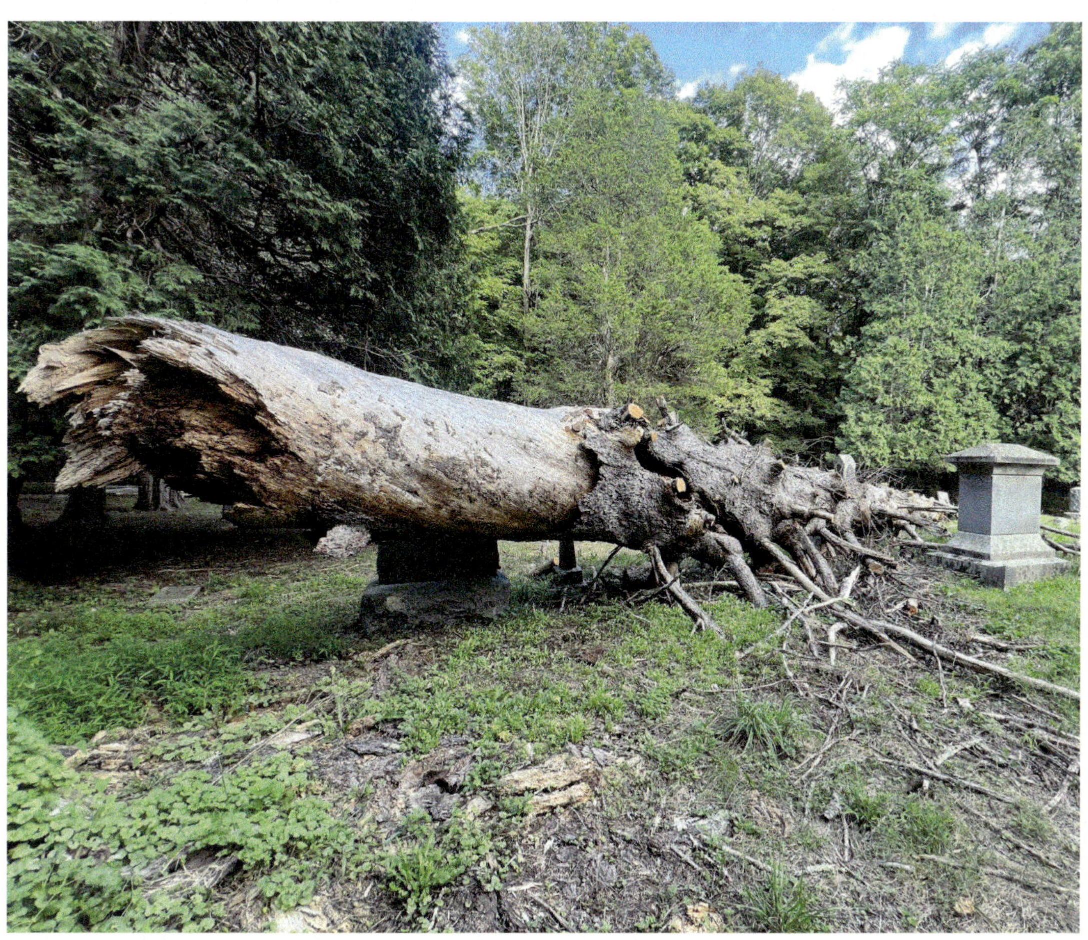

My visit to photograph Walpack Cemetery isn't the first time I've visited. I started going to Walpack around 2020 when many places were closed due to COVID. I knew I wanted to include Walpack Cemetery when this book was pitched to me. The cemetery is maintained by the township and is generally in very good condition, aside from this fallen tree.

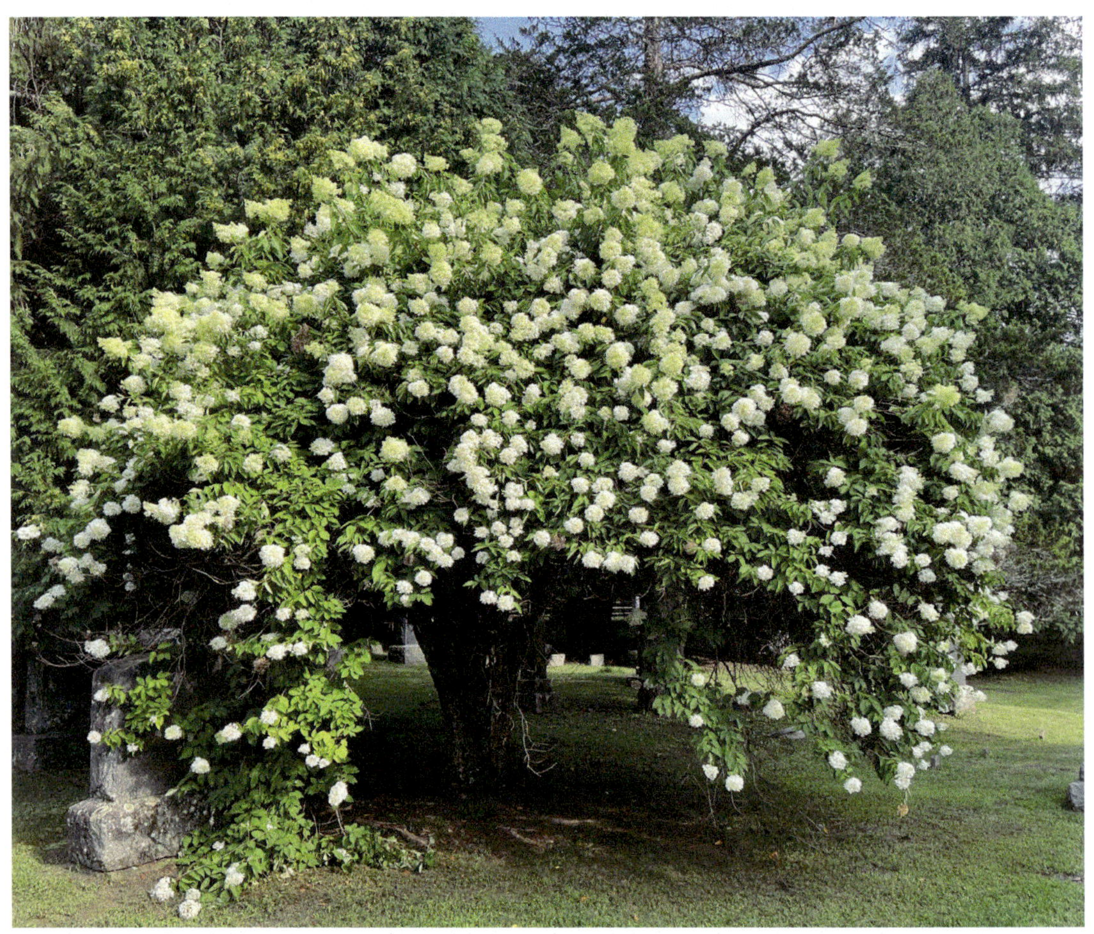

Walpack Cemetery is beautiful and feels like a garden. You can also visit the rest of the abandoned town and the church is sometimes open for events.

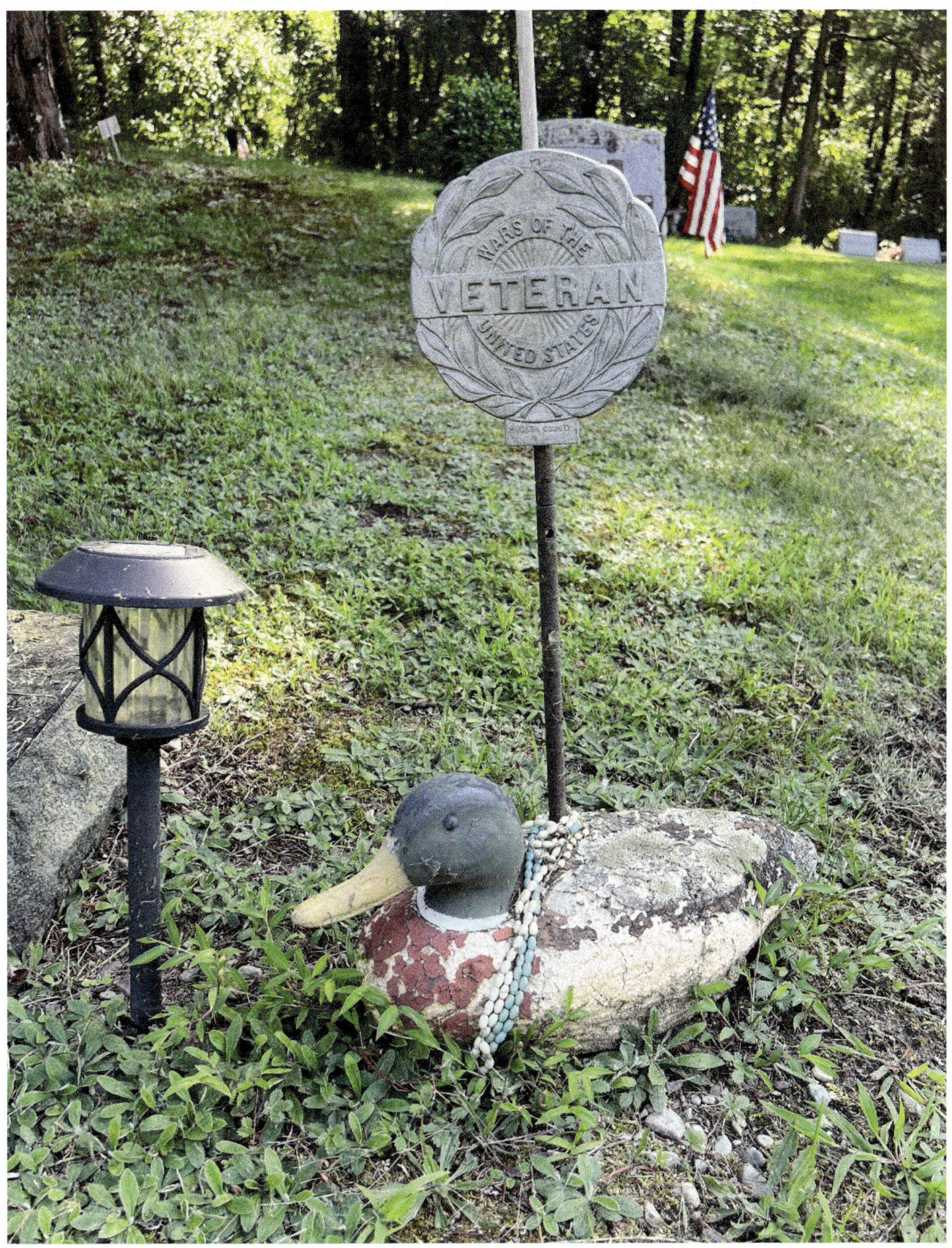

There have been recent burials at Walpack, I found stones and temporary markers dating to the early 2020s.

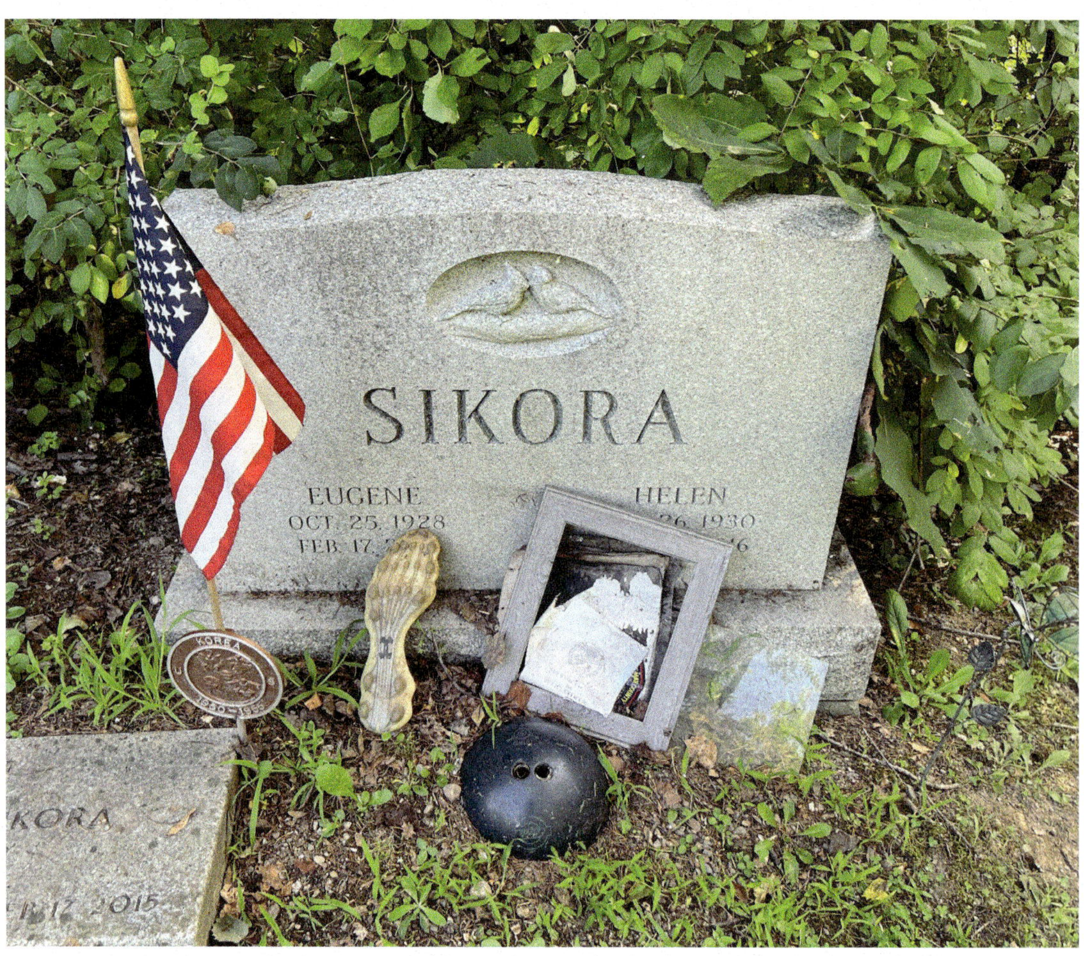

The one road to the cemetery was washed out when I visited, and the bridge that takes you directly to the cemetery was closed for vehicles. There was a third way to get there but that would have added an additional thirty minutes to the route. I can't imagine what it's like coordinating a burial here. The graves are well tended, and the families still leave mementos for their loved ones.

ENDNOTES

Chapter 1

1 Kaminski, F. V., "Morris County Gravestones: 'Little Lost Cemetery'," *The Genealogical Magazine of New Jersey*, vol. 50, (New Brunswick, N.J.: Genealogical Society of New Jersey, January 1975), p. 25.

2 Feith, E., and Capone, S., "Gone But Not Forgotten," *Morris County Historical Society Website*, January 17, 2023.

3 *Ibid.*

4 Ruse, L., "Woman Honors Father at Parsippany's Little Lost Cemetery," dailyrecord.com/story/news/local/2016/12/13/woman-honors-father-parsippanys-little-lost-cemetery/95374390/, December 13, 2016.

5 Kaminski, *op. cit.*, p. 25.

6 *Ibid.*

7 Ruse, *op. cit.*

8 Kaminski, *op. cit.*, p. 25.

9 Feith, *op. cit.*

10 *Ibid.*

11 Kaminski, *op. cit.*, p. 25.

12 O'Donohue, J., *Old and Forgotten Cemeteries of New Jersey: Morris County Part I.* (North Charleston, S.C.: Createspace Independent Publishing Platform, 2015), p. 39.

13 Kaminski, *op. cit.*, p. 25.

14 Ruse, *op. cit.*

15 Feith, *op. cit.*

16 Ruse, *op. cit.*

17 *Ibid.*

18 O'Donohue, *op. cit*, p. 41.

Chapter 2

1 Larini, R., "Eight Early city Residents Now Rest in a Deeper Peace," *The Central New Jersey Home News*, (July 8, 1980), p. 9.

2 Sarapin, J. K., *Old Burial Grounds of New Jersey: A Guide* (New Brunswick, N.J.: Rutgers University Press, 1994) p. 43.

3 Mickula, P., "Findings–Historical and Genealogical Research, Loews Cemetery Plot," *Report for the Cultural Resource Consulting Group*, 2005.

4 Weird NJ, "Mary Ellis Story Is One For the Movies," *Asbury Park Press* (Asbury Park, N.J.: June 29, 2014), p. A6.

5 Larini, *op. cit.*, p. 9.

6 "History of Miss Ellis' Grave–New Brunswick's Most Romantic Spot," *The Daily Home News*, (New Brunswick, NJ: August 18, 1918).

7 Larini, *op. cit.*, p. 9.

8 *Ibid.*

9 Talmont, N., "Gravestone, Clippings Last of Romance," *Central New Jersey Home News,* (New Brunswick, N.J.: June 10, 1956), p. 22.

10 Mickula, *op. cit.*

11 *Ibid.*

12 Talmont, *op. cit.*, p. 22.

13 "History of Miss Ellis' Grave–New Brunswick's Most Romantic Spot," *op. cit.*

14 Mickula, *op. cit.*

15 King, A., "Precious Privacy Hers Forever," *Central New Jersey Home News* (New Brunswick, NJ: August 21, 1966), p. 45.

16 Sloane, C. D., *The Last Great Necessity: Cemeteries in American History* (Baltimore, MD.: Johns Hopkins University Press, 1991), p. 29.

17 Sloane, *op. cit.*, p. 70.

18 Talmont, *op. cit.*, p. 22.

19 King, *op. cit.*, p. 45.

20 "History of Miss Ellis' Grave–New Brunswick's Most Romantic Spot," *op. cit.*

21 Talmont, *op. cit.*, p. 22.

22 "History of Miss Ellis' Grave–New Brunswick's Most Romantic Spot," *op. cit.*

23 Cole, L., "The Legend of Mary Ellis Who Still Awaits Her Betrothed," *The Sunday Times* (New Brunswick, NJ: October 17, 1926), p. 12.

24 *A Directory of the City of New-Brunswick for 1855* (New Brunswick, NJ: 1855), p. 18.

25 Weird NJ, *op. cit.*, p. A6.

26 Martin, A., "A Sentimental Developer Saves a Grave," *New York Times* (New York City, N.Y.: November 6, 2005).

27 Larini, *op. cit.*, p. 9.

28 *Ibid.*

29 Mickula, *op. cit.*

30 Larini, *op. cit.*, p. 9.

31 Sarapin, *op. cit.*, p. 43.

32 Mickula, *op. cit.*

33 Larini, *op. cit.*, p. 9.

34 King, *op. cit.*, p. 45.

35 *Ibid.*

36 Mickula, *op. cit.*

37 *Ibid.*

38 Larini, *op. cit.*, p. 9.

39 *Ibid.*

40 Mickula, *op. cit.*

41 Larini, *op. cit.*, p. 9.

42 Weird NJ, *op. cit.*, p. A6.

43 *Ibid.*

44 Larini, *op. cit.*, p. 9.

45 Weird NJ, *op. cit.*, p. A6.

46 *Ibid.*

Chapter 3

1 Lynwander, L., "Newark Journal: An 'Amazing Cemetery' and Its Role in History," *The New York Times* (New York City, N.Y.: April 24, 1994) Section 14NJ, p. 2.
2 *Ibid.*
3 Senkevitch Jr., Dr. A., "Mount Pleasant Cemetery," *National Register of Historic Places Inventory–Nomination Form* (Newark, N.J.: Newark Preservation and Landmarks Committee, May 1986).
4 Lynwander, *op. cit.*, p. 2.
5 Senkevitch, *op. cit.*, section 8.
6 *Ibid.*
7 "Woodside's Mt. Pleasant, a Cemetery of Rural Beauty," knowingnewark.npl.org/woodsides-mt-pleasant-a-cemetery-of-rural-beauty/, January 30, 1997.
8 Senkevitch, *op. cit.*, section 8, p. 4.
9 Senkevitch, *op. cit.*, section 7.
10 Senkevitch, *op. cit.*, section 8, p. 4.
11 *Ibid.*, p. 5.
12 *Ibid.*, p. 4.
13 *Ibid.*, p. 6.
14 *Ibid.*, p. 5.
15 Senkevitch, *op. cit.*, section 7, p. 9.
16 Senkevitch, *op. cit.*, section 8.
17 Senkevitch, *op. cit.*, section 7, p. 4.
18 *Ibid.*, p. 3.
19 *Ibid.*, p. 4.
20 *Ibid.*, p. 7.
21 Senkevitch, *op. cit.*, section 8, p. 9.
22 Lynwander, *op. cit.*, p. 2.
23 Senkevitch, *op. cit.*, section 8, p. 9.
24 Senkevitch, *op. cit.*, section 7, p. 8.
25 *Ibid.*
26 *Ibid.*, p. 9.
27 *Ibid.*, p. 10.
28 "Woodside's Mt. Pleasant, a Cemetery of Rural Beauty," *op. cit.*
29 *Ibid.*
30 Senkevitch, *op. cit.*, section 17, p. 6.
31 "Woodside's Mt. Pleasant, a Cemetery of Rural Beauty," *op. cit.*
32 Senkevitch, *op. cit.*, section 7, p. 17.
33 "Woodside's Mt. Pleasant, a Cemetery of Rural Beauty," *op. cit.*
34 Lynwander, *op. cit.*, p. 2.
35 "Munn," *The Evening News* (Newark, N.J.: January 2, 1892), p. 9.
36 *Ibid.*

Chapter 4

1 Nonestied, M., "Burial Reform at the Jersey City and Harsimus Cemetery," gardenstatelegacy.com/files/Burial_Reform_at_the_Jersey_City___Harsimus_Cemetery_Nonestied_GSL12.pdf (Newark, N.J.: Garden State Legacy, Issue 12, June 2011).
2 Sloane, *op. cit.*, p. 142.

3 *Ibid.*, p. 35.
4 *Ibid.*
5 Faber, E., "Here's What You Might Find at an Oddities Market in a Historic Cemetery," abcnews4.com/news/offbeat/heres-what-you-might-find-at-an-oddities-market-in-a-historic-cemetery, October 12, 2021.
6 Sloane, *op. cit.*, p. 34.
7 *Ibid.*, p. 2.
8 *Ibid.*, p. 17.
9 *Ibid.*, p. 31.
10 *Ibid.*, p. 63.
11 Nonestied, *op. cit.*
12 Eaton, H., *Jersey City and its Historic Sites* (Poughkeepsie, N.Y.: A.V. Haight 1899), pp. 44-45.
13 Eaton, *op. cit.*, p. 44.
14 *Ibid.*
15 Faber, *op. cit.*
16 Eaton, *op. cit.*, p. 45.
17 *Ibid.*
18 *Ibid.*
19 *Ibid.*
20 Edgecombe, M., Personal Communication, April 20, 2024.
21 Nonestied, *op. cit.*
22 Sloane, *op. cit.*, p. 31.
23 *Ibid.*
24 *Ibid.*
25 Sloane, *op. cit.*, p. 70.
26 *Ibid.*, p. 32.
27 "An Act to Incorporate the Jersey City and Harsimus Cemetery," *Acts of the 55th General Assembly of the State of New Jersey* (Trenton, N.J.: Joseph Justice 1831), pp. 87-89.
28 *Ibid.*, pp. 87, 89.
29 Nonestied, *op. cit.*
30 D'Auria, P., "Meet the Man Who Brought an Abandoned Historic Cemetery Back to Life," nj.com/hudson/2020/02/meet-the-man-who-brought-an-abandoned-historic-cemetery-back-to-life.html, February 7, 2020.
31 Edgecombe, *op. cit.*
32 *Ibid.*
33 *Ibid.*
34 Eaton, *op. cit.*, p. 45.
35 *Ibid.*
36 Nonestied, *op. cit.*
37 *Ibid.*
38 Edgecombe, *op. cit.*
39 Nonestied, *op. cit.*
40 *Ibid.*
41 Eaton, *op. cit.*, p. 45.
42 Nonestied, *op. cit.*
43 *Ibid.*
44 Nonestied, *op. cit.*
45 *Ibid.*
46 Fink, J., "Answers Still Sought About Deteriorating Cemetery," nj.com/hudson/2008/05/answers_still_sought_about_det.html, May 23, 2008.

47 Susco, T., personal communication, April 20, 2024.
48 Faber, *op. cit.*
49 Fink, *op. cit.*, May 3, 2008.
50 *Ibid.*
51 *Ibid.*
52 *Ibid.*
53 Nonestied, *op. cit.*
54 Fink, *op. cit.*, May 3, 2008.
55 D'Auria, *op. cit.*
56 Fink, *op. cit.*, May 3, 2008.
57 *Ibid.*
58 LaMonica Egar, M., personal communication, April 20, 2024.
59 *Ibid.*
60 *Ibid.*
61 Fink, J., "New Day For Jersey City Cemetery," nj.com/hudson/2008/06/new_day_for_jersey_city_cemete.html, June 13, 2008.
62 La-Monica, *op. cit.*
63 Fink, *op. cit.*, June 13, 2008.
64 Faber, *op. cit.*
65 *Ibid.*
66 Nonestied, *op. cit.*
67 Faber, *op. cit.*
68 D'Auria, *op. cit.*
69 La-Monica, *op. cit.*
70 *Ibid.*
71 Susco, *op. cit.*
72 Parrillo, R., "Goat Gardening at Jersey City Cemetery," nj.com/inside-jersey/2016/07/chow_time_at_jersey_city_cemetery.html, July 23, 2016.
73 *Ibid.*
74 La-Monica, *op. cit.*
75 D'Auria, *op. cit.*
76 La-Monica, *op. cit.*
77 *Ibid.*
78 *Ibid.*

Chapter 5

1 Stochel Jr., W. R., "Piscatawaytown Burial Ground," Metuchen-Edison Historical Society (Edison, N.J.: Edison Greenways Group) pp. 1-3.
2 Edison Greenways Group, "Piscatawaytown Burial Ground GPR Project Report" (New Brunswick, N.J.: October 2021).
3 Edison Greenways Group, *op. cit.*, p. 5.
4 *Ibid.*, p. 5-6.
5 *Ibid.*, p. 7.
6 *Ibid.*, p. 5.
7 Stochel Jr., *op. cit.*, pp. 1.
8 *Ibid.*
9 Edison Greenways Group, *op. cit.*, p. 5.
10 *Ibid.*, p. 10.
11 *Ibid.*

12 *Ibid.*, p. 4.
13 *Ibid.*, p. 10.
14 *Ibid.*
15 Stochel Jr., *op. cit.*, p. 1.
16 *Ibid.*, p. 2.
17 *Ibid.*
18 *Ibid.*
19 Hunt, Dr. E. M., "Metuchen-Edison Historical Society Record of Burials in Piscatawaytown Grave Yard as of October 28, 1880."
20 Stochel Jr., *op. cit.*, p. 2.
21 *Ibid.*
22 Husted, H., "Abigail Sharp: New Jersey's One Witch," njstatelib.org/abigail-sharp-new-jerseys-one-witch/, July 17, 2024.
23 *Ibid.*
24 *Ibid.*
25 *Ibid.*
26 *Ibid.*
27 *Ibid.*

Chapter 6

1 Johnson, D. K., "The Mexican Lindbergh," *Aviation History*, vol. 32 (Leesburg, VA: HistoryNet, November 2021), pp. 10-12.
2 Barra, A., "Mexico's Lindbergh," *American History* (Leesburg, VA: HistoryNet, April 2015), pp. 59-63.
3 Johnson, *op. cit.*, p. 12.
4 Barra, *op. cit.*, p. 59.
5 *Ibid.*
6 *Ibid.*, p. 60.
7 Johnson, *op. cit.*, p. 10.
8 Barra, *op. cit.*, p. 60.
9 *Ibid.*
10 New Jersey Department of Environmental Protection, "Carranza Memorial Site Overview," nj.gov/dep/parksandforests/historic/carranzamemorial.html#:~:text=Carranza%20Memorial%20Historic%20Site%20Overview&text=Tragically%2C%20while%20flying%20back%20to,the%20site%20of%20his%20crash.
11 Johnson, *op. cit.*, p. 10.
12 Barra, *op. cit.*, p. 60.
13 *Ibid.*
14 New Jersey Department of Environmental Protection, *op. cit.*
15 *Ibid.*
16 *Ibid.*
17 Barra, *op. cit.*, p. 61.
18 *Ibid.*
19 *Ibid.*
20 *Ibid.*
21 Johnson, *op. cit.*, p. 12.
22 Barra, *op. cit.*, p. 61.
23 Johnson, *op. cit.*, p. 12.
24 New Jersey Department of Environmental Protection, *op. cit.*

25 Barra, *op. cit.*, p. 61.
26 *Ibid.*
27 Johnson, *op. cit.*, p. 12.
28 Barra, *op. cit.*, p. 61.
29 Johnson, *op. cit.*, p. 12.
30 New Jersey Department of Environmental Protection, *op. cit.*
31 Barra, *op. cit.*, p. 62.
32 Johnson, *op. cit.*, p. 12.
33 Barra, *op. cit.*, p. 62.
34 New Jersey Department of Environmental Protection, *op. cit.*
35 Whomsley, M., "Carranza Monument: New Jersey Honors an International Good Will Aviator," *WPA Highlights Magazine* (January 1937), pp. 39-41.
36 Barra, *op. cit.*, p. 62.
37 *Ibid.*
38 Whomsley, *op. cit.*, p. 41.
39 Emilio Carranza Death Certificate, July 14, 1928.
40 Whomsley, *op. cit.*, p. 41.
41 Johnson, *op. cit.*, p. 12.
42 Whomsley, *op. cit.*, p. 39.
43 Barra, *op. cit.*, p. 63.
44 New Jersey Department of Environmental Protection, *op. cit.*

About the Author

Janice Phillips is a licensed funeral director, who has also worked as a freelance artist, and sold taxidermy at an oddities store. Born in New York City and raised in New Jersey, she developed an appreciation for cemeteries after attending a preschool at a church with a colonial graveyard. In her spare time, she enjoys urban exploration, horror movies, and pulling over for every interesting cemetery on the road. You can find more of her original photography on Instagram: @scarinasvault.

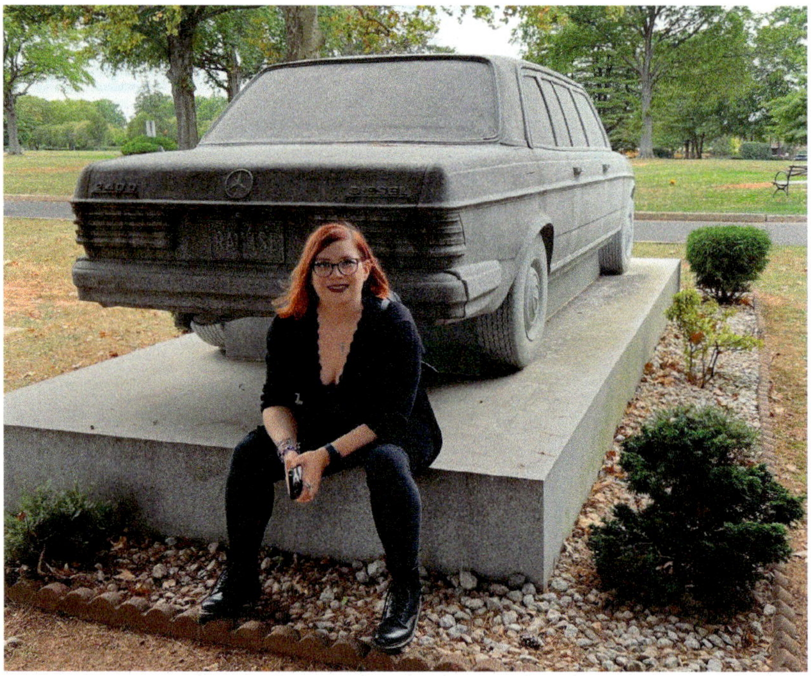

(Taken by Michael Nagy)